P9-BAW-054

Florence Whiteman Kaslow and Associates

Issues in Human Services

Jossey-Bass Inc., Publishers
San Francisco • Washington • London • 1972

ISSUES IN HUMAN SERVICES
A Sourcebook for Supervision and Staff Development
by Florence Whiteman Kaslow and Associates

Published and copyrighted in Great Britain by
Jossey-Bass, Inc., Publishers
3, Henrietta Street
London W.C.2

Library of Congress Catalogue Card Number LC 72-83965

International Standard Book Number ISBN 0-87589-137-3

Manufactured in the United States of America

JACKET DESIGN BY WILLI BAUM

FIRST EDITION

Code 7222

The Jossey-Bass Behavioral Science Series

Preface

Although relevant articles on supervision, in-service training, and staff development have appeared in journals, and books are available dealing with organization theory, group interaction, and training design, there is a paucity, indeed an absence, of recent major books on supervision and staff-development practices in human-service agencies. Recently, in trying to prepare a bibliography for a graduate course in supervision and staff development, I became acutely aware of the fact that such books are virtually nonexistent. The impetus for *Issues in Human Services* developed from my felt need for a volume that would deal with this crucial facet of social service, namely, the preparation of staff members to deliver services efficiently and effectively.

Because the philosophy and methodology of one-to-one supervision have been amply covered in the literature, I decided not to make these particular topics the primary focus of *Issues in Human Services.* I chose, instead, to treat supervision and staff development from a holistic framework: to try to cover many views and approaches, to examine the validity and appropriateness of each view and the dilemmas of each. In order to achieve this perspective, I asked leading educators and practitioners to become contributors. Each agreed that a book on this topic was timely and needed. I chose each for his special expertise and brought together people in several related disciplines, including social work, sociology, education, and psychology.

I have arbitrarily separated *Issues in Human Services* into two parts, the first dealing primarily with history and philosophy and the second dealing specifically with practice settings and problems. However, theory and practice in human-services delivery systems are so integrally interwoven that isolating them, even for analytic purposes, is impossible, and they dovetail in many chapters in both parts.

Felice Perlmutter sets the stage with a historical analysis. She traces supervision from its inception as a training tool for ensuring quality service to clients; through the period of mandatory individual supervisory conferences; through the recent past, when these conferences were challenged; to the present, when new types of staff members are demanding more viable training approaches.

In Chapter Two, Alex Gitterman presents three models of education—curriculum-centered, student-centered, and integrative—and compares these models with their counterparts and offshoots in social work supervision. The model followed by a supervisor prescribes the kind of supervisory sessions he holds, his relationship to his supervisees, and the subject matter of conferences or meetings. Although Gitterman's discussion is primarily theoretical, he gives examples from practice for illustrative purposes.

In Chapter Three, Archie Hanlan addresses the administrative aspects of supervision by taking a fresh look at function, structure, and process. He argues that new approaches to supervision may increase agency tensions and complicate existing arrangements and relationships if function, structure, and process do not accommodate and support innovation in supervision.

Recently, paraprofessionals have been the cause of much confusion and controversy. Willard Richan (Chapter Four) identifies the key issue: the underlying fear of the potential of this new cadre of workers. He recommends setting up meaningful and acceptable training programs that open up new career opportunities for the poor and make the services of indigenous workers available to members of the community.

In Chapter Five, Eugene Royster directly confronts the dilemmas encountered today by black professionals. He offers a trenchant, perceptive assessment of the special difficulties of the "marginal man" whose responsibilities to his agency and to his community conflict.

Class and ethnicity come under scrutiny in Chapter Six, by Alfred Kutzik. He traces the influence of these factors on the supervisor and the supervisee and relates socioeconomic status and national origin to patterns of hiring and promotion, the introduction of supervision, and later to professionalization.

The issues treated by Hanlan, Richan, Royster, and Kutzik are touchy and frequently ignored or glossed over. They are controversial and go deeply into personal, professional, and organizational relationships, the concealed biases, attitudes, and policies that mitigate against change. Each candidly articulates concerns that each agency must come to grips with.

In Chapter Seven, I give an overview of the philosophy and practice of group supervision. I use a Parsonian framework for formulating the instrumental and expressive goals of a supervisory group within the agency system. I look at the teaching-training, quasitherapeutic, administrative, and consultative functions of the supervisor and consider how these can be fulfilled through small-group unit supervision. I also take into consideration the cost of supervision, a little discussed but vital concern.

Chapter Eight, by Matti Gershenfeld, is a natural companion to the material on group supervision. It considers the adaptation of the laboratory approach to in-service training to the social-agency setting. Gershenfeld raises some disturbing questions as to why more agencies have not used the laboratory approach, particularly when a substantial body of data attests to its vitality and feasibility in staff development.

Part Two brings together descriptions of current practice in a variety of settings. Ruth Cohen describes a two-year demonstration project with graduate students in a geriatric center. Although such was not the intent, her chapter illustrates the philosophy and practice of group supervision.

John Main, Eugene Cohen, and Sidney Eisenberg and Wilbur Finch discuss supervision in the juvenile court, in a federal psychiatric setting, and in a public-welfare agency, respectively. Each of these huge, bureaucratic institutions is in a continual state of flux and is the target of public and legislative scrutiny and criticism. Agency practice is regulated by law as well as by many policy rulings. The supervisors' tasks are multifaceted, staff are rarely homogeneous, and rules change rapidly. In these three chapters, it becomes evident that the one-to-one model of supervision continues to flourish and perhaps to be preferred in some agencies. The crucial issues are the validity and appropriateness of supervision at all, the competence of the supervisor, and the flexibility of agency policies for introducing and testing new training modalities.

Several questions reappear throughout *Issues in Human Services.* One question concerns the best balance of individual and group supervision. Another question concerns whether staff groupings should be homogeneous or heterogeneous and why. A third question concerns whether the various supervisory functions of administration, teaching, staff development, and consultation should be lodged in a single individual. Pervasive themes are the need for experimentation with new training approaches and the need to build mechanisms for feedback and ongoing evaluation. Most contributors agree that collegial structures and peer-group supervision merit serious consideration as alternatives to hierarchical structures.

In *Issues in Human Services,* I make no attempt to be internally consistent. To do so would distort reality; consensus does not exist in the human services today. If it did, innovative supervisory endeavors would not be under way. I hope that this collection of viewpoints succeeds in drawing together existing knowledge in the field of supervision, in teasing out the implications, in reaching new conclusions, in formulating new directions, and in stimulating the reader to use supervision effectively. If so, the goals of the contributors have been realized.

The preparation of *Issues in Human Services* required the assistance of a number of people. I wish to express my gratitude to the contributors, who worked so diligently to write original chapters of high quality and to meet deadlines while teaching or rendering social services. The freedom which they all extended to me to edit the drafts was a support, as was their continuing belief in the importance of this book. I would also like to express my gratitude to Roseanne Orner and Caroline Thomas, who patiently typed the manuscript and offered words of encouragement.

Finally, the deepest appreciation goes to my husband, Solis, and our two children, Nadine and Howard, for their patience, understanding, and cooperation during the long nights when I sat in the office writing and editing and for all their playful encouragement to hurry up and finish "the book."

Philadelphia
September 1972

FLORENCE WHITEMAN KASLOW

Contents

Contributors

EUGENE COHEN, *assistant chief, Social Work Service, Veterans Administration Outpatient Clinic, Philadelphia*

RUTH COHEN, *district director, services to older persons unit, Jewish Family Service of Philadelphia; lecturer, School of Social Work, University of Pennsylvania*

SIDNEY S. EISENBERG, *professor of social work, Sacramento State College*

WILBUR A. FINCH, *doctoral student, University of California, Berkeley*

MATTI GERSHENFELD, *lecturer, Temple University Department of Psychoeducational Processes*

ALEX GITTERMAN, *instructor, School of Social Work, Columbia University*

ARCHIE HANLAN, *professor, School of Social Work, University of Pennsylvania*

FLORENCE WHITEMAN KASLOW, *associate in social work and psychiatry, Department of Psychiatry, Hospital of University of Pennsylvania*

ALFRED J. KUTZIK, *professor, School of Social Work, University of Pennsylvania*

JOHN MAIN, *professor, Department of Sociology and Anthropology, West Chester State College*

FELICE PERLMUTTER, *professor, School of Social Work, University of Pennsylvania*

WILLARD C. RICHAN, *professor and associate dean, School of Social Administration, Temple University*

EUGENE C. ROYSTER, *professor of sociology and department chairman, Lincoln University*

Issues in Human Services

A Sourcebook for Supervision and Staff Development

CHAPTER 1

Barometer of Professional Change

Felice Perlmutter

The following acerbic statement touched a sensitive nerve of the profession of social work. "The day after the bomb fell the doctor was out binding up radiation burns. The minister prayed and set up a soup kitchen in the ruined chapel. The policeman herded stray children to the rubble heap where the teacher had improvised a classroom. And the social worker wrote a report; since two had survived, they held a conference on interpersonal relationships in a time of intensified anxiety states" (Saunders, 1957, p. 56). Although a comfortable response was to laugh it off as a clever bit of sophistry, the more important response was to reflect upon the crucial issue raised. Why was the public image of social work negative, reflecting its internal arrangements rather than focusing on its humanitarian values and the vital social functions it performed in modern American society?

I believe this problem can be illuminated by an analysis of the function served by supervision, a carefully refined and methodically defined process. I regard supervision in social work as an indicator of growth and change in the profession. Its development relates both to the external social context in which social work is practiced and to the internal context of changing theory and practice. Supervision is identified as a key variable in this analysis because social work stands alone among the professions in its use of supervision beyond the educational or training phase. In fact, social work has been designated a semiprofession largely because of its use of supervision (Etzioni, 1969).

Emphases and orientations in supervision have varied over time, but a basic definition can accommodate these variations: "Supervision has been the traditional method of transmitting knowledge of social work and skill in practice from the . . . experienced practitioner to the inexperienced student or worker" (Burns, 1965, p. 785). The variation in definition ranges from scientific management to psychotherapy, indicating the shifting historical focus of the profession. The supervisory process has been able to accommodate statements as disparate as the two which follow. "The ultimate object of all supervision is to increase efficiency. . . . This principle of scientific management is as applicable to philanthropic agencies as to the world of business (F. Watson, 1922, p. 477). Contrast this efficiency approach with the following approach emphasizing the worker's development: "Workers carrying responsibility for the program of social . . . agencies are persons too, and what happens to them in the interrelationship is essential to the carrying out of the programs . . . and must be put to the same searching tests" (Williamson, 1950, p. 2). Thus, supervision in social work combines two major components, administrative and educational. Both functions are usually carried by one supervisor.

Whereas the existing literature on supervision is concerned with content and methodology, our interest here is structural, focused on the issues raised and the functions served by the supervisory process. Although content and structure are inextricably intertwined, content is explored primarily as it elucidates the structural aspects. My consideration is limited to supervision as part of the work situation, not supervision performed in conjunction with academic training.

In this chapter, I do not intend to discuss general issues of American social welfare and social-work practice. However, we must give our attention to a few selected issues important for an understanding of the process of supervision.

First, the profession of social work is interstitial. It serves both the client in need and society at large. Much attention has been paid by the profession to its role as advocate (Ad Hoc Committee on Advocacy, 1969, pp. 16–27). This issue is complex, for the social worker's function is defined by and his salary is paid by an agency (be it public or voluntary) which receives its sanction from and is accountable to the community, although his services are offered to a client in need. Similarly, Parsons (1964, pp. 374–375) views law as an interstitial profession in that it is "not only 'oriented to' but to an important degree '[integrated] with' the structure of political authority" in that "the laws for which it is responsible are official enactments of the state." In contrast to social workers, attorneys are hired and paid by their clients, an arrangement which guarantees their independence and autonomy. This point is of fundamental importance. (A radical plan for client independence through a client voucher system, based on a model similar to that of law and medicine, has been proposed—Piliavin, 1968, pp. 34–41.) The implication of this relationship for social work supervision is that the professional can be controlled by the organization and is not fully autonomous, and supervision is the administrative vehicle through which this control is exercised.[1]

The second important issue we must consider in dealing with supervision is that in contrast to the professions of law and medicine, whose major tool is applying internalized knowledge and skill, social work frequently dispenses external resources such as money. Whereas the resources of the former are infinite (cannot be used up), the resources of the latter are usually scarce (Toren, 1969, 177–178). Furthermore, because the external resources are not the social worker's property but belong to the community, social work is further vulnerable to community control, exercised in the agency through supervision.

[1] As physicians and lawyers move into bureaucratic structures to serve their clients (for example, community legal services and community health services), changes in autonomy will undoubtedly be evident.

A third issue is the dilemma which exists in the tension between humanitarian sentiment and professionalism, namely, objectivity. "There is a tendency for a profession, as it begins to stress the scientific and the technical, to get out of touch with human life. . . . Social work without service would be lame, but without values it would be blind. It can never reach the point of scientific objectivity . . . characterized . . . as 'impersonal.' . . . It will always have an element of the subjective, the personal, and the emotional" (N. Cohen, 1957, pp. 558–559). Supervision has increased objective, professional, neutral role performance, succinctly formulated as the development of the professional self, with a focus on the difference between the client and worker as a means of achieving professionalism (Robinson, 1949, pp. 12–13). This emphasis is congruent with Parsons' theoretical formulation regarding the neutral and functionally specific role of the professional; but it is at the expense of the primary, spontaneous, and emotional relationship of the early settlement house worker and friendly visitor. It is interesting to note that the caseworkers in the professional family agency in Manchester, England, attempt to combine both the primary and secondary forms by living in the agency, in the style of the early settlement house workers, while offering their neighbors a formalized professional service.

The fourth, and last, issue concerns the conflict between social action (reform) and social service (adjustment). Although both streams are basic to the history and evolution of social work, the supervisory process has focused on improving service and technique as a specific and clearly defined objective with the unanticipated consequence of neglecting reform. Supervision has diluted the worker's direct responsibility for and involvement in social action and reform because "established agency channels" have been viewed as the appropriate initiators of action. A study of the social-work practitioner in policy formation confirmed this thesis (Fraley, 1966; Pray, 1945, pp. 3–6). Let us now examine the process of supervision against the background of these four issues.

Historical Framework

Social-systems theory offers a general vantage point for an analysis of a particular social system, in this case the profession of social work. Two fundamental premises underlie this analysis: social systems are open systems and must be examined in their environmental context (Katz and Kohn, 1966, pp. 19–29); and a "genetic and developmental approach" with an emphasis on "origins and growth stages" is necessary for understanding the system (Selznick, 1957, pp. 141–142). Formal organizations in general and social-welfare agencies in particular are sharply affected by their social context, and their development is accordingly stimulated by the changing texture of the environment (Emery and Trist, 1965, pp. 21–32).

Classical social-systems theory suggests that every social system must meet four functional requisites: latent pattern maintenance, integration, goal attainment, and adaptation (Parsons and Smelser, 1965, pp. 16–18). The most fundamental requisite, and the one most resistant to change, is latent pattern maintenance. Therein is located the value framework, and "a social system's first functional requirement is to preserve the integrity of the value system itself," an activity which "proceeds continuously and independently of the system's larger adjustments" (Smelser, 1959, p. 11). Integration involves the establishment and maintenance of a harmonious relationship among parts of the system. Goal attainment refers to the ability of the system to define and attain specific goals in relation to the environment, and adaptation involves the external facilities and resources the system needs in order to achieve its goals. The adaptive facilities are broad enough to achieve a plurality of goals.

Although every system must simultaneously meet these four functional requisites to maintain equilibrium, our interest is in their function vis-a-vis development and change in the system. Consequently, I suggest a different application of the four system requisites, based on a phase-movement theory of group development (Hare and Effrat, 1968). Three phases of group development are herein specified.

In Phase I the dominant concern is with values and ideology (latent pattern maintenance), which must be made explicit as the initial formalization process occurs. This is the basic system problem at this stage since "A value *pattern* then defines a *direction* of choice and consequent commitment to action" (Parsons, 1968, pp. 135–160). Thus, the value pattern, operative from the embryonic phase of formation, sets the overall framework for the total social system. Although the values in part coincide with those of the broad social system, they may be disparate or more specialized in a particular sphere. Because values are enduring and least susceptible to change, they maintain their basic integrity through the developmental process, although the interpretation of the values and the emphasis placed on them vary in each successive phase. For example, within the framework of broad American social values, such as equal opportunity and minimal federal-government activity, cogent values are selected in regard to social welfare, such as the alleviation of poverty and the focus on individual adjustment (Wilensky and Lebeaux, 1958, pp. 33–41).

Phase II emerges as a result of changes in the external conditions which stimulated the initial development of the system and changes in the internal growth requirements. The primary functional requisites are now adaptation and integration. Given the value framework of the first stage, the system seeks to develop its techniques and to obtain relevant information in order to increase its resources and to improve performance of its central task. This shift results in an emphasis on means rather than on ends.

The third phase is again stimulated by change in the external environment and in the internal requirements of the system. Attention is focused on goal attainment and reclarification of objectives. Although the redefinition can be handled within the broad limits of the basic ideology of the system, more emphasis is now placed on less firmly grounded "precarious" values than on acceptable secure values (Clark, 1956, pp. 327–328). For example, the secure value regarding experienced professional performance can be questioned by precarious new and innovative styles of social work. In the third developmental phase, the system must move from an internally oriented posture back to an externally directed one as a sense of dissatisfaction emerges in relation to its position in society.

I examine the history of supervision in social work using this framework: Phase I—the beginnings of the profession (1870–1910); Phase II—the emergence of professionalism (1910–1950); Phase III—professionalism reexamined (1950–1970).

Beginnings of the Profession, 1870–1910

The value pattern which shaped the development of the profession of social work was clearly demarcated in the first phase of development. A clear-cut dichotomy emerged based on the structural foundations of the settlement house movement on the one hand and of the charity organization society (COS) on the other. The unifying ideological bond was the common concern with man and his plight in a modern industrial society. Yet separate and distinct value patterns were operative in these two organizational forms, and these patterns had far-reaching implications.

The COS was a logical development of a laissez-faire system which accepted the philosophy of self-reliance (Wilensky and Lebeaux, 1958, pp. 33–41). Thus, poverty was associated with personal inadequacy and defeat, and the role of the COS was to help with love and kindness, through identification with clients and uplift. "The enlightened benevolence of the present age . . . bids us give the poor 'not alms but a friend.' I would ask rather for both: alms are needed; but alms, to do real and lasting good, must come, and be known and felt to come, from a friend" (Charles J. Bonaparte, quoted in Pumphrey and Pumphrey, 1961, p. 190). "The best means of doing the poor good is found in friendly intercourse and personal influence. The want of money is not the worst evil with which the poor have to contend; it is in most cases itself but a symptom of other and more important wants. Gifts or alms are, therefore, not the things most needed—but sympathy, encouragement, and hopefulness" (R. E. Thompson, quoted in Pumphrey and Pumphrey, 1961, p. 177). Thus, the focus of COS workers was on the case, the individual, the family.

By contrast, the settlement house movement was sociologically oriented, focusing on the labor movement, economic reform, and community needs. "The very name, Neighborhood Guild, suggests the fundamental idea which this new institution embodies; namely, that, irrespective of religious belief or nonbelief, all the people, men, women, and children in any one street . . . in every working-class district in London shall be organized into a set of clubs . . . to carry out, or induce others to carry out, all the reforms—domestic, industrial, educational, provident, or recreative—which the social ideal demands" (Stanton Coit, quoted in Pumphrey and Pumphrey, 1961, p. 194).

These differences in philosophical orientation shaped the working relationships of the volunteers of the COS and settlement house movement. In the former, the approach was to formally guide new workers through the use of selected teaching materials, to emphasize learning by experience, and to accept the worker's need to identify with clients. The focus was on the development of skill in terms of its impact on the individual beneficiary.

Learning in the settlement house took place through observation and mutual exploration by equals. The field was social-science oriented, and a high value was placed on the interaction between social science and settlement house experience. The focus was on the importance of feedback to the general culture (Pumphrey and Pumphrey, 1961, pp. 202–203).

Supervision had its earliest development in the COS model. Interestingly, before 1890, all persons in the charity organization movement worked and learned together; however, by 1890, the introduction of a paid staff crystallized the differentiation of the experienced and the inexperienced worker (Burns, 1965, p. 785). The argument which justified the use of money collected by the charity societies for staff salary rather than for the poor is historically important because it helped change the system from a voluntary field to a profession.

> One lesson which few charitable societies have had the courage to teach as boldly as they should is that money for the poor can be spent in no better way than in providing workers who are always ready with the personal touch, who can best train volunteers and develop all charitable resources. . . . We use all the money that comes to us from subscriptions solely for salaries and other matters of administration, and we believe that money so used intelligently confers more benefit on the poor than money given for material relief. Material relief is a dangerous remedy; it must be administered with the greatest caution, just as in medicine we must be cautious in using nux vomica, arsenic, and similar drugs. They are beneficial if properly used, but deadly otherwise. . . . This is why we try to get first-rate persons as our officials and are constantly trying to raise the standard [Brackett, 1903, pp. 104, 107].

During this early period, the training of the worker was accomplished through various forms other than supervision. Although training was viewed as best done through lessons of experience from workers, in reality there were not enough trained workers to do the job. Consequently, the COS in New York City began to offer six-week summer institutes for COS staff. Other forms of training included weekly conference meetings, first described by Zilpha Smith from Boston as an opportunity to help the friendly visitors be more successful with their work. The program was voluntary, with group participation as the vehicle of learning (Pumphrey and Pumphrey, 1961, pp. 203–207). Another important tool for self-development was the *Manual for Visitors among the Poor* of the Philadelphia COS. The manual identified specific roles for the visitor and gave suggestions for successful contact. For example, not only did it discuss the personal style and attitudes of the visitor (for example nonpatronizing, sympathetic, and sensitive) but it also suggested use of community resources (for example, neighbors, hospitals, parks, and legal counsel) (Pumphrey and Pumphrey, 1961, pp. 176–181).

These devices sensitized the COS movement to the need for more effective methods of training. The conscious use of supervision consequently emerged and reflected the value placed on experience as the base for instruction. Interestingly, the structural form of supervision which was established in the first two decades is still the central mode (Burns, 1965, p. 785). This form includes regular, planned, and private conferences between supervisor and worker based on the worker's written records of his cases.

The value pattern of the COS movement thus shaped the emerging profession of social work in this first phase of development. The distinction between paid, experienced workers and volunteer, inexperienced workers led to the formulation of supervision as a device for improving service to individuals in need. The value pattern of the settlement house movement, oriented toward sociological and economic concerns, was not discarded but served as a minor, secondary influence in the emerging profession.

Emergence of Professionalism, 1910–1950

The theoretical framework specifies that Phase II emerges as a result of both external and internal requirements and that the system now must solve the central functional problems of integration and adaptation. Consequently, the system strives for the development of a harmonious relationship among its parts, while it simultaneously seeks to develop techniques and to increase its resources in order to improve performance of its task (which in turn reduces internal tensions).

From 1910 to 1950, the internal forces for change within the profession were compatible with the external forces in the larger social system. The social sciences were achieving importance in the academic sphere; these disciplines emphasized that social scientists and professionals should be value free and objective. In addition to this new value orientation emanating from the social sciences came the application of its body of knowledge, mainly in small-group process and dynamic psychology. Consequently, social reform activity was no longer viewed as a valid basis for professionalism (Wilensky and Lebeaux, 1958, p. 328), a position which supported the emerging interest in the individual client and his personal problems (especially because public agencies designed to focus on broad social problems were now in existence). The Freudian revolution was also well under way at this time and receiving broad acceptance on the American scene. Thus, the theories provided by the social sciences and analytic psychiatry filled the theoretical vacuum which existed in the profession. External resources required by the adaptive sector of the system were thus available in the form of intellectual formulations. These contributions were especially valuable because the profession was evolving from practice to theory rather than from theory to practice (Boehm, 1965, p. 644).

Because social work was actively identifying itself with the therapeutic professions, a malaise existed vis-a-vis its position. This new and self-conscious profession began to seek recognition, status, and authority. Simultaneously, the fact that social workers were performing therapeutic roles validated their status as society accepted this new professional activity. In addition, the new and untried public-welfare programs, which had yet to establish their credibility, required that persons filling the supervisory and administrative positions be well esteemed as professionals.

Perhaps the earliest crucial impetus for professionalism was provided by Flexner's paper "Is Social Work a Profession?" delivered at the 1915 National Conference on Charities and Corrections. But overall, Flexner concluded that social work was not a profession because it did not meet several of the basic criteria of professions. These criteria were: "professions involve essentially intellectual operations with large individual responsibility; they derive their raw material from science and learning; this material they work up to a practical and definite end; they possess an educationally communicable technique; they tend to self-organization; they are becoming increasingly altruistic in motivation" (Flexner, 1915, p. 581). Flexner accorded recognition to the social work profession for achieving only the last criterion. "Finally, in one respect in which most professions still fall short, . . . the rewards of the social worker are in his own conscience and in heaven. His life is marked by devotion to impersonal ends" (p. 306).

This critique undoubtedly stimulated conscious internal structural change in this struggling profession as Flexner was calling attention to a fundamental problem. These sources for change and the system's response are schematically presented in Table 1.

Table 1. EMERGENCE OF PROFESSIONALISM

Sources of Change	*Functional Requisites*	
	Integration	Adaptation
External	Social stability	Social-science knowledge Psychoanalytic theory
	Status for social work	New social-work services (public and psychiatric)
Internal	Quest for professionalism (status, power)	Therapist model
	Interdependence of worker and supervisor	Techniques and skills

Supervision became the tool for meeting the requirements of professionalism because there was little scientific basis for the role of the social worker. Supervision fostered cohesion and integration for the profession and for the larger system as well. Thus the social agency could be viewed as a microcosm of American society as all classes were involved in its operation, including the upper-class board of directors, the middle-class professionals, and the lower-class recipients of service (Robinson, 1949, pp. 148–149).

For the profession internally, the supervisory process fostered interdependence among the parts. The emphasis on technique and skill furthermore became the means by which the adaptation function was fulfilled because adaptation focuses on improving the performance of the central task, in this case service to clients.

The combined educational and administrative role of the supervisor was accepted without question in the second phase of professional development. While educational supervision emphasized the worker's learning in response to the unique and intangible aspects of his job, administrative supervision focused on transmitting to the worker relevant information about the agency, its requirements, rules, and regulations. With this development, social work committed itself to "learning while doing after the completion of formal training" and perfected "the unique tutorial program of supervision in which the . . . emotional and intellectual strengths of the . . . worker [are] amplified and weaknesses overcome" (Pumphrey and Pumphrey, 1961, pp. 286–287). "One never gets over needing this help" (Williamson, 1950, p. 42).

It is interesting to note an attempt on the part of leaders in the profession to demarcate the worker's growth and learning in order that the effectiveness of the supervisory process could be improved. Three stages of practice were specified. The worker with one to three years of experience needs to find his level of practice, rooting himself in the field by checking with others, rather than seeing how different he can be. The worker with three to five years of experience can be helped to develop his special gifts along with basic training. But emphasis is placed by agencies on building a well-rounded team in preference to exploiting individual talent: "While always ready to give special recognition where it is due, no staff can stand the singling out of one kind of ability. . . . Teamwork and a composite of abilities must be taken into account" (Austin, 1950, pp. 155–166). The worker with five to ten years' experience has real competence. After ten years, leadership for the future could be expected. Thus, the most striking and important aspect of the supervisory process was the dependence it engendered as the supervisor "assumed responsibility for the worker" (Hutchinson, 1935, p. 45).

The ultimate impact on the profession of this conscious refinement of supervision was that it eventually became equal in status and required as many financial resources as the direct service to clients. "By the end [of the 1930s] supervision was considered to be another specialized skill" (Pumphrey and Pumphrey, 1961, p. 287). The economics of supervision and direct casework service were examined in an important cost study in a casework agency in 1953 by Hill and Ormsby (p. 168). They reported that 42 percent of the costs were for interviewing (direct service to clients) and that 52 per cent of the costs were for processes related to supervision (recording, conferences, and consultations).

In addition to the educational and administrative functions, a third component was actively discussed and frequently included: therapeutic supervision. Although this aspect was always problematic and a consensus was never reached, it was an important dimension in the development of supervision.

> In other fields of clinical training it may be possible to lay more emphasis on . . . objective and concrete findings. . . . But it is certain that in work with family relationships this is never possible. The very conditions to be met are so common to us all and the personal reactions so emotionally upsetting to many of us that genetic relationships must always be borne in mind. The inescapable conclusion from this study is that adequate supervision of students in the mental hygiene field involves a certain amount of therapeutic approach. It is essential . . . that this be kept to a minimum and related only to casework failures or blockings [Lowrey, 1934, pp. xi-xii].

Although Lowrey limited the therapeutic function to a minimal level, this component of the supervisory process received other weightings throughout the next two decades. Wilson and Ryland (1949, pp. 534–538), in the first definitive group-work text, emphasized the therapeutic role. They defined the supervisor's function in terms of helping the worker: (1) to understand himself and change attitudes and behavior which block effective relationships; (2) to focus on his needs; (3) to strengthen his ego and ease a severe superego; and (4) to handle psychological transference and projection (namely, seeing the supervisor as a parent figure).

Thus, between 1910 and 1950, supervision became the tool for the development of professionalism. The profession was concentrating its efforts on defining and validating its position, and consequently the writings of this period focus on the definition of the supervisory process.

Professionalism Reexamined, 1950–1970

"We must always return more than we receive; the return is always bigger and more costly. . . . To give is to show one's superiority, to show that one is something more and higher, that one is *magister*. To accept without returning or repaying more is to face subordination, to become a client and subservient, to become *minister*" (Mauss, 1967, pp. 63, 72). As specified by the theoretical framework, the next phase of the developmental process was stimulated by both internal and external events: Supervision as an integral educational process in social work had the unanticipated consequence of fostering dependence in some workers; and, at the same time, the larger social system clearly did not accord social work the same recognition and status that were accorded to the other professions. Attention became focused on a reclassification of the objectives of the profession and of the agencies through which service is given, that is, the focus riveted on the goal-attainment function. Although the basic value pattern of the profession was not called into question, emphasis was placed on the less firmly grounded precarious values as the basic issues of the profession (discussed at the beginning of the chapter) came sharply into focus.

The writings in the professional literature in the 1950s revolved around two issues in relation to supervision: dependence versus autonomy, and administrative structure. Underlying these issues was the fact that the accepted and secure value of having the older, experienced worker as teacher and model for the new and inexperienced worker was at risk. Emphasis was placed on the precarious value of innovation and fresh approaches to service. Meyer (1959, p. 336) noted that not only was dependence an intraprofessional matter between supervisor and worker but the tendency to form dependent relationships was perpetuated on an interprofessional basis with colleagues in medicine, law, and psychiatry (1959, pp. 260–264). Vinter called attention to the hierarchical structure which centralized authority at the top, even though the complexity of the task and the discretionary role of the worker required a downward delegation of authority.

Predictably, new structural designs were developed to accomplish the objectives of supervision. A major suggestion was to separate the administrative function from the educational function: a person vested with power to evaluate, promote, or discharge a worker could not simultaneously perform the crucial educational task. A second suggestion was to restructure the educational process by abandoning the one-to-one supervisory relationship pattern. Specific proposals included a variety of organizational forms, all based on the principle of collegiality rather than authority. For example, because the M.S.W. implies competence, supervision for those with a master's degree should be used as a resource, available but not imposed (Scherz, 1958, pp. 435–443). Group supervision should be developed based on peer group learning and consultation, not group process or group therapy (Judd, 1962, pp. 96–102). Use of worker's records as the basis of learning and supervision should be replaced by observation as well as by direct help and teaching (Miller, 1965, pp. 83–89). Supervision should be time-limited with the objective of developing self-reliance and leadership.

Interestingly, in spite of the internal awareness of the need for change in the supervisory process, the implementation of change can be attributed directly to the external events of the 1960s. First, the civil rights movement and the anti-poverty program had a powerful impact as they raised questions regarding the interstitial nature of the profession. Specifically, the identification of the worker with agency function or middle-class society's dictates was viewed as incompatible with the primary requirement of meeting clients' needs. The demand that the worker function as the client's advocate required a loosening of the structure of supervision, which served a controlling, status-quo–oriented function.

Second, the constraints of professionalism were questioned as the community-organization method emerged. "In accepting a political mission, social workers in general and community-organization workers in particular . . . have to accept the fact that at this point in history social work is closer to the social-movement end of the continuum than to the 'professional' end" (French, 1967, p. 18). If professionalism was being questioned, the process of supervision was necessarily at risk.

Third, new recruits into social work were frequently participants in and products of the counterculture, ready to reject traditional forms in the quest for a more equitable society (Roszak, 1969). They were not too easily socialized into the profession and served as a strong impetus for change of an already crumbling structure.

Finally, newly developed, publicly funded programs (for instance, the community mental-health centers) as well as emerging public-welfare social services stimulated a new debate concerning the form and function of supervision in a radically revised context (Kneznek, 1966).

Thus, supervision was sharply questioned and structurally revised as a result of the reexamination of professionalism, its objectives and methods, in the third phase of development.

Summary and Conclusions

This chapter has examined the historical development of supervision from a structural-functional point of view, with an emphasis on the issues raised and functions served for the profession of social work by the supervisory process. A theoretical framework of phase development has guided the analysis.

Phase one was identified as "the beginnings of professionalism, 1870–1910." The primary problem in this period was the specification of a value-pattern which would shape the development of the profession. Thus, the ideology of the charity organization society was dominant with its emphasis on the individual client and the social worker's role as developed and improved by experience. The ideology of the settlement house movement, which stressed social science and economics, became a secondary theme.

The second phase, "the emergence of professionalism, 1910–1950," focused on the integration of the profession both in the fostering of harmonious class relationships for the larger society as well as the internal interdependence of parts (namely, the supervisor and the worker). The adaptive requirements of this phase were met as the profession sought to develop techniques and to increase its resources in order to better perform its task, which in turn served to reduce internal tensions.

The third phase, "professionalism reexamined, 1950–1970," emerged as a result of internal and external dissatisfactions with the supervisory process and its consequences for the profession. Consequently both the means and ends of the profession were reexamined in relation to the changing social context. Specific structural changes in supervision resulted.

This analysis points up the often unanticipated and ironic consequences of structural aspects of social systems. Supervision was formalized as the vehicle for the development of professionalism, but in reality it served the opposite function. It encouraged and perpetuated dependence and prevented the acceptance of social work as a full-fledged profession both internally and externally.

CHAPTER 2

Comparison of Educational Models and Their Influences on Supervision

Alex Gitterman

In reviewing the literature of educational philosophers and psychologists, a variety of critical theoretical issues consistently emerges, particularly the nature of motivation, learning, and teaching. In this chapter, I group these issues into three distinct models: (1) the subject-centered model; (2) the student-centered model; and (3) the integrative model. I trace the history of the models and examine their respective educational ideologies. The specification of major concepts provides the opportunity for building theoretical links to the literature of social-work educators and theoreticians. Three parallel social-work supervisory models emerge: (1) organization-centered models; (2) worker-centered models; and (3) integrative models. I also trace the history and ideology of each of these models. Finally, I assemble excerpts from supervisory conferences to illustate the practical and operational implications of the divergent theoretical models.

Subject-Centered Model

The subject-centered model can be identified with the early philosophy of mental discipline. According to this doctrine, education reflects a process of disciplining or training minds. Consequently, mental exercise, particularly in difficult or abstract subjects, strengthens the cognitive faculties in a manner almost analogous to muscles being strengthened by lifting weights. Firm self-discipline was regarded as essential to learning; the desired outcome, according to Morris Bigge (1964, p. 21), "consisted of harmonious development of all of one's inherent powers so that no one faculty was overdeveloped at the expense of others."

The Socratic teaching method is associated closely with the mental disciplinarian. Knowledge is perceived as inborn and available, but requiring expert questioning for the purpose of recall. Consequently, the Socratic teacher skillfully asks students leading questions until they identify and recognize "correct" answers. Highet (1950, p. 88), describing Socrates as a master teacher, explains: "Here the teacher does not talk. He asks questions, and the pupil talks. But the questions are so arranged as to make the pupil conscious of his own ignorance and to guide him towards a deeper truth, which he will hold all the more firmly because it has not been presented to him ready made but drawn out of his own mind." An interesting example of the Socratic method is provided by Broudy (1963, pp. 12–13). He uses an illustration in which Socrates attempts to teach a slave boy a complicated theorem. After asking various leading questions, Socrates asks: "Are you prepared to affirm that the double space is the square of the diagonal?" To which the slave boy responds: "Certainly, Socrates." The illustration suggests that the boy learned to respond, "Certainly, Socrates," rather than to acquire a knowledge of a complicated theorem through complex deductive logic. In essence, whether learning took place beyond following the cues of the teacher is questionable.

Thus, the Socratic method perceived knowledge as being inborn, requiring leading questioning for the purpose of recall. But, John Locke, in the seventeenth century, questioned the conception of innate faculties. He perceived the mind as being empty at birth, a *tabula rasa,* and believed that ideas were arrived at through the senses. He perceived knowledge as emerging from sensory experiences and his writings thus shifted focus from mental discipline to the formation of habits. He perceived man as being morally neutral and psychologically passive. He wrote (1912, p. 70): "In the reception of simple ideas, the understanding is for the most part passive. . . . As the bodies that surround us do diversely affect our organs, the mind is forced to receive the impressions, and cannot avoid the perception of those ideas that are annexed to them." In essence, Locke and his disciples identified the mind as a storing house for external sensory impressions (see Scheffler, 1965, pp. 131–143). The learner remains passive; the soul of teaching was the feeding of organized sensory stimuli. Thus, the teacher had the responsibility and the power of organizing the sensory experiences and shaping the passive learner. Locke (1959) pointedly describes his conception by asking the question: "Let us then suppose the mind to be . . . white paper, void of all character, without any ideas; how comes it to be furnished? . . . To this I answer, in one word, from experience. . . . Our observation . . . supplies our understanding with all the materials of thinking." Johann Herbart further advanced the Lockean philosophy. (See Herbart, 1901; Eby, 1952, ch. 18.) He wrote (1895, p. 120): "The soul has no innate natural talents nor faculties whatever. . . . It has originally neither concepts, nor feelings, nor desires. It knows nothing of itself and nothing of other things; . . . [it has] no laws of willing and action and not even a minute predisposition to any of these." However, he believed that ideas were active, constantly connecting with other ideas, dynamically controlling sensory experience. He referred to this process as apperception (1895, pp. 63–64). In sum, the mind was conceived of as insignificant compared to ideas, in fact, the mind was "little else than the battleground for contending ideas" (Adams, 1897, p. 50).

Because Herbart attributed to ideas the essential power of seeking out companion ideas, or banding ideas together, frequent repetition became a central teaching principle as a key to the formation of habitual responses. A primary teaching function was the selection and arrangement of subject material, primarily through the use of elaborate lesson plans which contained both appropriate questions and answers. Teachers were expected to identify what their students needed to learn, and students were expected to conform to the prescription.

Near the beginning of the twentieth century, Edward Thorndike and John Watson introduced a behaviorist psychology. They differed from their predecessors in that they became more interested in the physiology of the body than in the association of ideas. This emphasis upon physiological processes was considered a crucial step in fashioning psychology into a true science. Thorndike attempted to link the mental process with its physical counterpart. Specifically, he perceived learning as the connection of stimulus and response. He assumed (1913, p. 1) that through environmental conditioning, specific responses were linked with specific stimuli.

> A man's nature and the changes that take place in it may be described in terms of the responses—of thought, feeling, action and attitude—which he makes and of the bonds by which these are connected with the situations which life offers. Any fact of intellect, character, or skill means a tendency to respond in a certain way to a certain situation—involves a *situation* or state of affairs influencing the man, a *response* or state of affairs in the man, and a *connection* or bond whereby the latter is the result of the former.

Consequently, the art of teaching was perceived in mechanical terms—a matter of giving and withholding stimuli which would produce or prevent certain responses. The teacher had within his provinces the power to produce positive movement and to prevent undesirable responses.

Watson, on the other hand, based his assumptions on the laws of physics and chemistry. (See Watson, 1924.) He was strongly influenced by Pavlov's experiments and supported the latter's finding that learning was a process of building desired conditioned reflexes through the substitution of reward stimuli. (See, for example, Hilgard and Bower, 1966, pp. 48–73.)

B. F. Skinner is a leading exponent of the contemporary stimulus-response associationist frame of reference. He moved away from Watson's concern for precise identification of physiological mechanism but continued the emphasis upon the linkage between stimuli and responses. Of interest to him was the provision of a reinforcement stimulus following the subject's response. In the application of Skinner's formulation to a class, the teacher provides external reinforcement like praise or gold stars when a student gives the correct response. Teachers control the educational process and through the use of reinforcement, develop fixed responses.

Basically, the theory attempts to predict and control human behavior. Learning is broken down into specific steps, and a schedule of reinforcement is developed in a progressive manner. Skinner suggests (1954, pp. 86–97) that the teaching machine is an efficient and productive device for education. Thus, if a teacher wants to teach any subject, he can analyze the specific behaviors involved and develop an instructional program for machine use (Skinner, 1958, pp. 969–977).

What do the above models have in common, and why have I chosen to group them together as subject-centered models? Philosophically, the models perceive people as being relatively passive and controlled by their environment. The doctrine of cause and effect underlies the frame of thought. The teacher controls the process of education through the selection of curriculum and the inculcation of material into the students. Jerome Bruner (1968b, p. 83) identified this doctrine as the "expository mode" of teaching in which the "pace and style of exposition are principally determined by the teacher as expositor; the student is the listener."

John Dewey (1947, pp. 4–5) describes this model of education as "one of imposition from above and from outside. It imposes adult standards, subject-matter, and methods upon those who are only growing slowly toward maturity. Learning here means acquisition of what is already incorporated in books and in the heads of the elders." It takes much into account, except "vital energy seeking opportunity for effective exercise" (Dewey, 1922, p. 84).

Learning is perceived as a logical, intellectual process. The subject matter is identified in its end form, separated from the context from which it emerged. Learning is described as the incorporation of generalized abstractions which are to be learned in a predefined order, in a given amount of time, through the skillful manipulation of the teacher. One method of teaching is through asking students questions to which the teacher knows the correct response. Nathaniel Cantor asks (1966, p. 67): "Then why ask the question?" His answer is: "To discover whether the pupil can repeat the teacher's or textbook's answer. This tests whether the pupil can repeat what the teacher knows."

Motivation for learning is considered outside the learner's capacity and within the power of the teacher. Man's behavior is viewed as the result of conditioning which produces reflex responses at the introduction of stimuli. Consequently, reward and punishment stimuli provide the basic motivation. Bruner (1968b, pp. 87–88) perceives this motivational process as unhelpful and uneducative: "Much of the problem in leading a child to effective cognitive activity is to free him from the immediate control of environmental rewards and punishment. Learning that starts in response to the rewards of . . . teacher approval . . . can too readily develop a pattern in which the child is seeking cues as to how to conform to what is expected of him."

Student-Centered Model

The student-centered model can be traced back to the works of Rousseau. Rousseau's philosophy was a response to the traditional educational theorist. Man was perceived by him as being good and highly active in relation to his environment. Basic evil emerged from society and from the constrictions which society placed upon the individual. Consequently, the child required protection from society. Rousseau admonished (1911, p. 6): "From the outset, raise a wall around your child's soul" in order that he not be engulfed by "the crushing force of social conventions." Rousseau's child is possessed by innate beauty which he needs to unfold naturally. The major responsibility of the teacher is to protect the child from external forces. "When our natural tendencies have not been interfered with by human prejudice and human institutions, the happiness alike of children and of men consists in the enjoyment of their liberty. . . . Nature provides for the child's growth in her own way, and this should never be thwarted. Do not make him sit still when he wants to run about, nor run when he wants to be quiet. If we did not spoil our children's will by our blunders, their desires would be free from caprice" (Rousseau, 1912, pp. 49–50).

Rousseau perceived teaching as an imposition of ideas or conventions upon the child. He equated learning with growth and development, and it could occur only when the child was left alone. "Give your scholar no verbal lessons; he should be taught by experience alone; never punish him for he does not know what it is to do wrong; never make him say 'Forgive me,' for he does not know how to do you wrong. Wholly unmoral in his actions, he can do nothing morally wrong and he deserves neither punishment nor reproof. . . . Therefore, the education of the earliest years should be merely negative" (pp. 54–57).

In assessing Rousseau's philosophy, one is struck by its reactive tone. Principles are oft stated in terms of what should not be done. Dewey (1947, p. 6) identified the dangers inherent in developing a new movement: "In rejecting the aims and methods of [the movement] which it would supplant, it may develop its principles negatively rather than positively and constructively."

Froebel, father of the kindergarten movement, identified himself with Rousseau's interpretation of the child-society relationship. Froebel's child was good and only became distorted by outer influences (1887, p. 121). Play assumed a central place in Froebel's schools (kindergarten means garden for children). He felt that through play, children reached out to the external world and exercised control and mastery over their environment. Play was important because it represented the first means of developing the human mind (Marenholz-Bulow, 1895, p. 67).

In the student-centered model, self-expression, growth, and development become both the desired means and the desired ends. The fulfillment of the child's developmental needs is the ideal. Dewey (1966, p. 9) captures the banner flown by this model: "The child is the starting point, the center, and the end. . . . To the growth of the child, all studies are subservient; they are instruments, valued as they serve the needs of growth. . . . Not knowledge or information but self-realization is the goal."

A typical slogan of the movement is : "We teach children, not subjects." An educational philosopher, Israel Scheffler, identified (1968, p. 38) the emerging dichotomy between subject and student. "Suppose I told you I had been teaching my son all afternoon. . . . You would have a perfect right to ask 'What have you been teaching him?' . . . Suppose . . . I said, 'Oh, nothing in particular, I've just been teaching him, that's all.' You would be at a loss to understand."

The subject-centered model and the student-centered model

seem to represent two fixed polar limits between which professional educators must choose. This conception is understandable. Dewey explains (1966, pp. 4–5): "It is easier to see the conditions in their separateness, to insist upon one at the expense of the other, to make antagonists of them, than to discover a reality to which each belongs. . . . We get the case of the child vs. the curriculum." He explains that this polarization of issues represents the history of man in which beliefs are formed in pairs, emerging as mutually exclusive either ors. Consequently, the history of education is fraught with "opposition between the idea that education is development from within and that it is formation from without" (Dewey, 1947, p. 1).

Integrative Model in Education

The integrative model emerges from two major concomitant influences in the early twentieth century—gestalt psychology and progressive education. The former originated in Germany. Max Wertheimer is credited with the initial formulation of the gestalt principles. (Kurt Koffka and Kohler are also credited with initial contribution. See Koffka, 1935, p. 35.) The major thesis is expressed in the word *gestalt,* which refers to an organized pattern, a configuration, a whole rather than isolated parts. "The gestaltists insist that the attributes or aspects of the component parts, insofar as they can be defined, are defined by their relation to the system as a whole in which they are functioning (Murphy, 1949, p. 288)." They perceived the relationship between man and his environment in relativistic terms. Thus, people, situations, or objects derive their characteristics from their relationship to other people, situations, or objects. For example, a homely girl, seen with homelier girls, appears pretty. Her attractiveness is judged in the context of the total situation.

Kurt Lewin popularized gestalt psychology in the United States. He attempted to make it scientific by using laws of physics and geometry, and he developed a cognitive field theory. His theory (1936; 1951) attempts to explain how people learn about their environment and themselves and how they use what they learn. The major theoretical principles are: (1) relativism; (2) human behavior is purposeful, and consequently intellectual processes are highly influenced by an individual's goals; (3) a situation must be described through the eyes of the perceiver (for example, a teacher must look through the eyes of a learner); (4) a situation must be grasped as whole—the field—and from there one can proceed to an analysis of its parts; and (5) events occur simultaneously and interdependently; whatever the length of time, everything goes on at once rather than one event causing another (Bigge, 1964, p. 21).

William H. Kilpatrick is recognized as the leader of the progressive-education movement (Tanebaum, 1951), and Dewey is its major spokesman. A. L. Cremin (1954, p. 24) credits Dewey with tracing the beginning of the movement to the work of F. W. Parker. Their philosophy was frequently criticized and equated with that of Rousseau. Consequently, some of their initial efforts were in differentiating their ideas from the student-centered model. Dewey (Tanebaum, 1951, p. vii) identified the planning and direction necessary in education: " 'Progressive education' . . . implies direction; and direction implies foresight and planning. And planning . . . implies taking thought." He pointed out (1966, p. 41) that the student needed a large degree of freedom but that he did not advocate turning children loose or simply indulging their needs. "All children like to express themselves through the medium of form and color. If you simply indulge this interest by letting the child go on indefinitely, there is no growth that is more than accidental. But let the child first express his impulse, and then through criticism, question, and suggestion bring him to consciousness of what he has done and what he needs to do, and the result is quite different." Kilpatrick also addressed himself (1926, p. 208) to the criticism that he favored allowing children to do whatever they wanted. "Suppose a child wishes to do wrong; then I wish him stopped, caught, redirected, educated in some way, so that (a) he shall learn that what he had proposed was wrong; (b) he shall learn why it was wrong. . . . Is this wishing him to do as he pleases?" Thus, freedom is perceived relativistically, as a means and not an end. Whether the freedom is meaningful, then, depends upon what is done with it and what purpose it serves.

Dewey, like the gestalt psychologists, attempted to develop an integrative philosophy. He identified the polarities between the subject and the child which carry over to other subdichotomies: discipline versus freedom; logical versus psychological; structure versus spontaneity; and conformity versus individuality. He urged that a middle position be taken, one that avoided both the extreme of authoritarian control and of total permissiveness.

For this integration to materialize, Dewey developed two major principles: experience and interaction. The philosophy of the first principle is based upon the existence of an organic link between education and personal experience. Education is perceived as a continuous process, moving from the learner's personal experience into an organized theory. Dewey urges the re-creation of the abstract world as a means of making studies have personal meaning rather than being merely symbolic memorization. He also urges (1966, pp. 11, 22) enabling students to involve themselves in problem solving and personally experiencing the living character of the abstractions.

The second principle, interaction, purports that subject materials have to be adapted to the needs and capacities of the student, and, concomitantly, the student has to adapt himself to the subject. For the student, this adaptation necessitates an active search, risk, and, at the same time, passive meditation and understanding (1947, p. 163). For the teacher, adaptation requires the ability to structure opportunities so that the student may interact with his environment (1938, p. 33).

Dewey suggests that the principles of experience and interaction do not in themselves represent education. Rather, the *quality* of the experience and the interaction determine education. Thus, we do not simply "learn by doing" (1947, p. 16). This idea brings us to a difficult question: What is quality education? What are the desired outcomes identified by Dewey and the gestaltist?

Several specific valued outcomes clearly emerge. First, through the reconstruction of experiences, the student learns by self-discovery or insight. He develops a sense of the context or the relationship between previously perceived isolated experiences. The realization belongs to the learner as he discovers the existing pattern. For example, one might introduce a young child into the world of colors by identifying the various color combinations in relationship to the primary colors. The teacher may impart his own "insights" or generalizations, but these do not represent insight for the child until he grasps the relationship himself. Alternately, one might introduce the child to colors by structuring the experience so that he has the opportunity to experiment and to make discoveries for himself, to experience an "aha" or insight.

Second, initial insights are frequently limited to a single experience. The child has gained a more valued experience, however, when related isolated insights are turned into a larger discovery or a higher level of abstraction and generalization. These generalizations serve as an umbrella for the previously isolated "ahas" and provide the opportunity to condense and transfer the learning.

> Emphasis on discovery in learning has precisely the effect on the learner of leading him to be a constructionalist, to organize what he is encountering in a manner not only designed to discover regularity and relatedness, but also to avoid the kind of information drift that fails to keep account of the uses to which information might have to be put. [Personal discovery] helps the child to learn the varieties of problem solving, of transforming information for better use, helps him learn how to go about the very task of learning [Bruner, 1968b, p. 87].

Thus, one condenses by generalizing and transfers by recognizing new ideas or situations as similar to other ideas or situations for which the thinking and behavior have been appropriate. For learning to take place, a change in the thinking processes must occur. Bruner (1968b, p. 77) captures the primary emphasis upon thought process: "Perhaps the fitting ideal is . . . the active pragmatic ideal of leaping the barrier from learning into thinking. It matters not what we have learned. What we can do with what we have learned: that is the issue."

The final valued outcome is the development of intrinsic self-directed motivation rather than externally received reinforcement. The latter restricts the learner as he is manipulated by the outside world, responding to the giving or withdrawal of love, grades, or gold stars. "External reinforcement may indeed get a particular act going and may even lead to its repetition, but does not nourish reliably the long course of learning" (Bruner, 1967, p. 128). However, the former requires the student to identify a purpose, a task to pursue. Intrinsic motives require that the learner be self-propelled to master his learning tasks and that the rewards come from the work and its fulfillment. Thus, curiosity and desire for competence become both the motives and the rewards: "The will to learn is an intrinsic motive, one that finds both its course and its reward in its own exercise" (Bruner, 1967, p. 128). The discovery or insight becomes the reward itself.

Social Work Supervision: Organization-Centered Model

The Organization-Centered or Administrative Model had its roots in the early 1900s when agencies were primarily involved in the delivery of direct, concrete services, like public assistance and child placement. The goal of professional practice was one of uplifting the unworthy to the level of righteousness of the social workers. Because social workers possessed the right values, they "knew" what was best for their clients. Concomitantly, the worker's supervisor possessed the essential practice knowledge, values, and skills; the worker was assigned the job of apprentice. The supervisor attempted "to make over the worker, usually in his own image, seeming to say 'Do as I do and you will be right' " (Williamson, 1961, p. 41).

The supervisor, the "expositor," offered his expertise. Supervisors engaged primarily in didactic teaching which emphasized general concepts rather than an examination of specific cases. "A person can learn to apply his knowledge to a variety of situations more rapidly, more effectively and more creatively when his learning is based upon general theories and ideas than when it is based on specific knowledge gained in one case which he attempts to apply to another" (Scherz, 1958, p. 438).

Just as in the subject-centered model, the worker receives abstracted generalizations removed from empirical experience. The supervisor maintains control over the process either by providing the "correct" responses or by "socratically" leading the worker to the predefined solution. The following excerpts are from supervisory records and represent the practice of experienced supervisors working in various settings. The excerpts illustrate the supervisor "telling" the worker the correct responses rather than helping him to develop his own answers. "It sounded, I said, as though she felt that the other types of activity we had discussed, e.g., bingo, music group, etc., were not 'social work.' She responded, 'yes, that's it, it's just not dignified.' I explained why we provided these activities—patient enjoyment, opportunity for patient to decide how activity was to be conducted, [and] fostering friendship." The supervisor convinces and attempts to talk away the problem rather than explore the meaning of "not dignified." A similar pattern is evident in the following: "She [the supervisee] commented how difficult it was for her and how a change to a 'new approach' of work was frightening. I [the supervisor] explained, '. . . by controlling the action of the group by preconceived plans and constantly directing its actions, she felt safe and secure; that the uncertainty which accompanies one in flowing with the unexpected of group process was frightening.' She responded, 'I guess so.' "

The supervisor's attempt to teach replaces the ability to listen and partialize the supervisee's fright. The final comment, "I guess so" reflects upon the supervisor's "smartness," namely, that it was not much help. However, this particular supervisor achieved some insight into her supervisory pattern by the end of the record: "I did it again —I wonder if I am getting any closer to finding out why I'm compelled to 'teach,' to 'tell,' to 'lecture,' to 'exhort.' I suppose there are several reasons. Probably a major one being a need to prove to the student that 'I know something.' 'I seem to be thwarting the acorn's effort to become an oak tree.' " One can sense the supervisor's struggle to move beyond his own need to "teach" and instead to become a skillful and sensitive cooperative agent.

The remaining quotes illustrate the "socratic" teaching method in which the supervisee is led to the "correct" responses.

> I [the supervisor] stated that since she was dissatisfied with the contract that emerged, what had gotten in her way of raising this with the group. She [the worker] said, "I was frightened," and I asked, "Of what?" She said that they were more powerful than the people she had worked with in a previous ward. I asked her to explain and she stated that these people had told her what they wanted and that she felt that she had to go along with them. I asked what she saw as the worker's role in establishing contract. She replied, "To help the group explore what they wanted to do." I asked whether exploring alternatives was not a part of the worker's role. She replied that she hadn't thought of it and became silent.

One can easily feel the pull of the supervisor's questions, leading until the supervisee identified the "correct" answer. The supervisee's experience of being manipulated ends with a powerless silence. At a later point in the conference, the same pattern is evident:

> I asked her what she thought she should do and she said that she would like to keep her contact with Mrs. A. centered

> around her committee work. I asked her how might she do this and she said by telling her. I agreed and returned to the record where the group discussed not knowing what monies were available to them and asked why she backed off during this discussion. She said because she did not have the answer. I asked whether the worker was there to give the answers and she was again silent.

The supervisor again has a point that she wishes to make but instead asks a leading question. Her opportunity to move closer to the supervisee's experience is lost and replaced by a generalization about the worker's role.

Supervisors confront a serious problem when they do not have the correct answers. Because they have accepted the role of teaching masters, the supervisory problem is reduced to disguising lack of expertise. Alfred Kadushin has identified the consequent wide variety of "games" played out in the supervisory process (1968, pp. 23–37). One supervisor developed the strategy of throwing back to the supervisee the difficult question. While the supervisee was struggling for his own answer, the supervisor quickly tried to figure it out also. In this instance, supervision is perceived as an exclusively intellectual experience in which both supervisor and supervisee "figure out" the correct answer. Underlying this conception is the false assumption that "knowing" is equivalent to "doing." Thus, although both may develop much knowledge, they lack specific skills for translating the knowledge into action.

Worker-Centered Model

The worker-centered model emerged from three influences: (1) the movement of private agencies into treatment services; (2) the impact of psychoanalytic knowledge; and (3) the bestowing upon the university the responsibility of education for the professions. The first two developments resulted in a need for specialized staff training. Consequently, agencies introduced an educational component into the supervisory role. The supervisor had to assume responsibility for the "teaching and development of professional methodology" (Austin, 1957, p. 569). Furthermore, as the profession incorporated the Freudian medical-treatment model into its philosophy, the worker's personality structure became a key supervisory concern. Williamson (1961, p. 41) identified the effect of this new knowledge upon supervisory practices. "[There was] a tendency on the part of the supervisor to overinvolvement with the personality structure and the personal problems of the worker. . . . At its worst, the concerns of the real client grew dim, and the worker tended to become the client who *must* have personal problems, for to seem to be without them might signify supervisory failure to uncover and treat."

The concern of the supervisor moved from the administration and delivery of concrete services to the development of self-awareness because the knowledge of the self represented the primary "requisite in learning to engage in a professional helping relationship." Self-awareness is specifically defined as "the capacity of an individual to perceive his responses to other persons and situations realistically and to understand how others view him" (Nathanson, 1962, pp. 31–39). The supervisor became engrossed with the worker's learning to "feel" the right way, to develop personal insights, and to develop his personality.

In the student-centered model, the emphasis is upon protecting the learner from society's constrictions so that he can unfold naturally. In the worker-centered model, the emphasis is on providing the learner with personal insights to move beyond his constrictions and to continually grow and develop. In both models, subject matter is nonexistent; the personality receives exclusive attention. In supervision, self-awareness is treated as a final objective rather than as an essential ingredient for a helping person. The "why" of one's behavior becomes the central concern. An excerpt from a supervisory conference record (in personal files of the author) illustrates.

> He [the worker] stated that he went up to see whether or not any or all of the group members would be coming to the first meeting. He further explained that the members expressed fear in riding the elevators alone so that he wanted to ride down with them. As I [the supervisor] listened, my feeling was that the worker was primarily motivated to visit the members prior to the meeting as a way of making sure that they came to the meeting and as a result of his anxiety to make a good impression. I wanted him to gain this insight into himself and thus asked, "Why did you decide to go by for them— What were you thinking and feeling?" He looked as if he had been "caught" and laughed nervously, and replied that he really hadn't thought about it, and just "decided on the spur of the moment to go up for them." I said, "But you had to think about it,

> what was underneath your decision?" He continued to look "caught" and seemed to resent my probing. I asked, "Am I making you angry by asking these questions?" He denied his underlying anger and insisted "I simply went up to pick them up and that's all." I asked him how he was feeling when he went by their apartments. He explained that he was looking forward to the meeting and felt they would appreciate his picking them up. I asked him to look at his record in which he stated "Today I went up to see whether or not any member would be coming. . . ." He agreed that he really didn't know and this was part of the reason he went. I said, "Right, one of your underlying reasons was to influence the members to come to the meeting. Can you get an insight into yourself from this?" He sat in silence. After a while, I continued that if he didn't try harder he would miss an important opportunity to get beneath the surface and gain some self-understanding. At this point, he looked totally lost and I found myself getting impatient.

As the conference continued, the worker finally manufactured an apparent insight: "Yes, I realize, I'll have to work at not being controlling and manipulating." However, this insight apparently lacks meaning because the worker is experiencing and learning from the supervisor how to manipulate and control.

Focusing exclusively on the worker's personality structure often leads to self-consciousness and emotional constriction. Workers become occupied with their own feelings rather than with the acquisition of essential technical skills and the incorporation of these into their own personalities. Furthermore, although the organizational model confuses the relationship between knowing and doing, the worker-oriented model confuses the relationship between feeling and doing. In sum, if a worker develops self-insight, he has not necessarily acquired the skills to perform his job.

As social workers became increasingly more dissatisfied with the limited conception of administrative supervision and being told what was best, and as they became equally dissatisfied with being psychologized and made self-aware, the profession, particularly in the 1950s and early 1960s, identified the major methods of dealing with supervisory practices. One school of thought recommended the structural separation of administrative and educative supervision; another insisted upon a better integration. The former claimed that "the natural antipathy between administration and teaching in supervision lies deep in the history of supervision as a process" (Wideman, 1962, pp. 31–38).

Lucille Austin, a key advocate of the separation of administration and education, insisted that the problem went beyond the difference between good and bad supervision. She argues (1956, p. 376) that administration, as well as education, "is a highly skilled operation demanding full attention and specialization. . . . The combining functions lead to a conflict of roles and confusion for the worker; . . . the worker could function more profitably if he were exposed to a variety of contacts with agency personnel, rather than limited to one relationship." Various professionals attribute the fostering of dependency to the educational supervisory functions. "Supervision as an educational process has been maintained in many instances long after workers should have achieved the professional maturity necessary for continued growth without intensive supervision. Many social workers . . . question continuing the educational aspects of supervision beyond the time when a practitioner has achieved sufficient competence to take responsibility for planning and implementing his own professional development" (Reece, 1961, p. 63). Thus, the natural question of an organization's need for "accountability" and a professional's need for "freedom" becomes polarized.

One consequence of this false dichotomy was the elimination of the educational function or its limitation. (See Henry, 1955, pp. 34–49; Wax, 1963, pp. 37–43.) Another consequence was the emergence of a new structural position: the consultant. The intent was to remove the controls and authority from the supervisor: to implement availability without control (Aufricht, 1955, p. 48).

Integrative Model in Supervision

Other professionals called for a better integration of the supervisory, administrative, and educative responsibilities. They perceived the supervisory process in unitary terms rather than either administrative or educative terms. They dismiss this dualism in a manner similar to Dewey's not accepting the child versus curriculum dichotomy. They seek to find the administrative tasks in the educational ones and the educational tasks in the administrative ones. The writings of Jeanette Harford reflect this point of view: "An agency has a responsibility for the totality of its services and . . . teaching and administration cannot be separated if they are a true expression of that responsibility" (1955, p. 52). What emerges from this integrative process is the emphasis upon assisting workers with acquiring essential administrative and the needed helping skills. Schwartz (1968, p. 14) reflects upon this assertion by asking a pointed question: "When you are dealing essentially with the business of the exchange, the so-called 'administrative' aspects, what are the skills that have to be taught and learned? And, conversely, when you are dealing with 'feelings,' what are they about? One must learn to see the what in the how and vice-versa." The crux of the supervisory experience emerges from the client service demands and the essential skills necessary to provide the service.

Two major interrelated functions unite in the supervisory experience: (1) helping the worker provide the service of the agency effectively and (2) assuring accountability for the provision of the service. In relation to the former, Williamson (1961, p. 21) states: "The ultimate objective of worker supervision . . . is to implement agency purposes and plans and continually to deepen the quality of the services through which the agency seeks to express its purposes." The latter function stresses assuring accountability of the staff's and agency's services to its board of directors, its community, and its clientele. By focusing on the job to be done, and in being held accountable, the supervisory process is perceived as integrative. (See Miller, 1971, p. 1497.)

As in Dewey's educational model, the integrative supervisory model addresses itself to the relationship between "knowing," "feeling," and "doing." The technical competence of the worker (what he does) is the major area in which the professional differs from the nonprofessional. Clients judge professionals by their helping actions, by their ability to be of service and to "do," not by their diplomas or what they "feel" or "know." The model insists that although a professional needs extensive knowledge and appropriate feeling, the major challenge is the transmission of these into helping techniques and skills. Schwartz (1964, p. 4) captures this relationship: "there are 'knowers' who cannot help anybody and there are 'feelers' who cannot put their feelings to use in the service of people. . . . the client is not interested in his worker's store of knowledge, in his aspirations for humanity, or even in his degree of self-awareness; always his questions will be: does he seem to know what to do for me, and has he been able to help me?" The supervisor must transmit his personal knowledge, intuition, and insight into creative and descriptive helping actions. The supervisory process is a microcosm of the helping process itself. The supervisor has to model that which he is teaching. This modeling requires the integration and methodological application of a complex variety of educational, administrative, and helping skills. The following excerpts (from personal files) illustrate a few of these skills.

> R came in at one o'clock and seemed worried. She stated that she was worried about her relatives' group. She didn't feel helpful, involved, connected, etc. She said loudly, "I just don't know what to do; I am at the end of my rope." (In previous conferences, I found myself either becoming overwhelmed by her despair and making psychological interpretations, prematurely reassuring her, or directly solving her concerns. I was determined to help her begin to assume greater responsibility for various practice binds). I said, gently but firmly, "in our first few conferences, we haven't looked at your records; you have a lot of material; let's look at your concerns more specifically. Why don't you begin reading the record?" She hesitated, stating that parts were left out and the recording wasn't really accurate about what happened; she forgets to record important things. I said firmly, but gently again, that she had recorded a lot of material—we should look at what was in there before we learned about what wasn't, and again asked her to begin reading. She paused, looked at me, and I encouraged her to begin. She shook her head in agreement and began to read clearly. She read the contracting at the beginning of the group and said that she wondered; is it OK? I asked her what she thought. She responded that her efforts were very specific, but she did talk too much. She thought some more and continued that she did get what she wanted and the people seemed to dig into their concerns right at the beginning. I added that I thought that her being very specific about many of their concerns certainly helped them make a beginning.

The supervisor struggles to reverse previous efforts at psychologizing the worker's problem, offering immediate reassurances, or teaching. He offers the worker a new method, one in which both have responsibilities, but each has his own role. The supervisor demands focus, clarifies the boundaries, and encourages the worker to examine her practice. The worker begins to assume responsibility and to direct the vital energy essential for any intellectual pursuit. The supervisor's emphasis upon a line by line examination of the record material sets the context of their exchange and keeps the work specific, concrete, and operational. As the conference continues, the worker becomes increasingly self-propelled, experiencing the freedom and reward of successfully directing her own inquiry.

> We got to the part of the record where one relative began talking about problems with unexpected bowel movements with the patient at home. The relative asked R a question to which she didn't know the answer. R offered to invite a doctor to the next group meeting. She read on, but I stopped her and said: "I feel that you have missed the relative's concerns. Let's go back into the experience. What were your feelings at that moment?" She began to laugh uncomfortably and spoke about the whole bowel movement business making her uncomfortable. I asked her: "What did you feel at that moment?" After a pause, she responded that at that moment she didn't really want to listen, get too closely involved with the relatives *re* giving patients digitalis. I responded that I could understand and suggested that she might have felt hopeless. "Like what good is talking about these things going to do?" She agreed, describing her anxiety and a sense of being trapped by it. After having her assume the role of the relative and obtain a "feel" for the specific underlying concerns, we role played different ways in which she might have reached for the member's concerns. She particularly liked her idea of reflecting the member's concern to the group, asking whether anyone else had similar concerns or experiences. I found myself being caught in her excitement as we both threw ourselves into the role playing. R searched the record for other places where she disconnected and suggested a doctor to "explain" the reasons behind problems, e.g., bowel movements, catheter, sex. She exclaimed: "Wow, I see how I ran away—that was really scary, but I do sense how I will do it differently next time." This felt good to me. I realized that my previous conference in which I lectured or solved questions must have been experienced by R as real aggressivity, an assault, rather than what I had intended, a giving of my expertise.

When supervisor and worker assume their respective responsibilities, they experience the opportunity to work freely and creatively. Their work becomes characterized by a common focus, a sense of purpose, and direction. The supervisor helps the worker to reexperience the situations in which she disconnected from her clients rather than discussing them abstractly. The reconstruction of experience provides the opportunity for both supervisor and worker to struggle to integrate the logical and psychological, the content and the affect. At the same time, the obstacles in the worker's practice become partialized into manageable pieces and then generalized into meaningful patterns. Finally, the supervisor becomes the model of the professional person that he is trying to assist the worker to become.

Conclusion

I have tried to group and interrelate three models of education with three models of social-work supervision in both theory and practice. I have an obvious bias toward the integrative model. In its complexity, the model is extremely simple; and in its simplicity extremely complex. It provides us with a rich perspective of the organic link between teacher and student, supervisor and worker. The process of learning and doing is presented as an active, ongoing pursuit, characterized by a focus, sense of purpose, and emotional energy. Both teacher and learner have a major function to perform. Their functions are interrelated, and when fulfilled, the outcomes of their joint efforts are greater than their individual contributions. In essence, learning and doing represent the process of life, and, in turn, life represents the process of learning and doing.

CHAPTER 3

Changing Functions and Structures

Archie Hanlan

This chapter analyzes and proposes a restructuring of social-work supervision through the concepts of function, structure, and process. These three concepts are employed here as analytic tools which cut across several theoretical approaches to social work. Specifically, the concepts go beyond the usual dichotomy of so-called diagnostic and functional approaches in social work. The three terms are used in many disciplines, especially in the social-science literature on administration, and they generate a particularly useful way of reexamining social-work supervision. This particular analytic framework should aid in explicating emerging trends in supervision which serve the values of the profession and its primary commitment to various consumer groups.

One central dilemma in traditional social-work supervision is an inherent value conflict. Both diagnostic and functional social-work educators have made reference to this conflict. For at least the past twenty years, social-work literature has clearly indicated dual functions in social-work supervision, namely, teaching and administration. For example, Lydia Rappoport (1969, p. 454) has said: "What may be laid down (by non-social–work administrators) as desirable program goals and procedures may be at variance with professional values and professional conceptions regarding the nature of and the needs of human beings."

This conflict between professional social-work values and administrative values has also been noted by Ruth Smalley (1969, p. 33). She has stated that social work must choose "whether it wants to be a single profession or whether it is to split down the middle with social planners and social administrators embracing one set of goals [and the] values and educational curricula to reflect those values and goals . . . [or whether it wants to focus on] social services delivered through direct-service method, articulating other values, goals, and [the] curricula that reflect them." Thus, two respected social-work educators operating on different psychological theories, Rappoport and Smalley, agree on a concern that the agency administrator will not reflect the values and goals of the social-work practitioner.

I will argue another hypothesis in this chapter. It is commonly assumed that social workers with a master's degree, whether they are in direct practice, a supervisory position, or an administrative position, share a basic set of professional values and goals. (See Hanlan, 1970, pp. 41–53.) Given this assumption, the central problem is to assure the attainment of those goals. (This chapter addresses itself only to holders of the master of social work degree and not to the more complicated issues related to baccalaureate and paraprofessional workers.)

Major Concepts

Three major terms recur in the social-work literature on supervision. Every author emphasizes one of the terms over the other. I intend to demonstrate the relatedness of the three concepts of function, structure, and process. Further, I will attempt to demonstrate that these terms, as they are employed conceptually by writers outside of social work, are used broadly and should enable us to gain a new perspective on social work supervision.

Function most frequently refers to specific programs and services provided by a particular agency in a particular community. Thus, agency function includes and subsumes the objectives and purposes of all forms of social-work practice in a variety of agency settings. Social-work supervision, for the purposes of this chapter, refers to the functions of a supervisor within the agency. For example, as previously noted, the traditional functions of a social-work supervisor have been teaching and administration. The concept of function has been employed in a number of classical works on administration including the writings of Chester Barnard (1938) and Herbert Simon (1957). Simon has cautioned (1957, p. 38) that an exclusive focus on "functions and lines of authority is completely inadequate for purposes of administrative analysis."

Structure has been used in social-work literature to refer primarily to the administrative and organizational aspects of a particular agency. It is generally agreed that structure should follow from agency function, that is, the administrative and organizational arrangements of an agency should flow from and facilitate the accomplishment of agency objectives and purposes. Again, this use of the concept is consistent with that of Simon, who uses the term *functionalization* to link objectives, functions, and work tasks (1957, p. 192). The organizational structuring of social-work supervision within an agency should, then, be a key factor in the accomplishment of the agency's functions and objectives.

The third conceptual tool, process, refers here to the dynamic, interactional network which occurs among participants within the context of the function and structure of an agency. Occasionally critics claim that social work is too concerned with process. Wideman (1962, pp. 78–85) states that this concern is justified in regard to social work supervision. In contrast, however, Simon has noted (1957, p. 3) that the structure and function of any organization can only be understood in terms of the kinds of processes identified here. Indik (personal correspondence with the author) indicates that function, structure, and process are "heavily overlapping in meaning." (See also Indik, 1968.) Further, more recent developments in administration literature suggest that an open-systems theoretical viewpoint requires more than the rational model of agency function and structure.

Thompson has stated that "the rational model of organization results in everything being functional—making a positive, indeed an optimum, contribution to the overall result. . . . [It is no] accident that such views are dismissed using the open-system strategy." (See Thompson, 1967, p. 6, or Sharkansky, 1970.) In open-system terms, social-work supervision, as a process, is part of a changing, adaptive, nonstatic system of human interactions.

In the language of administrative and organizational theory, function and structure refer to rational, formal organization. Process refers to the informal organization, group dynamics, and decision-making behavior. Thus, as modern administrative theory requires the employment of all three concepts simultaneously in order to approximate an accurate view of an administrative system, a similar systems approach is required if we are to analyze and accurately reevaluate supervision. Only through a recognition of the interdependence and necessity for all three concepts can we provide ourselves with an integrative, holistic approach.

Functions

The dual functions of teaching and administration in social-work supervision have been described and accepted to some degree for the past two decades. Although an occasional article has called attention to tension in these dual functions, the general emphasis has been, as Wideman says (1962, p. 85), on "integrating the two functions." The major exception is a critical and innovative proposal by Lucille Austin (1956). Strangely, few social workers have pursued the creative suggestions she made. Before considering Austin's proposal, let us outline the usual supervisory functions.

The administrative function exists as a result of the agency's need for fiscal and service accountability. Accountability is necessary within the agency, to boards, and to the community at large. The supervisor serves in a managerial and hierarchical capacity. The worker is clearly accountable to the supervisor in his duties, and the supervisor is responsible to the next person up in the vertical line of command. The teaching function of the supervisor bears directly on the enhancement of the individual worker's professional knowledge and skill in providing service to clients. Presumably, one goal of teaching is to increase the autonomous practice of the social worker.[1] Thus, teaching is a matter of competence and not subject to hierarchical review in most professions.

From a systems point of view, the dual functions of the supervisor are interdependent with the functions of the agency as a whole. Thus, if the agency's function is to provide marital counseling, but not child placement, the supervisor's teaching function is already partially determined by the agency function. As suggested earlier, however, a sole concern with function can produce a narrow and distorted view of an agency. For example, many voluntary and public agencies are having to redefine their traditional functions because of growing pressure from community groups and funding sources, and as a result of an increasingly unstable administrative environment (Hanlan, 1971, p. 198). In this context, the functions of many social agencies cannot be assumed. The functions for which the agency was originally established may no longer be relevant or appropriate. For example, even the long established Community Service Society of New York has proposed a radical redefinition of its function in the community (*Social Work,* 1971, p. 3). This example dramatically illustrates that goals and objectives do not remain static and that agency functions are subject to change with redefinition.

The functions of the supervisor are also directly affected by this uncertainty and change. The merger of a number of small independent, sectarian agencies in Philadelphia under one administrative organization is one illustration of how the change in functions has broad ramifications throughout all levels of the organization (Barnett, 1971). In this particular case, the tension was particularly noticeable at the level of the first-line supervisor. The situation became critical when supervisors who formerly performed casework teaching functions were now required to train their staff and themselves in a wide range of community-organizing functions.

The move toward the separation of eligibility determination

[1] Autonomy has been defined by some social workers as existing when "the major portion of responsibility and decision-making in a case is left to the person carrying the case, rather than to a hierarchy of administrators." See Comess and O'Reilly (1966, p. 82).

and service in county welfare departments provides another dramatic example of a major change in agency function which directly alters the function of the social-work supervisor. (See Fisher, 1971, pp. 468–474.) In this instance, the separation policy requires that the supervisor no longer be allowed to determine eligibility for financial aid. This change has a cycle of interrelated effects in the organization. We can no longer automatically assume that the traditional functions of teaching and administration will continue to go hand in hand.

Structures

Just as agency function has determined supervisory function, agency structure determines supervisory structure. In the past, supervisory structure has tended to be the traditional, bureaucratic pyramid, the worker at the bottom reporting to the supervisor, and the supervisor reporting on up the line. As we have already noted, this structure is inappropriate for the teaching function and has created much tension. Clearly, we have not allowed function to determine structure. That is, if we were consistent in carrying out supervisory teaching, we would have long ago provided a nonhierarchical structure. Major goal displacement can and does occur with especially dysfunctional consequences. Wasserman (1971, pp. 89–95) has noted that in a hierarchical structure, "the supervisor's function had little or nothing to do with social-work values, knowledge and skills."

Partly in response to such dysfunctional arrangements, social-work literature indicates that some agencies have attempted to experiment with new ways of alleviating this inherent tension. Group, in contrast to individual, supervision has been advocated as a way of strengthening professional competence and autonomy among social-work peers rather than between superordinates and subordinates. (See, for example, Appleby and others, 1958, pp. 18–22; Fitzdale, 1958, pp. 443–450; Judd and others, 1962, pp. 96–102; Apaka and others, 1967, pp. 54–60.) Most of this literature stresses the goal of increasing the autonomy of the practitioner rather than changing the structure of supervision itself. Apparently, the more experienced workers in an agency get together spontaneously for group sharing, consultation and supervision, without making any formal, permanent structural revisions in the role of the supervisor within the agency. Group supervision stops short of basic structural changes and does not deal with pervasive problems. It may, in fact, complicate or add to existing structural tensions. The United States Army is one of the few examples of an agency which clearly and consistently followed up a separation of supervisory functions with an explicit and compatible organizational structure. Devis (1965) finds the function and structure of social-work supervision in the army compatible with Austin's suggestions and holds that the teaching and administrative functions for military social work have been clearly divided with separate administrative structures for each function. Devis claims an increased morale, autonomy, and effectiveness for the social-work practitioner. Civilian social work has made no such clear-cut distinctions nor followed them out with the logical, structural requirements for a social agency.

Studt (1965, p. 164) did suggest a downward delegation of the supervisory role into "the staff work group [for] leadership in program planning rather than the unilateral representation of upper authorities. Such a staff work group [becomes the collegial] reference group to which each member is responsible, encouraging each person to perform his function in service in a manner that is consistent with the commonly defined goals and enriching his understanding of the total service process." Although this idea is compatible with some of the emphasis placed on group supervision, Studt carries the idea into a more operational agency structure.

The division of administrative and teaching functions in supervision cannot be rationally considered unless one also attends to the structural requirements of such a separation. Austin proposes (1956, p. 381) that when the teaching function is separated out, it should be considered a staff development function. She emphasizes that the staff development position would become a staff, not a line, authority position. In such an arrangement, the teaching function is not hierarchical. Austin argues (p. 380) that "if the staff members who traditionally have been responsible for supervision were relieved of their administrative assignment, not only would they be able to give fuller attention to the education of the practitioner group, but they might conceivably have some time available for casework practice."

Austin's proposal is clearer in regard to teaching than it is in regard to administration. She goes on at some length in specifying the responsibility for evaluating the worker's performance. The social-work supervisor as administrator would "work directly with the casework staff and with students both for group meetings and through individual conferences for the purpose of developing and interpreting program, formulating policy, and of setting work requirements" (p. 381). Austin suggests, but does not spell out, the major structural changes that will have to occur within the agency to facilitate the division. She does appear to be one of the first proponents for the clear-cut separation of the functions, without a specific plan for the structuring of those separate functions.

To what extent can we justify the administrative function as a special social-work activity? Following through on the previous public-welfare illustration, if the determination of eligibility for financial aid were considered solely a supervisory administrative function, what would be the basis for requiring a professional social worker to perform this function? In terms of the needs of clients and humanizing the aid service, it would seem that social work has a special claim. But few social workers are trained in terms of the efficiency of aid payments and managerial and technical knowledge for facilitating fiscal procedures. It could well be argued, however, that a social worker with some managerial expertise would be of particular value to welfare clientele as well as to the agency.

Apparently, changes in agency and supervisory functions have not been accompanied by clearly thought out changing structures. One must then question the effectiveness of the change in functions not only from the staff's point of view but also from the point of view of increased effectiveness in service or the dysfunctional consequences of these modifications for people receiving the services of the agency. Apparently, the time is ripe for a clear cut separation of the teaching and administrative functions. Experimentation with a variety of approaches is called for. Studt's idea of delegating administrative responsibilities to the staff work group is compatible with the experiment of Kahle, who decentralized authority and responsibility to a collegial structure in a family-service agency (Kahle, 1969, pp. 21–28). The structural change must not become an end in itself for staff. It should rather be made for the purpose of improved services to clientele.

Process

If it is true that many agencies, faced with the need to change and adapt their functions and agency structures, have not yet experimented with new forms of supervision, an examination of supervision as a process may lead to additional clues for bringing about this desired change. Process is defined here as the transactions occurring over time between or among participants, usually a social worker and clients. Process in supervision encompasses comparable transactions between social worker and supervisor. In a larger sense, however, the process in a systems view, refers to the total, organized network of interpersonal relations between individuals and among groups within a social agency. Thus, rational delineations of function and structure are constantly subjected to and bounded by less rational influences of staff and clientele. Social-work supervision, then, is a process focused on the supervisor and social worker, but constantly impinged upon by interpersonal events.

In a study of two social agencies, Blau and Scott (1962, p. 115) concluded that the supervisor is "the connecting link between the formal organization and the work group." A broad view of the process of supervision, then, enables us to perceive the critical interplay among function, structure, and process. From this perspective, supervision is a critical level of the organization for understanding these interactions and for making any rational efforts to achieve desired changes in a social agency.

In the earlier illustration of merged sectarian agencies, many, if not all, of the conflicting forces which followed agency changes in functions seemed to converge on the supervisor. At that particular level of the organization, one could view the impact of client, staff, and administrators in the effort to restructure an agency and provide increased contemporary services in the community.

This conceptualization of process serves as a sensitizing idea similar to that of collective disturbance noted in the studies of efforts to develop therapeutic communities in psychiatric hospitals (Caudill, 1958). Evidence suggests that unless we are sensitized to some of these factors and variables, efforts at reform and change can have exceedingly dysfunctional consequences. In the efforts to reform psychiatric hospitals, the resistance to change has been so severe that it has caused major upset and disorder among patients. Administrative changes were accompanied by increased suicidal attempts (Stotland and Kobler, 1965). We must seriously heed the unintended consequences of efforts to reform psychiatric hospitals. Social agencies can be changed only by careful attention to function, structure, and process. Reform efforts must be based on first-hand knowledge of the nature of the supervisory process in a specific agency, on the flexibility and dedication of the staff, and on the ability to perceive the total social and client system of that agency.

Change

Apparently, one reason for the hesitation in confronting a clear-cut separation of administration and teaching is that it has not been possible to perceive and act upon function, structure, and process simultaneously. Social agencies are mini-communities made up of formal and informal components. These make the accomplishment of planned change complex and difficult. Yet, there is a growing body of knowledge about planned organizational change. (See, for example, Bennis, Benne, and Chin, 1961; Zald, 1970.) At the very least, we can anticipate some points of resistance and some dysfunction in planning agency changes.

Social work seems compelled to follow the model of other professions, especially in regard to the increased autonomy of the practitioner. It seems inevitable that the teaching functions will eventually be completely removed from the administrative function. Indeed, the term *supervisor* may no longer be appropriate because the term has clearly become linked with administrative and hierarchical responsibility. In a consistent definition of the teaching function, the supervisor is more of a consultant. Austin called this new supervisor a staff development person. Whatever he is called, he no longer has administrative authority over the worker for learning. Consultation implies a nonhierarchical relationship in which the worker has the freedom to accept or reject advice. Some maintain that the worker is free to determine when and where he receives consultation, and this type of autonomy and responsibility of the practitioner *is* assumed in most professions (Abrahamson, 1967, p. 8).

With all of the teaching responsibilities removed from the first-line or unit supervisor, the remaining duties are primarily or solely administrative. The remaining duties approximate those of a supervisor or foreman in industry. I disagree with Austin's proposal that this new administrator continue to have some direct responsibility for the caseworkers' performance. Such an arrangement undercuts the function of the staff development person and leaves the caseworker with his role undefined and ambiguous between staff members to whom he is accountable. I see him as responsible for reporting only on the routine job performance of staff, for conveying agency policies and rules, and for insuring that administrative reports and other information (such as caseload size) are available to agency management. The accountability for casework expertise or any other social work practice expertise should be located in the staff development person and not in the administrator.

Austin ties the need for a professional social work administrator to the retention of some casework responsibility in that position. I feel that professional education in social work is still required for the new breed of administrator but that a different kind of social work education is indicated. I agree with Rappoport and Smalley that such a social worker must be socialized toward a firm commitment to social work values and goals. This socialization alone provides an insufficient knowledge base for any form of social work practice, including the position of the new administrator. Specialized education is needed in the area of administrative theory and management. A variation of the clinician–executive, proposed for psychiatry, could easily be developed for the social-work administrator (Levinson and Klerman, 1967, pp. 3–15). Some schools of social work are now experimenting with varying mixes of basic social-work education and specialized education in administration. (See Neugeboren, 1971, pp. 35–47.)

Separating out the administrative function requires new educational and practice content for the professional social worker who administers services to clients. A plethora of social work literature presently exists calling for a more rational use of manpower resources both in education and in practice.[2] I wish to emphasize the need for acting quickly and for developing and introducing a rational approach.

The efforts to strengthen the professional practice of social workers by redefining the function and structure of supervision will also entail an inescapable redefinition of the roles for which social workers are educated and which they practice. Clarifying the function

[2] Recent changes in the social welfare field "require both more and better qualified social work staff with advanced education for clinical practice, planning, administration, and policy roles, and others with baccalaureate degrees or less for many direct service roles." (See, for example, Pins, 1971, pp. 5–15.)

of teaching in supervision and separating out that function as a distinct one in its own right, also involves a redefinition of the administrative functions which remain. Unless social workers are willing to abandon administrative functions to business and public administrators, we will need to move rapidly to educate for and identify expertise. By educating workers in administrative theory and management theory as well as in the work programs and services themselves, we may lay a claim as a profession to a *special* expertise regarding administration in social agencies.

Conclusions

I suggest that much of the social-work literature on supervision written in the past two decades has focused on function, structure, or process at the expense of perceiving the interrelationships among the three. Except for group supervision, which has not dealt with the structural problems within an agency, and military social work I find few examples which resolve the many dilemmas which have long been identified with social-work supervision.

If we are to accept the full consequences of the creative ideas of Lucille Austin and finally separate the functions of administration and teaching, then our professional responsibility to ourselves and our consumers requires that we take a view of the total system of an agency. This view calls for new knowledge and skills. We must legitimize a wider range of professional roles than we have thus far granted ourselves. If our mission as a profession is to improve and extend services, then perhaps we can agree that the major issues are substantive and not ideological. A purpose of this chapter has been to demonstrate that the concepts of structure, function, and process are matters of basic knowledge more than they are ideological issues within the social work profession. The presumed value conflicts between social-work administrators and practitioners is neither an ideological nor substantive issue if we are clear that we are educating and practicing in all areas to achieve the larger values and goals of the profession.

CHAPTER 4

Indigenous Paraprofessional Staff

Willard C. Richan

Indigenous paraprofessionals are indigenous to the population which is the target of the social service. They may be drawn from clients of service systems or potential clients or may simply be persons who are in like circumstances and essentially peers of the client group. Although the social service clientele comes from a wide range, economically and socially, the focus here will be on low-income and minority groups.

The subject of indigenous paraprofessionals tends to be discussed in ideological and emotional terms because it goes to the heart of the dilemmas surrounding professionalism both within social work and in society. To put it simply, professional social workers are threatened by the notion that persons outside the pale should have a distinctive function within the social services. The issue is not the classic problem of job competition in its literal sense; however, this element, too, may become increasingly important in view of the tightening job market in social work and the professionalization of the bacculaureate-level worker.

More to the point is the threat posed to social work professionalism per se. We have pinned our claims to professional status on special expertise—expertise requiring intensive education at the graduate level. The assertion that persons of limited education can do the same work as professionals as well, or in some cases better than the professional, challenges claims to professional recognition. (For statements which neatly summarize the nub of the claim and the counterclaim, see "Case Conference on the Neighborhood Subprofessional Worker," 1968, pp. 7–16.) I refer here to *para*professionals, literally alongside or going beyond the professional, a more accurate sense of what I am talking about than the term nonprofessional.

A more subtle threat than that to professionalism stems from the fact that the workers are indigenous. Although the layman has always figured prominently in social work, we have made a distinction between giver and receiver. Typically, the benefactor has been from the middle and upper-middle class, moved by a feeling of obligation toward and a desire to help those less fortunate and implicitly less adequate. As social work has become professionalized with the replacement of the unpaid philanthropist by a bureaucratic functionary and the development of specialized education, this spirit of *noblesse oblige* has persisted.

At the same time, social workers worry about elitism. They chide one another for professional arrogance, and they criticize other professions which are too castelike. The dignity and right to self-direction of our clientele are basic threads in our value system. We speak of client self-determination, suggesting that professional authority in social work is open, flexible and amenable to the client's wishes. And yet, client self-determination has had a special meaning—self-determination must be within the limits of agency policy and professional guidance; it must never coerce or manipulate the worker.

It has become evident to social workers that such attitudes create a formidable barrier to the populations they are seeking to reach. The problem becomes especially severe when a previously captive population ceases to be captive, as when assistance recipients are no longer required to relate to social-service workers. For the social work professionals, this problem is more serious than organized political pressure by client groups which is directed at the service bureaucracy itself; social workers are aware that they will quickly become an expensive surplus commodity if there is no demand for their services.

Client mistrust and resentment of large service bureaucracies and welfare professionals pose additional problems. These resentments may be attitudes as American as apple pie, for they have been shared historically by farmers and city workers, Northern immigrants and Southern natives, conservative businessmen and radical activists. But their expression has been particularly sharp among low-income urban blacks and other minorities since the 1960s (Cloward and Epstein, 1965, pp. 623–643). In the stridency of the antagonism, one can miss an important fact: the urban poor do not merely reject what social service systems have to offer. Were this so, one would have simply seen an abandonment of the poor by significant elements of the social services during the 1960s. But the severity of the confrontations is related to the fact that the antagonists have been aware of their dependence on the hated system for fulfilling vital needs. (See, for instance, findings of the Kerner Commission, 1968, pp. 283–288.)

Thus, the use of indigenous paraprofessionals involves dilemmas for both professional social workers and low-income client populations. The social workers fear the implications of an expanding role for those indigenous to the client population; yet they need what the paraprofessionl can bring and offer. Likewise, the client population resents, yet needs, the social service bureaucracy. The respective dilemmas make the role of the indigenous paraprofessional viable and at the same time complicate it.

Functions

Understandably, both career opportunities and enhancement of overall personal functioning have come in for major attention as social workers have considered the use of paraprofessionals drawn from the ranks of the disadvantaged. But although these dimensions are important and cannot be overlooked, my focus is primarily on the indigenous worker as a resource. To consider him anything else would inevitably lead to an unreal work situation. Supposedly, the purpose of hiring anybody is to use his talents and energy for explicit ends. The person who is hired primarily for therapeutic effects or for manufacturing a career is being used; the difference is that in the latter instances, the ends are not so likely to be explicit.

An old failing of many Americans is to set higher standards of usefulness for the poor than those which prevail for the rest of us. We are all familiar with patronage jobs which demand primarily that one deliver votes on election day, with subsidies to gentlemen farmers for not growing crops, and with other ingenious sorts of boondoggling. Why should the poor be different? Why should we not create work primarily for their benefit? The poor do not necessarily have to make themselves useful, but the social services should make creative use of their talents; the system is sorely in need of this relatively untapped source. We must be aware of both humanizing and dehumanizing elements in the work situation and seek to enhance the former and lessen the latter. Likewise, developing meaningful career lines and avoiding dead-end jobs is important—both for the worker and for the ultimate effectiveness of the social services.

It is useful to distinguish between two sets of functions in considering the use of indigenous paraprofessionals. Those which I call organization-related functions facilitate the internal operation of the service system. Alternately, community-related functions mediate the relationship between the service system on the one hand and clients and potential clients on the other. Especially in the case of low-income clientele and large service bureaucracies, there are inherent strains between these respective sets of functions.

To understand organization-related functions, let us take an overview of the internal dynamics of the organization. In carrying out its mission, any institution spawns a great array of specialized work roles. Persons recruited to these roles must have the necessary expertise or develop it on the job. They must have sufficient motivation to do their work. The respective roles must be integrated so that the organization can function as a whole. A key element is communication, both oral and written. Another is authority, which involves both insistence upon adherence to specific requirements and reciprocal patterns of relationship between persons in different statuses. I do not mean to imply that formal rules are never broken. Workers frequently devise their own informal rules. But the innovations are selective, and the tendency is still to maintain the forms of authority even when its reality is weak. Members develop an identification with the organization. The desire to get ahead is one motivating factor, but it is not the only one.

What kinds of people are best suited to serving organization-related functions? People who have the requisite skills and knowledge, of course. But also needed are individuals who communicate effectively, orally and in writing, in the language of the organization; individuals who observe the forms and to a large extent the substance of authority; individuals who can be relied upon by their colleagues (for example, are punctual and consistent in their behavior); and individuals who identify with the organization and want to get ahead according to the rules. These are kinds of behavior which are highly prized and therefore are rewarded. But these same behaviors and the accompanying attitudes can alienate the key constituencies an organization is seeking to relate to: the poor, for instance. Nor is the disaffection only one way; the worker who fits these criteria finds it hard to identify with the poor.

It is a serious mistake to attribute all the problems between social service organizations and their clients to cold, punitive, unresponsive agency personnel. The forces at work are much broader and more fundamental than that. When indigenous paraprofessionals provide a bridge between the organization and low-income clientele, it is within a limited context. This is an important caveat as we turn to the subject of the *community-related* functions; frequently, a romantic tone creeps into discussions of this dimension. Is the community-related function of the indigenous worker primarily to recruit new clients, to cool out restive neighbors, to act as advocate in their behalf, or to bring about basic institutional change? Depending on where one looks in the literature, it can be any or all of these functions. (See Miller and Riessman, 1968, pp. 203–214; Houston, 1970, pp. 291–299; Atkeson, 1967, pp. 81–89.)

But a fairly consistent set of functions can be inferred from certain characteristics cited by various authors. These functions include familiarity with lower-class and ethnic minority life styles, identification with the client community and its aspirations, spontaneity, informality and warmth. (See Brager, 1965, p. 36; Cudabeck, 1969, p. 96; Goldberg, 1969; Grosser—cited in Grosser, Henry, and Kelley—

1969, pp. 12–39, 116–148; Lowenberg, 1968, p. 69; Riessman and Hallowitz, 1967, p. 1410; Hardcastle, 1971, p. 57; Levinson and Schiller, 1966, pp. 95–101.) Thus, the indigenous worker is seen as offsetting what are perceived as dysfunctional elements in service bureaucracies: lack of identification with the poor and their interests, aloofness, coldness, and formality. If one adds the implicit and sometimes explicit expectation that the indigenous worker will align himself with community residents against the service system, we have an obvious conflict between organization-related and community-related functions.

Dilemmas of Marginality

Were we dealing merely with two sets of functions and related worker attributes which were equally prized and equally rewarded in our society, our problem would be relatively simple. Indigenous persons with the respective attributes or the potential for developing them could be channeled to tasks involving the corresponding functions. But our society is highly bureaucratic and success is associated with qualities and life styles which lend themselves to organizational life.

The aspiration to move upward on the social ladder appears to be virtually universal even among those who fail to obey the necessary ground rules. (See, for instance, Hannerz, 1969; Liebow, 1967, pp. 29–71.) Surely, those low-income individuals motivated to become paraprofessionals have a strong desire for status. Also, one criterion for recruitment of indigenous workers is evidence that they have achieved mastery over their own problems, a quality associated with mobility aspirations. But the selection process aside, the influence of the work environment on the indigenous worker, once inducted, is especially powerful. Inherent in the work situation are strong forces inducing an organizational orientation, and precisely this orientation can defeat a major rationale for using indigenous workers, that is, their identification with the client community, their informality, and their spontaneity.

Because organization-oriented workers fit in comfortably with the rest of the staff, agencies may prefer them to the more troublesome community-oriented workers, and they may even fail to see any problem in selecting the former only. The workers can then fulfill another function for the organization: window dressing. Window dressing is not a total loss; it does allow a select few persons to make it in the system. But if an agency is truly interested in connecting with its client community in meaningful ways, the problem remains.

A number of solutions have been suggested. Let us look at two. Brennan (cited in Richan, 1969, pp. 202–211) proposes that paraprofessionals be hired on a short-term, "planned replacement" basis to avoid the problem of contamination. Aside from keeping the paraprofessional "pure," the approach would capitalize on the natural zeal which one finds in the initial stages of a project but which later fades. Brennan bases his thesis on experiences with middle-class paraprofessionals. But it is one thing for suburban housewives and college students to move rapidly in and out of social service jobs, and another for low-income clients in search of stable employment to do so.

An alternative solution to the problem of organizational seduction, proposed by Hardcastle (1971, pp. 60–64), is insulation of indigenous paraprofessionals from the rest of the agency by placing them in special units. Although this approach might avoid socialization of the paraprofessional to the professional culture, it would almost certainly insulate the organization from the influence of the paraprofessionals. To offset this problem, Hardcastle suggests placing such special units in close administrative proximity to the top. But how would paraprofessionals view this compartmentalization? Would they see it as protection against organizational contamination, or simply as blatant segregation? And for those who aspire to a career, would not the special unit constitute a dead end?

Given the fact that employment as a paraprofessional does indeed represent an opportunity to make it (a major appeal in recruitment), it is the worst form of exploitation, nay, enslavement, to cut off avenues of advancement, either by rapid turnover or encapsulation, in hopes of keeping the indigenous workers unspoiled. In reality, the poor are part of a society which rewards some statuses and behaviors and punishes others. They have a right to share those rewards insofar as possible.

Are we, then, faced with an impossible dilemma? Must we choose (on the one hand) between providing avenues for the legitimate mobility aspirations of poor people, who by becoming more career oriented become dysfunctional to efforts of the social services to relate effectively to their client communities, and (on the other hand) freezing people out of opportunities for advancement in order to keep them relevant? If we think only in static terms, the answer is probably, yes. If, instead, we visualize a continuous process, in which some indigenous workers move up a career ladder and are replaced by new recruits, while others continue to find satisfaction and acceptance as "middle men," the picture is less dismal.

The desire to make it in the work world varies from one paraprofessional to the next. Presumably, young workers and family heads are more strongly impelled to climb career ladders than older, unattached persons. (Halpern found this difference among older and younger Navajo Indian aides. See Halpern, 1971, p. 46.) This difference is appropriate and the variations should be allowed to occur freely and naturally. The worker should not be stigmatized for "deserting his people" or for disdaining middle-class values of getting ahead. But the social forces pushing toward upward mobility are powerful, and, as I said previously, most indigenous paraprofessionals share these aspirations.

The link between upward mobility and alienation from one's former associates and cultural roots is neither universal nor inevitable. Workers can maintain their identification with the interests of the client community as they rise in the organization. The central factor in the degree to which indigenous paraprofessionals can keep this identification is probably the organization itself. Lowenberg found (1968, p. 69), for instance, that the rapidity with which workers took on professional behavioral norms and lost their indigenous character was related to whether the agency was traditional or innovative in its orientation. If the paraprofessional perceives that the organization both recognizes and values the strengths in the client community and prizes his own special contributions, he is free to remain true to himself and to his community. If, however, he detects, through overt and subtle cues, that his professional coworkers derogate the client community, he seeks to disassociate himself from patterns and ties which are dysfunctional to his aspirations.

Changing the Service System

The crisis of confidence between the social services and low-income populations has been caused primarily by social demands on these systems and the characteristic features of the systems—the personnel taking their cue from their working environment. A handful of indigenous workers does not create a bridge to the poor unless there is a basis for it, the readiness of the organization to go more than halfway in the bridging process.

The nature of the crisis is not simply attributable to bureaucratic tendencies that foster mistrust and resentment among poor people, although these tendencies are part of the problem. The function of many social service organizations is basically repressive and exploitative; the clients' resentment is real, based on an accurate perception of the nature of the service relationship (Piven and Cloward, 1971). Organizations vary in the extent to which they are repressive and exploitative. My basic assumption here is that they are capable of becoming less so. This assumption casts the bridging function in a different light, for it cannot consist merely of staff responsiveness, warmth, and informality. The organization as organization has to identify with the aspirations of the poor, and that means the political and economic aspirations as well as the social aspirations. Essentially, then, the rapprochement between the organization and the client community must take place in a genuine realignment of the interests of the organization and in the day-to-day working relationships of staff and clientele.

Let us consider the two levels on which this realignment has to happen: top leadership and line staff. A firm and open commitment at the top to responsiveness to the aspirations of the client community is necessary (but not sufficient) for an effective relationship. People at the executive and board levels need to support the bridging function, including the role of the indigenous paraprofessional in facilitating its occurrence.

But the best laid plans are often sabotaged within the agency infrastructure, especially when the agency is dominated by professional norms which run counter to the desired thrust. The resistance to meaningful utilization of indigenous paraprofessionals can be formidable indeed. I have already cited some sources of resistance. There is the threat inherent in the notion that the relatively uneducated possess valuable expertise. This contention defies the historic emphasis of social work that formal, professional education is essential for developing skill and knowledge. Inclusion of paraprofessionals as staff members also necessitates bridging the social barriers between helper and those formerly seen as those to be helped.

Other causes of resistance among professional staff include the failure of indigenous workers to conform to middle-class values of punctuality, obedience, and gentility; their personalized approach to clients and violations of confidentiality; and the perceived disloyalty of these workers to the organization. And, let us face it, class and race prejudice exist, too. Resistance is not the only problematic response of professional staff. Some staff members glamorize the indigenous worker, encourage him to take on responsibilities which are beyond his abilities, or use him in their own battles with the administration. (See Hallowitz, cited in Richan, 1969, pp. 165–177; Pruger and Specht, 1968, pp. 21–32; Denham and Shatz, cited in Richan, 1969, pp. 178–187; Beck, cited in Grosser, Henry, and Kelley, 1969, pp. 66–79.)

To an extent, such reactions can be dealt with by helping professional staff to understand on an intellectual level the purposes of using paraprofessionals, their role in the organization, and the special attributes they bring to the job. But obviously, sheer knowledge, although important, is of limited value. Beyond it are more stubborn and elusive attitudinal factors.

Structuring in collaborative working relationships, using professional-nonprofessional teams, and otherwise capitalizing on role complementarity are devices for reducing staff resistance. Training programs using group-interaction methods may also help, although they need to be applied thoughtfully and selectively. Experience with teams of professional and paraprofessional workers is not clear cut. Neugeboren (1971), found the combined teams to be more effective in work with clients in a neighborhood setting than were units made up exclusively of professionals or paraprofessionals. But Lefton and associates (1959, pp. 822–828) found that hospital teams which cut across professional lines had a negative effect on the morale of the paraprofessionals.

All of these approaches must deal with two dimensions of staff resistance: perceived costs and benefits, and perceived legitimacy. If professional workers view involvement with paraprofessionals as threatening to their vital interests (monetary rewards, career advancement, prestige) they resist such involvement. If compensations and administrative reassurances are built in, this source of resistance lessens. Conversely, if costs are attached to resistance (negative evaluation by supervisors, alienation of peers), staff members find they cannot afford the luxury of their antagonism. But, we are dealing with a profession which is highly ideological: social workers are constrained to rationalize their interests in terms of universal values. This dimension, legitimation, tends to be overlooked by many organizational analysts. Aside from manipulating costs and benefits, such normative factors have to be considered. Because professionalism is identified essentially with an elitist orientation, the professional worker can justify exclusion of paraprofessionals on grounds of maintaining standards of practice. But, if the social work literature and other bearers of the cultural values espouse as a higher form of professionalism one which prizes inventive uses of the talents of clients and their peers and propounds the model of the professional as trainer, consultant, and enabler, the justification of exclusionary attitudes is weakened and a responsive orientation is supported.

The more romantic view of the indigenous worker is harder to deal with because it may be based on genuine openness to change and identification with the client population. The danger is in the sense of failure and possible backlash if indigenous workers cannot meet high expectations. (See Denham and Shatz, cited in Richan, 1969, p. 184f.) But, although the problem is real enough, excessive enthusiasm is far less frequently problematic than are excessive pessimism and resistance.

Both these problems, romanticism and resistance, become particularly troublesome as indigenous workers are seen as having a role in directly influencing the organization and its staff. This influence is frequently mentioned as one of the important payoffs of using paraprofessionals (Houston, 1970, p. 293; Brager, 1965, p. 34; Riessman and Hallowitz, 1967, p. 1410; Garcia, 1971, pp. 274–278). Professional staff thus are expected not only to work effectively with the indigenous worker but also to learn from him; a related function is to help alert the system as a whole to problems in its relationship to the client community. This heightened awareness is indeed one of the exciting potential effects of using indigenous paraprofessionals. In fact, were the organization and its professional staff to be unchanged by the influence of the indigenous worker, we would have a situation analogous to an illicit love affair: lots of fun while it lasts, both parties a bit older and wiser for the experience, but not much to show for it in the end.

An important part of helping both top leadership and professional staff make the most of the experience, then, is preparing them for the fact that the bridging works two ways. Logical, if not emotional, acceptance of this reciprocity in advance may mitigate the negative attitudes that are bound to emerge. Hopefully, the change can be seen positively, as enhancing both the professional effectiveness of staff and the viability of the organization. Current awareness in the field of the problem of class and cultural barriers (admittedly, still largely intellectual) helps to get this point across to the organization.

Clarifying Roles

The indigenous paraprofessional has to be helped to gain a realistic view of his educative function vis-a-vis the organization. He may need to be helped to overcome lack of confidence and a sense of awe in the presence of an "omniscient" professional staff and an "omnipotent" administration (Hallowitz, 1969, pp. 166–177). Conversely, he must be clear about the limits of his role and the expectations of him.

Ambiguity and confusion are the surest roads to trouble (Denham and Shatz, cited in Richan, 1969, p. 183; Lefton, Dinitz, and Pasamanick, 1959; Abels, 1969; Christmas, 1966, pp. 410–419). Good supervisory and training practice necessitates that any worker know what is expected of him. But the question of expectations becomes especially vital for those who are unfamiliar with the cultural shorthand of bureaucratic systems.

Major problems which arise from role uncertainty are: unrealistic expectations about power and prerogatives on the part of the paraprofessional; competition between professional and paraprofessional; and frustration and a sense of failure when the indigenous worker cannot deliver on what he believes to be his mission. Administrators are not always able to spell these problems out precisely. It is wisest, at least, to be honest about that fact. No amount of advance orientation eliminates all role ambiguity; ultimately, the only way to be truly aware of the problem is to experience it. Part of the function of the trainer and supervisor is to be prepared for the inevitable crises which come up and to be ready to step in when necessary.

One can increase role clarity by assigning tasks which lend themselves to clear job descriptions. The more one can fashion jobs which use the tangible skills possessed by the indigenous worker, such as his knowledge of a distinctive culture, facility with a foreign language, and access to information not readily available to others, the easier it will be to clarify expectations. Clearly delineating the paraprofessional's tasks also makes easier the job of interpreting to the rest of the agency the special value of using the worker. The indigenous worker then knows that he is relied upon by the agency to help carry out its function in a way helpful to the client community. Other staff members not only recognize his value but are less likely to feel that their own functions are usurped.

Here, however, a further distinction should be made. Knowledge of a foreign language is likely to be a self-contained asset; rarely is the paraprofessional expected to teach the language to other staff members. But knowledge of a group's cultural values and life style can readily be shared with other staff members and should be, for such knowledge affects the ability of the organization to be responsive and sensitive. This expectation needs to be spelled out at the outset, so, for instance, an indigenous worker does not hold onto such special knowledge as his personal property. Education of colleagues does not put the indigenous paraprofessional out of a job because he will continue to have easier access to the client community and its secrets than does the professional worker.

Tangible skills and knowledge can be acquired in other areas as well. Indigenous workers trained to help people apply for benefits, provide child-care services, or carry out auxiliary activities for professionals have salable skills. These skills are complementary to professional roles, and a desirable interdependence between the two is achieved.

The emphasis on tangible skills is not intended to suggest a narrowly delimited involvement of the indigenous worker either in the agency or in the community. Rather, such skills are a credential in a world familiar with specialized work roles. Hopefully, from this base, the paraprofessional can expand his horizons to include the aforementioned bridging function in its broader sense, including interpreting the needs and aspirations of his community to the agency.

A role which is potentially exciting, and difficult to carry out, is that which essentially parallels existing professional roles in the same or other agencies but represents significant departures from standard practice. For instance, lay mental health aides and lay advocates closely attuned to low-income people, their life styles, and their needs may point the way to radically new and more relevant modes of operation by psychiatrists and lawyers. Established professional elites quickly sense the threat to their status quo. Such analogs of the professional role increase the possibility of conflict, but these are nonetheless tangible contributions with specific programatic objectives.

As role expectations become diffuse, the problems of implementation multiply. A general rule of thumb is that the more the roles of the workers are ingrained in their daily lives and those of their neighbors, the greater the likelihood of success. Examples include outreach and client recruitment, organizing and social action activities, role modeling, and family-surrogate functions. The major problem in such cases, as I discuss later, is the danger of oversocializing. As the indigenous worker gets further away from home base, for instance, when he sits on deliberative bodies dominated by civic and professional elites, he is increasingly likely to be in over his head. There are exceptions to this general rule; every ghetto, for example, has its charismatic leaders who are masters at negotiating with politicians and civic leaders. But more typically, the indigenous paraprofessional thrust into such alien and poorly defined situations is vulnerable to manipulation or simply serves the familiar window-dressing function.

Some illustrations may help to make these notions clear. Let us begin with roles which capitalize on specific and identifiable talents possessed by indigenous workers. One project in the Southwest used Navajo Indians as interpreters, drivers, and guides (Halpern, 1971). Their value in bridging the language barrier was obvious. Similarly, having grown up in the area, they were familiar with the geography and could get around more efficiently than professionals could. They also knew the cultural landscape: the Navajo form of greeting; thought patterns related to language patterns; and subtle aspects of the indigenous life style. In some instances, they were taught other organization-related skills such as welfare eligibility procedures and health-care routines. Thus, these paraprofessionals had tangible and visible assets, unduplicated by professional expertise: a solid base for a more extended and less tangible bridging function. The extent to which these broad dimensions were used varied markedly among agencies.

Tangible roles which closely parallel established professional roles are illustrated by the use of lay advocates for senior citizens in a program sponsored by California Rural Legal Assistance (CRLA).[1] These advocates must be at least fifty-five years old, that is, indigenous to the age group being served. They represent the full range of social classes and educational and occupational backgrounds. Their function is specific: to represent the interests of aggrieved older persons in dealing with social service institutions. Health care, for instance, looms large as an object of concern in this program and further helps to clarify the advocates' functions.

The role of advocate is new to most CRLA paraprofessionals, and they must be trained from the ground up. Ineptness or ignorance is costly. The boundaries between the lay advocates and the lawyers are clear: when formal litigation is involved, the professionals take over, although even here lay advocates are frequently engaged in ancillary roles (for example, fact gathering). The indigenous quality of the paraprofessionals is primarily valuable in what it symbolizes to the clientele, and it may also facilitate the ability of the advocate to identify with the plight of his client. This latter factor is of great import, for typically the attorneys in legal-service projects are young and have relatively little interest in the problems of the elderly.

Mental health and public welfare are two other fields in which indigenous paraprofessionals have taken on roles analogous to the professional roles. These areas of expertise are more amorphous than in advocacy, and distinctions between the respective roles of professional and paraprofessional are cloudier.

Cudabeck (1969, pp. 93–99) describes a project in which former AFDC (Aid to Families with Dependent Children) recipients acted as welfare aides, sharing the same cases with regular caseworkers. From the outset, the caseworker retained overall accountability. But aides were found to have special assets: they could communicate more readily with resistant clients; they understood life-style dimensions which puzzled caseworkers; and their general spontaneity made working relationships easier. On the one hand, they could engage in long,

[1] I am indebted here to Philip C. Lang, director of social services, CRLA Senior Citizens Project, for his comments and written material.

drawn-out, relaxed conversations with suspicious clients; on the other hand, they could be direct in confronting clients without seeming overbearing. A measure of the extent to which case workers valued the aides is the fact that once workers used an aide, they tended to ask for them repeatedly. One factor which helped make these aides acceptable was the core of tangible functions they performed in behalf of clients (for example, linkage with community resources and counseling around specific problems such as housing and nutrition).

The mental health field has done much experimentation with indigenous workers. (See, for example, Riessman and Hallowitz, 1967; Christmas, 1966.) As these paraprofessionals are involved in essentially socializing functions under the close supervision of clinical personnel, it is almost impossible to avoid a one-sided transaction. The professional wisdom relates to precisely those facets of life in which the indigenous staff member presumably can make the greatest contribution. Thus, in a professionally oriented socializing operation, the inputs of the amateur are simply no match for those of experts. The mental health professionals are geared to defining potentially arguable questions so as to preclude argument. This tendency to define the arguing process in clinical terms (that is, interpreting a challenge not on its merits but as a symptom of the challenger's functioning) can effectively rule out criticism of existing assumptions from the start.

Thus, the sharpest and least negotiable differences between the client community and the professional elite are brought into direct confrontation. Furthermore, in this confrontation, the traditional ground rules for settling controversies (burden of proof, clarity of language, empirical evidence) are ruled out of order. Just as the professionals tend to corrupt the process in a clinical direction, the paraprofessionals may corrupt it along ideological and political lines. Not surprisingly, some of the fiercest conflicts involving indigenous paraprofessionals have been in mental health settings. Planners should not necessarily write off mental health as an arena for indigenous paraprofessionals, but they must be aware of the pitfalls.

Finally, let me say a word about the avowedly political role of the indigenous worker. There is a tendency for politically based controversies to move in one of two directions. Either the change agent moves in quickly and gains concessions before being eliminated (either through expulsion or cooptation) or the community successfully demands a share in the control of the operation. Given the realities of financial resources, such take-overs are doomed to be short-lived in most instances. One should not forget Hallowitz' warning (1969): "Growing up in the ghetto makes one neither a political genius, necessarily, nor committed to a basic shift in power relationships." I am not suggesting, however, that the indigenous worker has no role in modifying agency policies and practices. He may well teach the agency and its staff better ways of responding to community need, alert those both inside and outside the organization to danger signals, and act as a mediator between organized groups in the client community and the agency. This role is most likely as he demonstrates, in more and less tangible ways, that he is truly functional to the interests of both.

Indigenous Worker as Learner

Up to this point, I have said little about training and supervisory processes. I have limited the discussion partly because purposes and institutional context are paramount, especially as one deals with paraprofessionals. I have, however, made several major points. One point is the crucial importance of clarifying the functions and roles of the paraprofessional at the outset. Another point is the fact that the agency leadership and line staff are at least as important targets of education as the indigenous workers. A third point is the danger of oversocialization, especially as it relates to organizational and community norms. Now we consider factors specifically related to the task of training.

Myths die hard. Take, for instance, the myth that ghetto home life lacks stimulation and that ghetto children are therefore culturally deprived and cannot handle abstract symbols. The fact is that ghetto children are exposed to and become familiar with all aspects of the adult world they will inherit, the pretty and the less pretty, much earlier than do their more protected suburban counterparts. To fail to understand subtle cues in one's social environment, and thus to inappropriately respond to peers or policemen, can literally be fatal. So the ghetto child learns. As for abstract symbols, the late Whitney M. Young, Jr., has written (1969, p. 56): "Aggressive black men, kept from respectable professions by the color bar, turned their talents to other, related avenues. I've met some people in the numbers racket who could have been great mathematicians. It takes a great natural gift to keep that many numbers in your head and to make complicated computations without once turning to a pencil and paper." One reason the myth persists is that ability is defined within a particular cultural context. The tools of assessment are indigenous to it. This context so permeates Western industrial society and has for generations that it is taken as universal. But even pure logic is *a* logic, rooted in particular patterns of language. I am not suggesting that this cultural context is bad. But we should understand that for the indigenous worker, it may be an alien context. The key word is *may*. Inevitably, the dominant culture permeates any minority culture, and many paraprofessionals are highly attuned to this dominant culture. But trainers must be prepared to apply different (*not* meaning more lax) criteria to ability and performance. Some tasks are not particularly appropriate for indigenous workers, at least not short of major training, in the course of which these persons may stop being indigenous.

An insidious factor is the tendency for lower-class and minority persons to believe the myth. Having been bombarded since early childhood with the message that they are unable to learn, they fulfill the prophecy. This self-fulfilling prophecy is the biggest reason why children in ghetto schools perform so abysmally; in effect, they and their teachers enter into a conspiracy to cheat them of success (U.S. Commission on Civil Rights, 1967, v. 1, p. 103ff.; U.S. Commission on Civil Rights, 1966, pp. 279–361 passim). The conviction that one is doomed to fail may express itself in different ways, such as passivity, bravado or a demand that evaluation by external criteria be waived.

The teacher must recognize the tenuousness of self-confidence in the indigenous worker and pace the introduction of substantive content to the readiness to absorb it. Small defeats can be devastating, for they may simply confirm for the learner his fear of failure. This process does not go on in a vacuum. Many professional staff members stand on the sidelines, waiting for confirmation of their own assumptions about the learning ability of the indigenous worker.

A key question is: Is what is being taught relevant? Many training programs devote substantial time and energy to matters of dress, punctuality, and basic attitude. And they should *as long as these factors have a bearing on the purpose for employing the indigenous worker in the first place*. Insofar as the avowed purpose is therapy or career preparation, they may indeed be germane. But, the primary function of the indigenous worker is to meet the needs of the organization and of his community. For instance, one group of welfare aides were valuable specifically because they thought nothing of engaging in long, rambling discussions with clients without regard to time, something the casework staff could or would not do. (See Cudabeck, 1969.) Middle-class rules of dress may make much sense or may create needless barriers between indigenous workers and community residents. But the worker who fails to show up at a hearing on time may thereby harm his client, and it is imperative for health aides to observe rules on cleanliness in a hospital.

A particularly troublesome issue is how much to emphasize confidentiality of information in the training program. This professional norm is ordinarily stressed by the organization and frequently disregarded by indigenous workers. Again, we have the question of relevance. We need to reexamine the purposes of confidentiality (protecting whom?) and be sure that it enhances the interests of clients. If confidentiality is relevant, the indigenous staff has to be clear about the reasons for the requirement and the consequences of violating it. Direct attempts to influence attitudes may be healthier than subtle seductions by the professional culture. But these attempts can still be irrelevant or counterproductive. One training program for community health workers at Temple University (undated) was addressed among other things to "the development of proper attitudes toward oneself, one's fellow employees, toward authority figures, and toward people one meets in interviews."

This program left no doubt as to what the proper attitudes toward existing health services and professionals should be. Criticism of medical and hospital care and medical personnel was treated as an issue of professional ethics. Oriented in part to preparing indigenous personnel for careers in the health field, the training material promised "unlimited opportunities in the wider aspects of the medical field to those who learned the proper attitudes."

What about inculcating attitudes of militancy and social change? Again the question is one of relevance. For a welfare rights organization *not* to preach assertiveness against the welfare system to both its workers and its clientele would be to defeat its central purpose. Likewise, the CRLA advocate who tells a client she should not take abuse lying down is helping her make necessary demands on the system. But for a mental health project gratuitously to preach radical activism to its community aides is another matter. It seems wiser to leave decisions about assertiveness up to the indigenous workers and clients themselves: not to stand in the way of their right to assert themselves (in fact, to stand ready to help them if asked to), but not to use them for some personal agenda either.

Indigenous workers are "strangers in a strange land." Regardless of the extent to which trainers, supervisors, and professional coworkers try to be helpful, the experience is bound to be trying. One way of mitigating these problems is to work with groups of indigenous workers. The process of mastering specific content can be accelerated through the judicious use of group teaching. (See, for example, Christmas, 1966.) More important, a peer group can help the individual resist pressure to give up his identity.

The notion of critical mass may have utility here. Glasgow, in discussing black and other minority students in a school of social work, refers (1971, p. 11) to the critical mass as the point at which there are sufficient numbers in the minority group to bring about a basic shift in the relationship with the institution. Translated to the indigenous-staff group, as long as there are only a token number in the agency, they do the accommodating. As their number increases to the point where the organization becomes dependent upon them for its ongoing operation, the interaction comes closer to being a true exchange.

If there is validity in what has been said up to now, some standard tools of authority have to go by the board. Typically, the greatest discretion is exercised by those in the top echelons of an organization and those with the most impressive professional credentials. The rationales are that the ultimate responsibility for what the organization does falls on those at the top and that those with professional training can be trusted to be self-directing. Both groups need the freedom to act in the light of their best judgment. As one goes down through the hierarchy, one finds work roles increasingly constrained and routinized. Standard tools for assessing performance at lower levels focus on quality and quantity of specified activities. One counts interviews, typing errors, and perhaps coffee breaks to determine who gets raises and promotions or who leaves the organization.

But I have been projecting here a function which requires a high degree of flexibility and autonomy. And assessment of specifics becomes difficult if not impossible because the indigenous worker operates in terrain which is foreign to the rest of the organization. One cannot, in such cases, simply waive accountability and assessment processes. Instead, we need to recast the whole concept of accountability in a different framework. Again, the question is relevance.

One starts with the purposes for using the indigenous worker. These purposes can be translated into specific outcomes. One then assesses with the worker at intervals to what extent the desired outcomes have occurred. In this context, meandering interviews, odd hours, and a casual manner may be associated with highly effective performances of certain functions. But assiduous attention to detail may be crucial for other functions, such as effective advocacy. Once the worker and the organization agree to some "contract," with definite ground rules which must be sensible and truly necessary, a breach of these cannot be ignored.

The morale of the rest of the staff is a problematic aspect of such flexibility. Professional social workers who have to sign in and out religiously, meet with their supervisors once a week, fill out endless forms, and pay outward respect to the boss are resentful of indigenous staff who observe none of these rituals. Good. That resentment may expose a great deal of bureaucratic nonsense for what it is and force the organization to rethink its rules and routines.

And is this rethinking not what this whole discussion has been about? For if there is a rationale for hiring indigenous paraprofessionals, including all the complications that it entails, it is to help organizations which have become encrusted inside and isolated outside to reexamine what they are doing and where they are going. This rationale is not simply the romantic vision of the noble savage leading the charge against the establishment. It is the hard-headed realization that once one opens the door to change, it can be hard to close it. Agencies which are so emboldened as to play around with indigenous paraprofessionals should beware. They might just find themselves becoming more responsive and relevant to that elusive entity called the client community.

CHAPTER 5

Black Supervisors: Problems of Race and Role

Eugene C. Royster

In this chapter, I will concentrate upon the analysis of the supervisory role in social work and in other helping professions from a sociological perspective. I will stress one approach to the investigation of a complex position in the delivery of welfare services. Although the position and functions of a social work supervisor have been said to be unique and therefore not amenable to either the assistance of social science technology or to analysis by social scientists, I assume the contrary. Specifically, the position of the first-line supervisor in the social welfare agency will be examined for those structural demands and problems that are found often in first-line supervisory roles in other organizations. I recognize, of course, that various social settings produce various kinds of impact upon similar position categories; thus, I will also focus upon other factors which lead to potential stress in any given situation. My prime concern will be an examination of stresses which relate specifically to the black supervisor and the interaction between race and role.

Examination of the supervisory role has both practical and theoretical importance. Although we must await the impact of forthcoming federal legislative policy changes, social welfare agencies are in the forefront of organizations which are becoming the focal point of social concerns and movements; that is, we are moving from an industrial to a service economy. Knowledge of the structure of such organizations and of the problems and prospects of the positions which compose this structure is imperative for the planning needed to equip these organizations to meet the challenges of the future. That this analysis is primarily conceptual or theoretical does not negate its relevance for practice. Relevant policy decisions are often made from such analyses. Although my analysis is presented from a sociologist's perspective, I believe that such an approach may be directly translated for use in the helping services. Sociology and other disciplines have generally neglected the application of their technology to problems of service organizations, except in terms of meeting their own theoretical perspectives. Social workers have been remiss in borrowing relevant data from the social sciences. However, remedies to this separatism are now being fostered by professionals in both arenas indicating the narrowing of this gap. Hopefully, interpretations and elements of this sociological perspective will add to the theory and knowledge of supervision.

General Perspectives

Historically, analyses of organizations in Western civilization have focused upon the role of the first-line supervisor. In particular, the position of foreman has been depicted as embodying the "classic dilemma" in modern organizations. This dilemma is the built-in structural demand which places the foreman in a marginal position between management and worker. As the marginal man in industry, the foreman deals directly with the worker and with management, having, in the ideological and in the practical sense, a foot in both camps. But the irreconcilability of the two "incompatible ideologies or systems of sentiment" (Miller and Form, 1951, p. 212) is a major source of this structural tension. In general, these structural stresses infringe upon all first-line positions, whether foremen or supervisors.

In addition to the structural factors which bring about tension, the holders of the positions are causal factors in the emergence of areas of conflict. Each individual in the hierarchical structure brings to it a set of characteristics or identities with corresponding role performances and expectations. These performances and expectations call forth patterns of behavior which may be in conflict with the demands of the position or the institution. More often, the interaction of role identities with those of other persons or with widely held norms, rather than with institutions, causes such conflicts. Examples of such factors leading to what may be termed traditional dilemmas or conflict are sex, race, and age.

Remnants of the ideology of the subordinate status of women suggest that the combination of a female supervisor and male workers produces a situation fraught with stress. Particularly in terms of a social appraisal of such a situation, it is feared that a woman in the role of supervisor lowers the status level of the job. On a more personal self-conception level, the woman supervisor represents the personification of the lack of domination and superiority of the male.

By extension, other situations, such as black supervisors with white workers or young supervisors with older workers are potential sources of tension. Although such combinations have been the subject of speculation and conceptualization for some time, it remains to be seen whether, in the light of recent social changes, they will continue to create such conflicts. Normative patterns which establish a hierarchy of superordinate-subordinate relationships are likely to continue long after they are legally discontinued and other leveling forces change the behavior usually assumed to be a result of these guidelines.

Problems and Conflicts

The argument presented has claimed the applicability of the analysis of the supervisory role across organizations. That there will be differences of degree or even of kind according to the types of organization considered is to be expected. Variations will occur and will have an effect upon the implementation and problems of the supervisor's role. This is the case with social work supervision.

Social work supervision has been characterized as uniquely

different from other supervisory positions. Its uniqueness is a result of two factors: (1) the continued use of supervision in professional activities even after social workers are professionally trained; and (2) the dual functions of education and administration carried by the supervisor.

Of these two factors, the latter presents the more discussed role conflicts. (See, for instance, Toren, cited in Etzioni, 1969, pp. 177–178; Wilensky and Lebeaux, 1965, pp. 237–238.) The former characteristic is challenged primarily on the basis of the reality of the need for such continued supervision for a group of professionals. The latter is questioned on two bases. First, it presents the conflict of the supervisor's role in helping the worker to grow in those skills and to acquire values necessary for appropriate helping performances while ensuring that he follows agency procedures and policies. Stated succinctly, it is a dilemma of professional values versus agency requirements. Second, it has been suggested that there is a conflict between the role of the supervisor as a teacher of performance and also as an evaluator of this performance. Nina Toren notes (p. 174), for instance, that the roles combined here can be equated with the combined roles of task leader and socioemotional leader of a group. Research into small groups has revealed that such roles should be separated to improve group effectiveness. To some extent, supervisors in other fields share these problems, but the nature of the helping process and the importance of the professional value system make the social work supervisor's position qualitatively different. He is not solely interested in increasing productivity. Let us consider other aspects of his role conflict.

Harold Wilensky and Charles Lebeaux (1965, pp. 237–238) have discussed some of the role conflicts which affect the social worker's professional behavior. Among these conflicting identities are: (1) professional values and standards of behavior versus agency values and standards; (2) individual humanitarian values versus agency norms; and (3) individual humanitarian values versus professional norms. The authors also note that for many workers, the conflict between these factors is seldom resolved, even after years in practice. The study of the effects of professional education and the cumulative effects of bureaucratization upon the resolution or accommodations of the worker to these conflicts would be a beneficial step in furthering our understanding of this and other similar occupational categories.

If we accept these role conflicts as illustrative of the social worker, then some of the conflicts which face the supervisor are illustrated, also. As difficult as it may be for workers to accommodate themselves to these role conflicts, the stress upon supervisors is greater. Not yet immersed in the ideologies and necessary concerns of upper echelon administrators, supervisors are constantly reminded by the workers they supervise of role conflicting ideologies, and they are expected to support the ideologies which make up one extreme of the role-conflicting situation.

Understanding the conflicting aspects of the supervisor's role and the role of the social worker is dependent upon recognizing the salience which various identities have for persons and upon recognizing the role-making potential inherent within the position. The two are interdependent factors in the complex analysis of the supervisor's role. Salience is the importance or degree of motivation imputed by the actor to the role identity which might be expressed. Role-making is the potential for a person to define his role within the limits set by the position.

One approach to understanding the importance of these concepts is to borrow the concept of task from the area of small-group research. Growing interest in the area of tasks has led to the realization that task dimensions have an impact upon group behavior and group properties. (For an extended discussion of tasks and their effects on group properties and behavior, see Shaw, 1971.) Although a delineation of the properties of tasks remains to be accomplished, some tasks call for cooperative behavior whereas others require competitive behavior. Tasks, however, may be studied in terms of how well defined they are or how objective they are. By well defined I mean how clear and definitive are the solution to a problem and the steps leading to it. For instance, the task of summing a series of numbers, some of which are held by various members of a group, is a well-defined task; the output is known, and the steps to the solution are known. Of course, group interplay and cooperation are not well defined. A group given the task of deciding on the morality of euthanasia has a poorly defined task with no objectively definable output and no objectively definable steps in the problem solving process that relate directly to the task. In general, the less well defined the task, the greater the opportunity for group members to determine their own actions in attempting to reach a problem solution, that is, to range widely in the role-making process. This situation exists in social work. To be sure, professional values, agency guidelines, and legal restrictions prescribe and proscribe the behavior of the worker. But within the rules of the game, the tasks and solutions are poorly defined. In fact, innovation may be highly prized. Salience of reference points and ideologies of the individual workers and supervisors play a part in defining the degree and type of variations which will exist between group members.

Black Movements and Social Work

The social welfare establishment and the vast complexity of its functioning reflect idiosyncracies which may negate generalization across occupational categories. In particular, the problem solving group involves worker, supervisor, other key agency personnel and to an increasingly greater extent, the client or consumer of services. The social work supervisor faces a qualitatively different situation than, for instance, the industrial supervisor who does not usually have to deal with the changes and challenges of a client population who impress upon him demands for behavioral modifications.[1] Although these demands are made upon supervisors in social agencies in general, they are heightened for the supervisor who is black. The thrust toward self-determination of the black community may have a profound impact upon the black supervisor and his supervisory role.

We recognize that black people do not all start from the same position of "blackness." Some blacks will start from a militant, separatist position, others from a militant but integrationist position, while others are characterized as "Oreos," black on the outside but white on the inside. Regardless of their individual interpretation and implementation of the black role, the black movement and its demands are a reference consideration in the determination of the behavior of the black supervisor. (See, for instance, Merton, 1957.)

The major revolution in American society during the past decade has occurred within the black community. (See Glasgow, 1971;

[1] Toren (cited in Etzioni, 1969, p. 180) has indicated that part of the supervisor's role is to be sure that the "worker adheres to the regulations prescribed by the community and the organization, which are sometimes incompatible with professional ethics or the humanistic enthusiasm of the young practitioner." If, by "community," the thrust of the client population or a particular subcommunity can be understood, then the issues raised in this chapter can be further understood. It should also be pointed out that the community and organization may be in conflict as well.

Billingsley, 1969.) Although this revolution has had practical, social, economic, and political results, its strength and vitality stem primarily from an ideological change or resurgence. A "black ideology" has emerged stressing black pride, black awareness, and a black way of looking at and interpreting the world. The "black is beautiful" concept, the revitalization of the role and dignity of the black man, the urge to an acceptance of and a pleasure in a black identity are aspects of the move to unite the black community in its struggle toward independence and self-determination, and in its combat with white racism. One of the major objectives of the black revolution is the movement of the black community from an open to a closed status. I use the term here in the Weberian sense. To Weber (cited in Henderson and Parsons, 1947, p. 137), closure means that outsiders are either excluded from the community or their participation is limited and subjected to conditions established by the community. The overriding concern is the closure of the black community despite wide variations in the approaches of its many segments. The thrust is for internal solidarity and cohesion so that a unified stance can be presented to the white power structure.

The impact of this movement is incisive to blacks as a group and as individuals. As the black community "gets itself together," ideological standards develop which guide the growth of individual and group values in racial relations. Thus, even if an individual does not adhere to these ideologies, the role of a black person is being redefined, and black behavior expectations are being developed. Although these expectations may be poorly defined, they exist as reference points in the evaluation of a person's behavior and are a constant, if implicit, companion to a wide variety of roles a black person may assume. These ideologies confront the roles of white people and white institutions with a new thrust, requiring a redefinition of how the dominant majority should act toward blacks and the black community. But now the definitions emerge from the black perspective.

Welfare Establishment

One of the purposes of community closure is to develop indigenous control over community resources. One of the most powerful institutions which has acted as a controller of the black community is the welfare establishment. With its ability to foster dependence, to invade the homes and private lives of recipients, and to regulate these lives, the welfare establishment must rank in the minds of the black community as a major threat to communal self-fulfillment. If a Jewish ghetto can be termed the gilded ghetto (Kramer and Leventman, 1961), then it is perhaps appropriate to call the black community the gelded ghetto. In the black community, the welfare establishment is seen as one of the perpetrators of this emasculation process. Practices which in the past have tended to inculcate white middle-class values and morality, practices which have enhanced the dominance of the black woman at the expense of the black male, and practices which have perpetuated the vicious cycle of poverty, discrimination, and racism are also part of the picture characterizing the relationship between consumers, social workers, the welfare establishment, and the community. As a consequence, the black community has begun to demand a more acceptable relationship, in terms of policies, programs, and personal treatment.

In recent years, the vitality of the black movement and the thrust of the black community's drive for more relevant services has been at least partly responsible for the growth in the number of black students in training for social work and other helping professions. In many ways, the black student confronting schools and programs of social work is a reflection of the confrontation taking place in society at large. Black students are challenging the assumptions undergirding theory and practice, the role of the welfare agency, and the racism which permeates the training for and the implementation of welfare programs. Through increased admission to schools of social work and efforts to challenge the welfare establishment, black students are attempting to establish a role for themselves in changing the institutional configuration within the black community. The increased use of students and paraprofessionals is one aspect of this movement. Both groups to some degree escape the socializing influence of the professional graduate school. They, especially, are looked to as interpreters of community patterns of ideology and behavior: as workers who can gain acceptance in the community as representatives of welfare institutions. Such changes in both the external and the internal systems have profound effects upon the role of the black supervisor.

Intraracial relations are becoming increasingly significant.[2]

[2] For a discussion of the problems inherent in the factors of black race and role on a more general basis, see Blackwell and Hang (1971).

Overriding all factors is the influence of the surge to self-determination by the black community. Changes in the relationship between the institution and its consumers are centered on the black supervisor. The supervisor is management, the managerial representative whose work most directly affects the consumers. But, according to the black community, if the supervisor is black then his blackness, not his agency ties, should be salient. The actions taken by the black supervisor should reflect the goals sought after by his black brothers. Black supervisors, like black workers, must demonstrate their loyalty to the black movement and the black community. They should be aware of what the black community is struggling for, of what the black person and the black family need, and above all, what the black has been denied through racism.

The conflict in the position of supervisor is most vividly experienced and seen in the relationship between black supervisor and black worker. For this reason, the conflict between agency or professional norms and the norms of the black community and its movement become exacerbated. Because the supervisor is management, he is caught between fostering agency norms and the black workers' concern for and, hopefully, championing of the cause of black clients. The possibility that conflict will materialize is great. Race and position are the major salient elements in the decision-making process. The black worker can often afford to take the role of the client and reflect client moods and desires; the black supervisor does not have this luxury. Reacting *only* as a black could be disastrous for the agency, its total clientele, the professional, the profession and, indeed, for the black community.

The role conflict between black supervisors and white workers is of relatively minor concern in this chapter. Certainly, as in traditional role dilemmas, there may be hostility between the superordinate black and the subordinate white. Although this problem may be serious in the social fabric, in my opinion the black thrust has taught us one thing, at least—that this hostility to black authority is a white problem more than black, just as it is a male problem more than female.

The black supervisor is in greater conflict over his commitment to the black movement. The greater the commitment, the greater the dilemma of whether to bring the white workers' racism into focus, and whether to teach and administer from a black perspective. The black supervisor must also decide whether or not to assign white workers to black clients, given the prevailing belief in much of the community that black workers are more effective with black clients and given the knowledge of racism within each white person. Often this problem leads to another problem: whether to appoint the less well educated black to a position in which he deals with clients or whether to appoint a white who is educationally better prepared for professional work.

Analogous issues are the dual problems of overidentification and countertransference. The black supervisor must be aware of the tendency to view the worker as an extension of himself and to perceive the relationship between black worker and black client as such an extension. Failure to take this process into account can seriously inhibit the supervisor's ability to assist either the worker or the client. In countertransference, the supervisor extends white stereotypes to black people and black life and the unique ability of the black supervisor to meet the needs and demands of the black community is seriously impaired. Although these factors do not fall within the topic of this chapter, they are, nonetheless, important factors for consideration. Certainly, other factors such as nonidentification and class differences are aspects of this problem area which should be considered when viewing the behavior of the black supervisor. (See, for instance, Calnek, 1970, pp. 39–46.)

Conflict with Black Nonprofessional Workers

In an earlier chapter, Richan discussed the general issues concerning paraprofessionals. Yet, it seems that a set of particular problems are to be found in the relationship between the black supervisor and the black indigenous nonprofessional. This nonprofessional is hired specifically because of his indigenous status and because of his ability to communicate through sharing the life style of the client population. Although training from the agency provides the worker with some skills which enable him to work within the bureaucratic structure, if he does not change his attitudes, he will retain his black orientation and community emphasis. Thus, a classic confrontation may exist between black agency staff members. The black supervisor embodies the ideology of the agency, is a product of professional training, and is a member of the middle class by virtue of his education, position, and salary. Blackness brings the supervisor and the nonprofessional together; but their blackness can also cause a crucial separation. The white establishment often thinks that being black assumes a knowledge of the black community. But such expertise is not automatic. The black supervisor should recognize this fact. But this recognition can lead to conflict over the self-perception of his black role and concern as to who is the task expert, regardless of formal position. The other role conflict which the black, as a member of management and the profession, may face is the decision regarding the socialization of the nonprofessional into behavior which is professionally more sound and useful for the agency. As a black, the supervisor can see the dulling effect of the training upon the black perspective of the indigenous person. The black supervisor must make a decision which cuts to the core of his training: whether to accept the tenets of the traditional approach or to recognize a black interpretation which may call for innovative approaches and new techniques.

Because the black supervisor is part of the management team and technically part of the decision-making process, the interaction between the black supervisor and the agency power structure is central. The black supervisor must deal with an agency whose practices and ideologies may be racist and with his role as black or professional in relation to it. The distinction between black and professional is not as clear in real life as it is on paper for there is overlap; there is a place for a professional who is black. But because so many agencies have hired blacks as window-dressing or as tokens, black supervisors often must thrust themselves forward as a means of visibly identifying blacks as a power force. To this extent, the black supervisor must place himself in a position where he can express the black viewpoint. But when he is vocal, the black supervisor comes into conflict with his role as a professional and as a member of management. All too often, the black supervisor attempts to change practices or to interpret the black vitality, only to find himself caught in the morass of the agency bureaucracy. At such times, the role conflict becomes most acute. To the degree that the black supervisor feels that he is a representative of black workers and the black community, the black supervisor may feel the strains of dissonance and retreat, either psychologically or physically. However, failure to bring about the changes which are perceived as necessary can also lead to a fixation with an alternative course of action. Although deviations from agency policy are part of the practice of workers, and supervisors often tacitly condone such actions, the press of the black movement may call for open support of such deviance. Indeed, the black supervisor might find it necessary to support either professional or community values. He is likely to be forced into a confrontation regarding his priority commitments by the black community. The resolutions of such conflicts are important as clues to possible future directions of the welfare establishment and the profession of social work. Implicit in the resolution should be clues to procedures for increased effectiveness in providing services to clients.

Summary

This chapter has looked at the role of the first-line supervisor in social agencies from a sociological perspective. The supervisor is subject to many of the traditional role conflicts of other institutional structures. The stress of marginality, part worker-oriented, part management-oriented, is found in the supervisory role in the social agency just as it is found in the industrial bureaucracy. A qualitative difference has to be taken into account with the supervisor in the social agency, however. In this case, a client population with an increasing voice in the determination of its own treatment differentiates the supervisor's dilemma from that of supervisors in the industrial complex.

The role conflict of the black supervisor is an example of this difference. The black supervisor finds role conflict in the traditional white-black relationship. But an even greater conflict exists today as a result of his role as a black, his role as a professional, and his role as a functionary of the agency. The impact of the black movement and its ideologies is manifest in all areas of a black's role behavior. For the black supervisor, the conflicts revolve around his position as a member of an agency which has, over the course of many years, supported many racist practices, practices which are denounced by the black community. As a professional, and as a black, the black supervisor is opposed to this position. As a professional, the values and norms into which he has been socialized are often in direct opposition to those of the agency, its practices, and the legal strictures which guide the agency. As a black, he is increasingly confronted by the values of the black community. The greatest conflict arises over the clash of professional and black values. I suggest that the black movement and a more unified black community provide a qualitatively different situation for the black supervisor and the black worker. They are expected to make a strong commitment to the ideology of their client community.

The discussion of the black supervisor has focused upon elements which are recognized, generally, as components of the role of a social worker as a practitioner caught in the middle. The role conflict of the black worker is an extension of these elements. I have offered no approaches to dealing with these conflicts. Of greater importance from a sociological perspective is the need to investigate them systematically. In particular, it is important to extend knowledge about intraracial conflict and accommodation. The investigation of the black supervisor in his relationship to the black worker and the black supervisor in his relationship to the black community is particularly needed. The perceptions of the black supervisor with regard to professional values versus black values, involvement in and belief in the black movement versus adherence to the agency and other factors will aid in understanding the role of supervisor. As changes which began in the 1960s come to fruition in the 1970s, such knowledge will assume increasing importance. The fact that whites are fleeing inner cities and leaving them to the black population, the increasing assumption of political power by black officials, and the increasing awareness and control of their destinies by black communities will bear heavily upon the determination of welfare policies and delivery of services in this decade. The increased enrollment of blacks in schools of social work and the increasing number of blacks working in the welfare establishment will have subtle yet profound effect upon the operations of that establishment and ultimately upon the profession of social work.

CHAPTER 6

Class and Ethnic Factors

Alfred J. Kutzik

Although the problematic social and cultural differences which typically exist between social workers and their clients have long been attended to by the profession, equally prevalent, although less evident, differences among social workers, particularly between supervisors and supervisees, have only recently begun to receive concerted attention. This concern has resulted mainly from the necessity for coping with the problems generated by the racial and class disparity between indigenous workers and professional supervisors in the antidelinquency, antipoverty, and community health programs of the past decade. Other developments during the same period have also focused attention on the heretofore little noted class and ethnic factors in social work supervision.[1] The in-

[1] Ethnicity is used here in the sense of "peoplehood," of any group which is defined or set off by race, religion, or national origin, or some combina-

creasing success which nonwhite, economically deprived minority groups have had in getting long established programs to serve them through line workers of their own background has been coupled with relative failure in replacing the entrenched white middle-class supervisors. Similarly, the increasing number of minority-group members recruited by schools of social work in recent years has resulted in more such students and beginning professionals being supervised by experienced practitioners of different social (ethnic class) identity.[2]

In the pragmatic manner characteristic of the profession's approach to all of its problems, the discussion of sociocultural issues has thus far proceeded largely on the basis of a logical piecemeal analysis of the experience of the last few years. The important problems posed by the supervision of indigenous workers by professional personnel and by the supervision of minority-group by nonminority-group personnel are here considered manifestations of the general problem of class and ethnic differences between supervisors and supervisees which have always characterized professional social work, including social agencies staffed entirely by superficially similar middle-class whites. The specific problems noted above are considered only the latest and most patent evidence supporting my contention that class and ethnic factors are as influential and sometimes more influential than organizational and professional factors in supervision. Consequently, this chapter employs a historical-sociological analysis to show how such sociocultural phenomena have affected social work supervision during the century of the profession's existence and to identify the means that have been or can be developed to minimize the negative and maximize the positive consequences of such phenomena.

From Charity to Social Work: 1840–1900

Before the last decades of the nineteenth century, practically no supervision existed of those providing social welfare services. Such

---

tion of these categories (Gordon, 1964, pp. 27–28). Social work supervision, despite the accepted understanding of this term among professional social workers to include both instruction and administrative oversight of subordinate by superior personnel, is used here exclusively in the latter sense. For similar usage see Miller (1971, p. 1494). Unless otherwise indicated, supervision is henceforth used to mean social work supervision.

[2] The combination of ethnicity and social class form the core of the individual's social identity (Gordon, 1964, Ch. 2).

services were so limited that they did not require much coordination and oversight. Despite its ubiquity, public assistance was so localized and minimal that it was generally administered by part-time unpaid overseers of the poor and, except in large cities, it was rare that even a single town clerk had public-assistance duties as his only responsibility. The many almshouses, workhouses, and "poor farms" established after 1820 each had a number of employees whose menial tasks had in some sense to be supervised, but no one provided what would today be considered social welfare services. The few institutions providing what were unquestionably such services for the orphaned and handicapped were too small and unspecialized for their noncustodial staff to have required administrative direction. This lack of administrative direction also held for the multitude of tiny charity societies manned by part-time volunteers. Such societies proliferated during the first half of the nineteenth century. The one welfare program before the Civil War which was of sufficient size and complexity to have clearly benefited from systematic supervision was the Association for Improving the Condition of the Poor, organized in more than two dozen cities after 1842. But despite the AICP's elaborate structure (cities were divided into districts, each of which had a volunteer "visitor" responsible for providing applicants with moral and practical advice as well as various forms of relief in kind contributed or collected by "members" under the general direction of a "board of managers"', there was no supervision of visitors. This was so even in New York City, whose AICP, servicing twenty-two districts with 278 sections, had a paid general agent and, until 1866, paid district secretaries who "did the administrative work for the districts and were expected to supervise volunteer visitors" (Becker, 1961, p. 385).

It has generally been assumed that, like most volunteers, AICP visitors were not supervised because they received no remuneration that could be used as the lever of administrative control. However, the essential factor may not have been the voluntary as opposed to paid nature of the position of visitor but the social identity of the incumbent. The constitution and early reports of the New York association, which served as a prototype for AICPs elsewhere, show that visitors were all dues-paying, contributing members whose socioeconomic status was similar to that of other members and not much below that of the managers and officers (*The First Annual Report of the New York AICP,* 1845, p. 5 et passim). In addition to the generally similar upper-class status of visitors, all other members and leaders of AICP were of a quite similar ethnicity: "The AICP movement was inaugurated by Protestants, controlled by Protestants, and supported by Protestants" (Watson, 1922, p. 91).[3] This common ethnic-class identity and the absence of acknowledged differentials in competence meant that proto-social workers (visitors) and quasi-administrators (managers) did not interact in a superior-inferior supervisory relationship. The most that could transpire between such social peers was advice from the more to the less experienced. And, indeed, the New York AICP had "Advisory Committees" which annually appointed district visitors and evidently proffered some advice to their appointees.[4] This system may seem like a form of "group supervision," but substantial criticism of a visitor's work, no matter of what quality, must have been ruled out because his support of the association (and that of his friends among its membership) would have been endangered by alienating him. Not surprisingly, if visitors could not be supervised by their peers, socially and organizationally inferior paid personnel also failed, despite being assigned this role by the AICP's founder and general agent (Becker, 1961, pp. 388–390). Not until 1877 was the first paid visitor hired by the New York AICP.[5]

Influenced by the example of supervision of paid workers by administrators in the charity organization societies that had been

[3] The accuracy of this generalization is only underscored by the fact that some Jews were always member-supporters of the organization. A very few Jews were visitors in its early years and one or two were committee members about 1900. Common ethnic-class identity of membership was (and is) the norm for welfare organizations, so that Jews were expected to, and generally did, participate in Jewish charities.

[4] Watson (p. 81) notes that "remonstrance was often necessary to prevent these [AICP] visitors from relaxing efforts at moral reform and . . . relying entirely upon almsgiving."

[5] Our contention that the common social identity of visitors, advisory-committee members, managers, and officers precluded supervision while effecting general conformity to association policy is supported by the little data available on the few visitors of different ethnic (and possibly class) background in the early days of the New York AICP. Of the four identifiably Jewish visitors in 1845, three were not only out of that office but no longer members by 1874. Evidently, they received more advice or less esteem than other visitors, among whom there was no such turnover.

established throughout the country after 1877, the AICP attempted to supervise their visitors. This effort met with little success, even in larger cities where the associations by 1880 employed the equivalent of executive directors ("general agents"). On the basis of two decades of experience in New York, Chicago, and Boston, a contemporary authority concludes (Devine, 1900, p. 180): "The volunteer visitors were found difficult to control; many lacked judgment; most of them were extravagant and often neglected to forward their monthly reports." He reports the typical complaint of the general agent of the Boston Provident Association who "used to say the visitors gave him more trouble than the applicants." The impossibility of having volunteer visitors supervised by paid administrators, despite the latter's greater competence based on experience and training, may be puzzling from an organizational perspective. However, from a sociocultural viewpoint, it is only to be expected that the superior-inferior relationship which earlier could not operate among social peers (visitors, advisory committee members, managers) could not now be imposed upon the same high-status visitors (usually businessmen or professionals) and lower-status paid agents, especially because the latters' wages were contributed to by their supervisees. The dysfunctional effects on AICP administration of the class differences between visitors and agents was not lessened by the fact that they were of similar WASP background. On the contrary, membership in the same ethnic group, with its own class structure and class-differentiated institutions, ranging from cliques to congregations, intensified the feeling of inappropriateness of supervision on the part of members of the upper strata working under members of the lower strata in one of the group's most publicized institutions.[6] The unprecedented need for administrative control of the expanded AICP programs during the decades of mass immigration and unemployment led to the use of paid visitors and other personnel who could be supervised, that is, individuals of social status no higher than that of their supervisors. Once this structural-

[6] The widely-distributed annual report, with its listing of officers, board and committee members, visitors, members, and their contributions—and agents and other employees—was a veritable social register of the Protestant community. The AICP's impact on the status of participants within this community is suggested by the observation of a contemporary that "their influence and their effect on public opinion was largely confined to Protestant circles" (DeForest, 1904, p. 20).

functional requirement was met, the AICP developed effective supervision. The New York association, despite its extraordinary size, was typical. By the turn of the century, it had over a hundred employees of various kinds, including several departmental "superintendents," the contemporary term for administrators. The superintendent's responsibilities included supervising subordinates.[7] Supervising was exclusively administrative oversight as indicated by the fact that in 1904 the key relief department had sixteen visitors, a visiting nurse, and two homemakers ("visiting housekeepers") as well as three admissions workers and a dozen office employees under a single superintendent. The latter appears to have been of nearly the same social class and ethnic identity as the visitors and visiting nurse but of higher status and different national-religious background than most of the "nonprofessionals," the normal sociocultural pattern of the administration structure of social agencies ever since.[8]

Despite the basic ideological commitment of the Charity Organization Society (COS) to volunteer "friendly visitors," from the first, in following the English pattern, they employed general and district agents. Unlike the situation in the AICP, this mix of high- and low-status personnel was not administratively dysfunctional for the COS. They neither intended nor attempted supervision of visitors by paid staff. Supervision was precluded by the philosophy of the COS movement. Its fundamental principle was that the inspiring example and counsel of the successful, wise, and industrious visitor was the essential means of uplifting the poor, ignorant, and indolent from degraded pauperism to self-respecting independent poverty. In the words of leaders of the COS movement: "Good men and women . . . each devoting a little of his time and thought and love to helping one or two of those who are down, you who are strong, give some of your

[7] Supervision in health or welfare during the nineteenth century meant the oversight of agencies by other agencies like the state boards of charity or charities aid societies. (See Brackett, 1903, p. 2 et passim.)

[8] For example, in 1904 the general agent, all six departmental superintendents, all seventeen visitors and six of eight nurses had English names; clerical staff included English, German, and Irish, more or less in order of job importance, and the lowest levels (messenger and office boy) held by an Italian and a Slav; unskilled caretakers and menial workers included some English, many Irish, and a few German, Scandinavian, and Slavic names ("Executive Officers and Employees," 1904, pp. 78–80).

strength to the weak. . . . You who love industry, teach it to the idle. You, in your strength of character, steady the stumbling" (Paine, 1874). "For every hopeless family there ought to be a helping, strong, wise person to undertake their education" (Lowell, cited in Devine, 1900, p. 180).

Because the superior character and wisdom of the visitor were assumed from his high socioeconomic position, there was nothing an employee of lower status—and, implicitly, inferior character and wisdom—could suggest to improve the "educational" service the visitor performed naturally. However, as in the AICP, the visitor could be and was advised by his peers. In fact, the district committees so characteristic of the COS performed this function more successfully than did the AICPs. A major factor in their success was that there was not in the early COS the constant conflict which plagued the AICP between visitors who preferred to give material relief and the organization's leaders who believed that moral example and instruction were the antidotes to pauperism. In the nineteenth-century COS, there was universal agreement that relief *caused* pauperism, and moral education alone could cure it. What the poor needed was "not alms, but a friend." Even after the terrible depression of 1893–1897, when the COS was forced to recognize that material assistance was necessary to prevent starvation, it still for some time considered relief a temporary expedient, secondary to the core program of "character building" of the poor through friendly visiting. Although the paid staff did not advise, much less supervise, visitors, they did assist them in their capacity as agents of the district committees, particularly in investigating the validity of applications for relief, whether to COS or the AICP. Far from being above the visitor in a supervisory role, the agent was a subordinate, serving rather than directing the visitor and district-committee members, an organizational relationship in congruence with their respective social positions. The district agents were themselves supervised by the general agent, but their shared social identity—middle- to lower-middle-class WASP—made this relationship unproblematic. Whether by accident or design, the fact that nearly all general agents were men and district agents were women made this superior-subordinate relationship more "natural."

These arrangements appear to have functioned well during the first decade and a half of the COS movement. But the unprecedentedly severe and lengthy depression of the mid-nineties necessitated the hiring of many new paid personnel and the recruiting of many inexperienced volunteers. The impact on COS staffing policy of the mass unemployment of the single year 1893 has been described as follows (Watson, 1922, p. 250): "Where possible, charity organization societies employed many extra workers and utilized volunteer visitors. The administrative work of the Associated Charities of Boston more than doubled during the year. In New York, the local society increased its work force about 50 per cent."

Although the newly hired agents performed satisfactorily under the tutelage of experienced staff, most of the unsupervised and largely unadvised new visitors did not (according to the canons of COS). "The experience of 1893–1894 taught many valuable although expensive lessons. . . . Foremost among these was the danger of large public [philanthropic] funds in the hands of those inexperienced in problems of relief. Even in the hands of the experienced, the tremendous congestion of work meant a lowering of standards. . . . Thousands who rushed in to relieve suffering in 1893–1894 'had no time to stop and learn that charity is quite a different thing than alms' " (Watson, 1922, pp. 263–264).

So great was the work load and so inadequate the supply and ability of volunteers to carry out COS principles that, for the first time, agents were used in large numbers as visitors rather than investigators: in current terms, as caseworkers rather than case aides. This upgrading in responsibility led to a curious development in supervision. Because the district agent assumed the function of the volunteer visitor, she was forced into the latter's position in the organization's administrative machinery and reported on her cases to the district committee for "advice." However, what had been advice or suggestions for volunteer visitors from their peers became supervision or direction for paid visitors from their social as well as organizational superiors.

The supervision of agents by district committees had already occurred before the Depression in the New York COS, for the enormous influx of immigrants into the city had made it necessary for agents to supplement or supplant the efforts of volunteer visitors in some districts. In 1892, for example, the district committee of the lower East Side reported: "No friendly visitors have been secured to lessen the burden of the agents, and the committee have felt themselves bound to a greater care and supervision of the cases in order to supplement more fully, by advice and counsel, the efforts of the agents."[9] Another district committee, which did have an adequate corps of nine volunteer visitors, reported that a large number of vagrants, who obviously could not be served by friendly visiting, had been "treated" by the agent, noting: "While the labor and responsibility of treating these homeless cases falls largely upon the agent, the committee has exercised a general supervision over them" (*Charity Organization Society of the City of New York Tenth Annual Report for the Year 1891,* 1892, p. 37).[10]

Despite phraseology indicating that it was the cases and not the agents being supervised, supervision of the latter was in fact taking place; subordinates were being directed and instructed by superiors.[11] This impossible administrative situation, with as many as fifteen lay de facto supervisors of a single agent still officially supervised by the general agent whose views must sometimes have conflicted with theirs, could not long continue. This set of circumstances evidently explains why there was so great a turnover of paid personnel around the turn of the century. The situation was undoubtedly one of the major reasons for the drive that developed at this time among most COS workers and leaders for staffing the organization entirely with paid trained personnel whose level of competence, not socioeconomic status, would be the sole basis of job responsibility. The negative experience with volunteers during the depression and the general acceptance by the developing social work profession of the theory of nonsubjective, social causation of poverty (Frankel, 1906, pp. 325 ff)—with all the economic, political, medical, and environmental factors involved—led

[9] The concluding quotation is from an article which discusses the COS personnel situation of 1893–1894: (Almy, 1895). For the overwhelming preponderance of paid staff over volunteer work in the New York COS at the Depression's end see *COS Statistics for December, 1897* (1897, p. 14).

[10] Agents had on a small scale served as visitors in New York and other charity organization societies from their inception (Kellogg, 1886, p. 452).

[11] This condition still existed a generation later when the district committees' weekly "case conference . . . composed usually of residents of the district" was characterized as follows: "The function of the case conference is, after hearing the reports of the professional worker as to the results of their investigation, to aid in the diagnosis of the more difficult family problems of the district" (Watson, 1922, p. 134).

to the establishment of formal training programs for social workers. The first of these programs was organized by the New York COS in 1898, and most of the seventeen schools of social work established in the next two decades were initiated and supported primarily by charity organization societies for their personnel. Along with the education these schools provided, the professional status which they conferred upon their graduates soon revolutionized supervisory practice in the COS (and strongly influenced other agencies who employed their students). No longer could unqualified nonprofessionals direct their work. The lay members of the case conference might advise, but only a professional could supervise another professional. Professionals now supervised nonprofessional workers including friendly visitors whether paid or unpaid.

The Family Service—Casework Field: 1900–1930

A supervisory system also existed within the public welfare sector, particularly in the large state institutions established in the second half of the nineteenth century. However, the classic bureaucratic pattern of superintendents overseeing officers overseeing employees had no influence upon nor was it influenced by the foregoing. In the settlement movement, which established neighborhood centers under private auspices in poor sections of many large cities beginning in the late eighties, there was practically no supervision among its collegial staff until the thirties and forties. Supervision in other social agencies was influenced primarily by the supervisory practice of such "casework" agencies as COS, AICP, and their successors in the family welfare field.[12]

A nationwide study of charity organization societies between 1911 and 1920 (Watson, 1922, pp. 467–479) found that the extent and nature of supervision of social service personnel varied greatly. Many small societies had none at all. The larger ones, emulated as far as possible by those with few resources, had a well institutionalized system of supervision for their paid personnel as well as some supervision of volunteers.

The new position of "case supervisor" was central to the supervision of paid personnel. Placed between the general and district

[12] For the "casework" origin of social work supervision see Robinson (1936, p. xii); Williamson (1961, pp. 41–42).

agents (now called "superintendents" or "secretaries"), the case supervisor was responsible to the former and supervised the latter. Although the case supervisor was technically supervised by the general secretary, this supervision as well as his own administrative oversight of other staff was minimal.[13] The case supervisor's job consisted in supervising the district secretaries, who, in turn, supervised the personnel in their districts.

On the basis of his reading case records and reports, the case supervisor was expected to "improve the quality of current treatment by frequent constructive criticism and suggestions." These suggestions were conveyed to the district secretaries at "regular personal conferences" and to some extent at (now advisory and educational) district case conferences, which the case supervisor attended "at regular intervals." Although the case supervisor had some contact with the paid visitors (now called caseworkers) at such district conferences, the workers were supervised by the district secretaries. This supervision followed the pattern described above, being based on case records and reports and taking place at individual as well as district case conferences. In addition, there were "regular meetings of [paid] visitors for the technical discussion of case and district work."

Although laymen were no longer involved in the supervision of social workers (as *all* paid service personnel were now called), for the first time in COS experience, the reverse was true. In some districts, district secretaries supervised volunteer visitors as nearly as possible in the same way as workers. In others, they were "supervised" by the "visitation committee of volunteers" and in a few districts by individual volunteers, although it is questionable whether such supervision was more than advice to peers from peers.

The difficulty in getting volunteers to accept supervision from workers is even more evident when it is remembered that the foregoing discussion describes practice in the best-staffed, highest standard societies. Most societies only had the traditional district case conferences. That some volunteers were being supervised by district secre-

[13] For the unimportance if not absence of supervisory responsibility of the general secretary see McLean (1927). The organization which published this book (and which McLean headed) was the successor to the field department of the Charities and Commons and the Charity Organization Department of the Russell Sage Foundation.

taries might suggest that the COS was more successful in overcoming the problematic social distance between them than the AICP had been. But this success can be attributed to the fact that many volunteers were now of lower status than in the past. An authoritative 1926 report (McLean, 1927) notes that volunteers were sometimes recruited as paid staff, evidently not from among the financially independent, high-status volunteers traditional with COS. By contrast, some workers, particularly at the district- and central-office level, came from higher strata of the middle class than those formerly typical of COS agents.[14] The consequent narrowing of the status gap between them, in conjunction with a common WASP background in most instances, permitted social workers to supervise some volunteers.

Although this development supports my view as to the importance of sociocultural factors in supervision, a concurrent development which appears to contradict it was far more significant. For now, many lower-status, non-WASPS were being employed as workers and, despite the generally higher status and different ethnicity of their supervisors, were being effectively supervised. This development is particularly pertinent to our discussion because these lower-middle- and upper-lower-class workers were largely of the same Irish and German background as most COS applicants, more or less corresponding to the indigenous workers of today. What accounts for their accepting supervision from personnel of a very different social identity? Does this acceptance negate the importance of class and ethnic factors?

But the class factor is not actually called into question, for the higher social position of supervisors and the lower one of supervisees conformed to and supported the superior-subordinate supervisory relationship, just as the earlier reverse situation conflicted with the district or even general secretaries' supervision of higher-status volunteers. Also the ethnic differences between district secretaries and workers, which had formerly hindered and often prevented supervision from successfully taking place, was no longer the almost insuperable obstacle it had been before the turn of the century.[15] The new factor which

[14] For example, see the biographies of Brackett, Bruno, Devine, McLean, and Veiller in the *Encyclopedia of Social Work* (1965).

[15] For example, in 1888, the New York COS had a district and assistant district agent with German names (Schnapp and Eisgren) and another assistant agent with a Dutch name (Plaatje), who were only briefly employed and did not

lessened the negative impact of ethnic differences (as well as that of class disparity) was training, particularly professional education.

Training of COS personnel had been practically nonexistent during the first two decades of the movement because they were considered agents carrying out the instructions of the board of directors and the district committee. There was more concern for the education of volunteers, particularly friendly visitors and district committeemen, for whom the district case conference was viewed as the primary educational mechanism. Whereas general agents attended the annual national and state conferences, district agents received no more than a brief orientation to their duties and the nature of their district on being hired. However, the traumatic experience of the depression of 1893–1897, when neither unsupervised volunteers nor untrained workers were able to function to the satisfaction of COS leadership, resulted in a fundamental change. Because volunteers were practically written off as untrainable and unsupervisable, the larger societies began organizing training programs for their many new paid personnel as soon as the depression ended. The New York COS, where an economist and university-level educator, Edward Devine, was appointed general secretary in 1896, led the way. Unsatisfied with the little he was able to develop in the way of training workers who were already carrying a regular work load, in 1898, one year after Mary Richmond's historic national conference call for a training school for professional social workers, Devine instituted a summer course for new and prospective COS workers. Soon, this program expanded into a full year course which merited the name of New York School of Philanthropy. Within a short time, thirteen schools of social work were organized by Charity Organization Societies in Boston, Philadelphia, and other cities. Increasingly during the next three decades, general and district secretaries were graduates of such institutions. By 1920, in accordance with standard professional practice, the latter were expected to instruct "new workers" in "the day's work of the society," namely, to orient them to the agency's programs and policies. In addition to this individual orientation, general or district secretaries were responsible for providing a deeper and wider orientation through

---

fill agent's positions when they became vacant in the next few years. There was one agent of German identity (Weidemeyer) but not a single Irish one for another decade.

classes "in which background is presented for technical training in the district and the relation of casework to community programs is made clear." They also were expected to arrange "seminars and study groups" for "old" workers "where problems of peculiar interest to themselves may be discussed under leadership" (Watson, 1922, pp. 479–480). By the midtwenties, in-service training for both beginning and experienced workers was so widespread that all paid personnel were conceived of by one authority as "trained, semitrained, and new" and he could state that "a society is not living up to its responsibility if it is permitting a situation to exist in which untrained workers are receiving no definite training and partially trained ones are not being guided along to further development." That this was general agency practice rather than merely professional principle is evidenced by the fact that many societies which had the resources to do so removed this heavy responsibility from the central or district secretaries and placed it on a new staff person called a "trainer" (McLean, 1927, pp. 76–77). It is not coincidental that workers of lower social status and different ethnicity than had heretofore been typical of COS personnel began to be employed and even attained district and general staff positions during this period. The worker's social position and ethnic identity were no longer important in determining his position and role in an organization in which the crucial relationships were now between profession and service-oriented staff rather than between job-oriented employees and their status-oriented employers. Because the basis of organizational positions and roles for staff had become competence in the provision of service, and because training (used here to include education) was both the main source and index of competence, it outweighed the formerly predominant sociocultural and ideological factors in COS personnel policy.

In addition to the function of conveying the knowledge and skills required for competence, training minimized the importance of class and ethnic factors through simultaneously inculcating the norms and values of the charity-organization field and, increasingly, of the profession of social work.[16] The common culture into which learners and teachers alike were socialized by training, particularly at schools of

[16] For the downgrading of ethnicity and class among intellectuals including professionals, see Gordon (1964, pp. 254–257).

social work, bridged the social distance which had formerly separated workers of various social identities.

As noted above, there had been a very few non-WASP agents or assistants who had worked briefly for the New York COS before the late nineties, but not a single one was Irish, (that is, a member of the major client group). One can only guess at the numbers of Irish "paid visitors" the New York COS was able to employ once its training program was started, but available records show that at least one of the twelve district agents between 1897 and 1905 and two of the eight or so bureau heads in the twenties were Irish.[17] Similarly, German and other non-WASP names began to appear among district and central staff with increasing frequency after the turn of the century.[18] Clinching the argument being advanced here (that the ethnic factor had become less important in supervision as a result of training) is the fact that in the twenties, these levels of staff included Jews—the white ethnic group most socially distant from the still WASP-dominated lay and professional leadership of COS.[19]

Nearly all the staff discussed in the previous paragraph, it must be remembered, were supervisors and had been supervisees of staff who were generally of a different ethnic identity and often of a different class background. Although training—and interaction in the same agency-professional social system—enabled staff to accept and benefit from supervision and offer it to others, other factors must have ac-

[17] Respectively Miss C. S. McCarty, John J. Murphy, and Ella A. O'Mara. Possibly a central staff member around 1905 named Kennady and a district secretary around 1915 named Quin were Irish.

[18] As early as 1905, Walter E. Kruesi was one of two assistant secretaries, second in command to the general secretary; Lilian Brandt was a department head. By 1914, Karl de Schweinitz was a department head, and in the twenties, Luise Kraus was a member of the central office staff. By this time, district secretaries included unmistakably German names (like Dessau and Neustaedter as well as probable ones like Bering and Dutcher). Although difficult to identify with certainty, a substantial number of names are probably of non-WASP origin, an outstanding readily identifiable one is that of the Italian-born Frank J. Bruno, who was a staff member from 1911–1914, before becoming general secretary of the Minneapolis COS.

[19] In 1926, when Bogardus found that Jews ranked eighteenth on his nineteen point social distance scale, Leah Feder was a district secretary and a year or two later Grace Marcus was a central staff member. Both were then faculty members of the COS's New York School of Social Work, a fact which underscored the role of professional education.

counted for the high degree of motivation even among those "on the receiving end" for engaging in this difficult relationship. The major factor was that supervision was the primary means of retaining or advancing one's position in the agency. Another significant factor was the way in which formal professional education had become geared to and to some extent combined with the COS's own administrative supervision. For, from the beginning, the schools of social work made practice work in an agency an integral part of the curriculum. When untrained or semitrained workers witnessed (often quite mature) students from the new high-status professional schools being regularly supervised by their (the workers') own supervisors, this acceptance naturally motivated them to participate in supervision.

The Settlement-Group Work Field: 1900–1930

A very different development than that of the charity organization casework field took place in the settlement-group work field although even more students were "supervised" in the latter. As noted above, until the 1930s, there was very little supervision of full-time settlement workers (called residents or staff). On joining the staff, new residents were loosely supervised for a short period of time by older residents, but never by volunteers. However, there was rather intensive continuous supervision by a staff of volunteers (also called nonresident associates). Why administrative practices so dysfunctional for the COS were functional for the settlements[20] can only be explained in terms of the different structures of their superficially similar organizational arrangements, particularly a work force of staff and volunteers.

In contrast to the COS, the early settlements had no boards of managers or directors and the staff were typically the social peers or superiors of volunteers. The founder-residents, who combined the roles of board and staff, were of such high socioeconomic status that they were singled out for criticism by Veblen as members of the leisure class. They were, in fact, mainly well-to-do women who had given up a life of leisure, social gospel-oriented ministers dissatisfied with the traditional ministry, and college students. Financially and administratively in control of the agencies they had created, it was the resident

[20] As evidence of the acceptance if not success of settlement staff supervision of volunteers during this period see the untroubled discussion of this subject in Woods and Kennedy (1922, pp. 436–437).

staff which set policies, including that of permitting part-time volunteers to participate in settlement work on condition that they did so under full-time staff supervision. This policy proved sound not only because volunteers were less knowledgeable and experienced than staff (which was just as true of the COS) but because volunteers were of a status no higher and often lower than staff (which was the reverse of the COS). For, although settlement volunteers were largely from the same upper- and upper-middle classes as staff, they were generally younger and less well-established and therefore in the lower strata of these groupings. Consequently, the social positions of staff and volunteers tended to conform to and support their organizational ones in the superior-subordinate supervisory relationship.

A national study of settlements conducted during the second decade of the century, twenty-five years after the first settlements were organized, found the still generally high socioeconomic status of staff was somewhat lower than it had been earlier. The great majority were, by then, on the settlement's payroll, indicating that few were persons of independent means as most pioneers of the movement had been. However, staff were still mainly "educated women" and professionals, now including doctors, lawyers, teachers, and ministers. Similarly, most volunteers were still on the lower rungs of such reputable occupations, but there were also others of less status: artists, musicians, and "craftsmen." As in the preceding three decades, the social and organizational positions of supervisors and supervisees tended not to conflict.

Of particular importance for this discussion, volunteers were considered to include students from "colleges, normal schools, institutions for teaching the practical arts, and schools of social work" (Woods & Kennedy, 1922, p. 46). So, far from encouraging staff supervision of staff, as in the COS and family societies, the example of school of social work and other student "volunteers" being supervised by staff reinforced the settlement norms of supervision of volunteers and nonsupervisory peer relationships among staff. Further, staff supervision of students influenced the supervision of all volunteers. That the latter included many current and recent students led to combining educational and counseling elements with the administrative core content of all volunteer supervision (Woods and Kennedy, 1922, pp. 436–437). While resembling the primarily educational-therapeutic supervision later developed in the family society casework field, settlement supervision of volunteers was essentially task-centered. Its educational and counseling components were behavioral, sociological, and political rather than psychiatric in orientation, and such components were secondary to and all-but-disappeared from the administrative content of settlement supervision once the volunteer was no longer a "neophyte." Both the initial and continuing supervision of volunteers was facilitated by their participation in the substantal inservice training programs characteristic of settlements from their inception, ranging from tours of the neighborhood to extensive courses.[21] Such training helped socialize into the agency and its supervisory subsystem volunteers of lower status than had earlier participated in settlement work. More significantly, by the twenties such training buttressed by monetary incentives brought into the settlements large numbers of part-time workers, obviously of lower status than the unpaid volunteers whom they increasingly replaced. This historic shift from volunteer to paid personnel was so strong that students, who now generally received stipends for doing "field work," were considered part-time staff. So again, staff supervision of students only strengthened the settlement norms of full-time staff as supervisors and not supervisees.

In a lengthy report on the settlement movement about 1920, the single sentence dealing with the supervision of staff reads: "Participation [by new residents] in clubs, classes, and societies, under experienced guidance gradually leads to positions of responsibility (Woods & Kennedy, 1922, pp. 422–433). Once a position of responsibility was attained, the regular oversight of the new resident by an older one ended. Although the absence of staff supervision was rationalized by the settlement principle of the democratic equality of all residents irrespective of their level of responsibility, it was due to the actual social, economic and educational equality of the early residents in combination with the nonbureaucratic structure of the small-scale, relatively unspecialized settlements of the 1880s and 90s. These social and organizational factors resulted in residents' relating to one another nonhierarchically, primarily through the now commonplace but then

[21] How extensive these could be is suggested by the seventeen-session course for volunteers of Philadelphia's College Settlement in the early 1890s. Woods and Kennedy discuss the training of settlement volunteers around 1920 in some detail (1922, p. 437).

novel mechanism of staff meetings. Reversing COS practice, such regular group conferences dealing with the administration of program as well as formulation of policy were no more than supplemented by occasional individual consultation. Even after settlements became larger and more specialized and persons of unprecedentedly low socioeconomic status joined their staffs, an egalitarian pattern of administration prevailed. This is dramatized by the fact that the settlements' executive directors (head residents or head workers), a position prevalent after 1900, although theoretically superior to and expected by both boards and professionally-oriented personnel to supervise other staff, did not do so.

> In the earliest [settlement] groups, a weekly meeting of residents decided details of cooperative housekeeping and outlined the program of neighborhood work. As settlements grew in size and complexity, it became necessary that some one assume continuous responsibility for the larger outline of administration and management. Under pressure of organization, settlements changed from a cooperative society to an institution in charge of a duly appointed executive. Many of the motives and some of the activities of administration on the cooperative system still [in 1920] remain. The more experienced residents still constitute the active cabinet of the headworker, and the resident body as a whole meets periodically to talk over problems of general concern. In many settlements, a variety of matters of practical procedure are referred to the whole group for vote, and the executives act in accord with the plans thus determined [Woods & Kennedy, 1922, pp. 433–434].

The implications of this passage were made explicit in the report of a study of thirty-four New York City settlements in 1927–1928 which concluded that among the responsibilities of the headworker "likely to be neglected" is "supervision of the staff" (Farra, 1935, pp. 498–499 and pp. 507, 528). With little if any administrative oversight of staff by their single superior, there was none at all by their organizational peers.

Ironically, although originating largely as the result of the uniformly high social status of early residents, these characteristic nonsupervisory administrative relationships facilitated the incorporation of lower-status individuals. By the twenties, most settlements' full-time staff included not only members of various middle-class strata but "men and women who know conditions under which artisans live through previous actual experience and count people of widely different fortunes and occupations among relatives and friends" (Woods & Kennedy, 1922, pp. 498–499). Strains between the relatively few staff of working-class origins and the majority of middle-class background were minimized by the absence of supervisory subordination of one individual to another in conjunction with the prevalence of peer group administrative and training activities characteristic of settlements.

The greater success of the settlements as compared to the charity organization and family societies in employing both part-time and full-time staff of differing class backgrounds was not only due to the factors discussed above. The multiethnic character of the settlement field played a part in this.

The early settlements were mainly founded and almost entirely staffed by WASPS. Although from the first there were a few settlements, particularly those organized by college and university people, which included non-WASPS, these were and remained atypical. However, from the first, there were also a few settlements founded and staffed by Jews, a pattern of organization increasingly typical of other groups as well after 1900. Despite the strong nonsectarian ideology of the predominantly WASP leadership of the field, many settlement-type neighborhood or community centers organized after the turn of the century were established and manned by non-WASPS. By 1922, there were dozens of such agencies "organized, administered and financed by Catholics" and over two dozen "organized and maintained by Jews." Although the staffs of the largest of these tended to be drawn from among the dominant Irish Catholics and "German Jews," smaller ones were formed and staffed by ethnic subgroups, as exemplified by the "Russian" Jewish community centers which proliferated after World War I.

In addition to the WASP character of most "nonsectarian" settlements, there were a substantial number of patently Protestant ones, among which were those of nondominant subgroups such as Lutherans. A few of the Protestant and nonsectarian settlements were founded and staffed by blacks. Entry into agencies of their own ethnic group by personnel of lower social status than the original staff was, of course, easier than entry into agencies whose staff differed in both ethnicity and class. The fact that personnel of other ethnic backgrounds found it possible to work for nonsectarian settlements to a greater extent than for COS or family societies[22] is attributable to such factors as the greater number of settlements and the less professionalized nature of settlement work. But unquestionably, among these factors was the settlements' administrative pattern of nonsupervision of full-time staff and task-centered supervision of part-time staff.

The form of administration developed by the settlements during the first half century of their existence continued to characterize them in the ensuing period.[23] Although just as authentic a part of the social work tradition, settlement administration, both supervisory and nonsupervisory, did not influence the profession as did that developed by the COS casework field. On the contrary, supervisory practice in the fields of group service and community organization was substantially influenced by the casework supervision due to the slower theoretical development of these fields and the not unrelated fact that almost all of the major schools of social work had been organized and were dominated (when not directly controlled) by the COS.

Heyday of Professional Supervision: 1930–1970

A development similar to that of the Protestant, "nonsectarian" charity-organization family-society field occurred in its Catholic and Jewish counterparts. The minority ethnic groups whose employment had been such a problem in institutions controlled by the WASP majority were beset by similar problems within their own ethnic subgroups, and they arrived at similar solutions. However, because of the various social situations and cultural orientations involved, solutions were first arrived at after 1930 by Catholics and Jews, even though these problems were just as long-standing as those of the WASPS.

Various American Catholic welfare institutions had existed from the early 1700s in which immigrants from France and their descendants played a leading role. But the key Catholic charities orga-

[22] For example, the Henry Street Settlement in 1932 included the following among its principal staff: Lillian Wald, Bertha Carter, Karl Hesley, Franklin Hanbach, Kathleen Cockburn, Dorothy Villiger, Robert Rubin, Helen Stevens, Ruth Canfield, Ethel Aaron, Eva Fry, Laura Elliot and Hedi Katz (*Directory of Social Agencies of the City of New York,* 1932, p. 735).

[23] For the continuing egalitarian approach to administration-supervision of settlement and related programs see Dimock and Trecker (1949, p. 24 et passim). For the continuing task-centered supervision of students, see Kutzik (1967).

nized in the late nineteenth century and dominant to this day were founded, controlled, and administered almost exclusively by the Irish until quite recently. The understandable difficulty of church-related institutions (based on the principle of "charity as an act of love" of the faithful Christian) in accepting the COS approach of "scientific philanthropy," performed by paid personnel greatly hindered the professionalization of Catholic charities. In addition to ideological factors, the long delay in adopting professional standards was due to a crucial difference between the program of the Catholics and the program of the "nonsectarian" charities. The latter were oriented towards case work counseling for families; Catholic charities were primarily concerned with providing institutional care for children and the aged, meeting both the cultural expectations and major welfare needs of their largely immigrant, working-class clientele at the height of unregulated industrialization. It is not surprising, then, that until the past several decades, these essentially Irish organizations rarely employed among their few paid personnel members of other more recent immigrant Catholic groups. The latter were not only ethnically different but generally of lower socioeconomic status than the board members and volunteers who—together with clergy assigned by the Irish-dominated hierarchy—administered the principal, diocesan Catholic charities. As in the early COS, both a cause and effect of this situation was the paucity of staff training. Although schools of social work were established at Catholic universities as early as 1914, these appear to have primarily trained Irish administrators for the Irish charity organizations. Only since the thirties, particularly since World War II, as Catholic social service has become increasingly professionalized (evidenced by the development of Catholic family-counseling agencies) have Italian, Polish, and other nationality backgrounds been increasingly employed and attained top administrative positions in diocesan agencies. As with the prototypical development in the "nonsectarian" field half a century before, the class and ethnic gap between board and staff, administrators and workers, and supervisors and supervisees has been bridged by professional training.[24]

[24] See the almost exclusively Irish names of the central and district staff of the Catholic charities of the Brooklyn and New York dioceses prior to the thirties and the general appearance of Italian and Slavic names among division and office heads in the *Directory of Social Agencies of the City of New York,*

Although the historical development of Catholic social service supports our view of the interrelation and impact of ethnic-class and professional-educational factors on social work supervision, the development of Jewish social service appears to contradict it. For, by the turn of the century, despite their low level of professionalization and general lack of training, the major Jewish charity societies, until then entirely administered and still controlled by "German" Jews descended from pre-Civil War immigrants from central Europe, were already employing substantial numbers of "Russian" Jews who were newly arrived from eastern Europe, not only as agents but also as executives.[25] However, this departure from the normal personnel pattern of charity organization, which prevailed among the other 98 per cent of the American population, was due to special factors affecting the tiny, insecure Jewish minority. Overriding the preference of the "German" leaders of these volunteer organizations to provide for the poor was the need for the Jewish community to "care for its own" effectively at a time of unprecedented Jewish immigration and explosively expanding anti-Semitism. At first, Americanized "German" Jews were hired as agents, but they were soon supplemented, when not supplanted, by "Russian" Jews. Although the charity society leaders and volunteers would have preferred to deal with "German" employees with whom they could better relate, the situation required "Russians" who could relate to and communicate with the predominantly Yiddish-speaking clientele and who could also serve as buffers against the demands of the well-organized, militant anti-"German" establishment "Russian" subcommunity.[26]

(1920–1972). To cite a single, crucial datum, indicating the eclipse of ethnic by professional factors in the staffing of Catholic agencies: By 1960, the executive director of Boston's Catholic Family Counseling Service was the non-Irish Rev. Joseph T. Alves, D.S.W.

[25] For this assessment of the state of professionalism and training see Bogen (1917, pp. 303–310, 335–336). See *Sketches of Jewish Communal Workers in the United States,* (1905), for background on the east European staff of major "German" charities, including Bogen himself, David Blaustein, Adolph J. Grubman, Isaac Spectorsky, and Louis Waldman. Waldman later became general secretary of both Boston's Associated Jewish Charities and New York's United Hebrew Charities.

[26] A dramatic example was the replacement of the "German" executive director of New York's Educational Alliance by the "Russian" David Blaustein over the issue of the place of Yiddish in the agency's program as a result of organized client pressures.

The difference between this development in Jewish social service and the "nonsectarian" family-service field can be seen from the fact that there was very little training and practically no supervision of workers by staff in Jewish family agencies until the late twenties. Until then, the predominantly "Russian" workers and even executives were generally considered agents of the "German" volunteers—called "friendly visitors"—and board and committee members who supervised ("advised") them.[27] In the thirties, the Jewish family agencies had to justify to the Jewish community their new emphasis on counseling service now that government had assumed the theretofore major relief function. These agencies also had to justify to the social work profession their *raison d'etre* now that nonsectarian casework agencies were beginning to employ and serve Jews. Thereupon, Jewish social service embarked on its since characteristic course of ultraprofessionalization, extensive training, and intensive supervision.[28]

At this historic moment, when the entire family–case-work field was finally united in seeking to attain professional standards, a fundamental change occurred in family-agency practice which is at the root of most subsequent problems in social work supervision. Staff training and supervision, always considered and treated as separate, albeit complementary, components of professional practice, were now combined. The traditional separation was epitomized by having different persons assigned as "case work supervisor" and "trainer" in the family societies of the twenties and was evident since 1900 in the overwhelming predominance of educational meetings, classes, and seminars for all staff over the individual orientation provided new workers by the district secretary. The separation of training and supervision was now eliminated as the result of several converging developments.

Until the twenties, social work supervision had been solely administrative oversight of the worker. The focus was so completely on the job that it was called casework supervision rather than case worker supervision. However, the new level of professionalization, evidenced

[27] For the agent status of workers around 1915, see Bogen (1917, pp. 300–315). For the continuing low level of professionalization and concern with justifying Jewish social service to the social work profession a decade later, see Cahn (1923). For the "enormous turnover" of personnel looking for positions in agencies with professional standards, see Taussig (1923, p. 49).

[28] For the beginning of supervision around 1930 in the Jewish Family Service of Philadelphia, see Eisenberg (1956, p. 27).

by the organization of the American Association of Social Workers in 1921, led the growing number of professionally trained supervisors to become dissatisfied with their essentially nonprofessional, bureaucratic role which, as our analysis indicates, devolved upon them in the course of the family-service field's divesting the lay-dominated district case conference of administrative control of paid personnel. In seeking a professional function for the nonprofessional role in which they found themselves, case-work–trained supervisors identified what they saw as the need to provide some form of therapy for the workers to help them overcome personal problems interfering with their work. In 1927, a national conference paper went as far as to advocate that the supervisor relate to the supervisee just as the worker "investigates and treats . . . the client" (Marcus, 1927, p. 286). This extreme position was shared by few, but the idea that truly professional supervision should in part deal with the worker's personal problems gained increasing acceptance. In addition to this minor quasitherapeutic function, another major new function was soon added to the administrative core of supervision—education. Then, within an astonishingly short time, this educational function subsumed the therapeutic function and replaced administration as the core of supervision. The first book on social work supervision expressed this phenomenon in 1936: "The word 'supervision' has become a technical term in social work with a usage not defined in any dictionary. Supervisors in a social agency are responsible for 'overseeing' the job in the generally understood meaning of the word, but they have, in addition, a second function of teaching or training workers under their supervision." This second function, however, was not considered secondary but primary, as the same author makes clear: "Supervision can be defined as an educational process in which a person with a certain equipment of knowledge and skill takes responsibility for training a person with less equipment" (Robinson, 1936, pp. xi, 53). The persons with less knowledge and skills were then identified as "students-in-training" and "apprentice workers." But this approach was soon extended to all workers who were not themselves supervisors (Robinson, 1936, p. xi; Williamson, 1950, pp. 19–20).

As has been suggested, a major factor in this extraordinary development which so radically and rapidly changed the nature of social work supervision was the need of professionals in a supervisory position for a professional form of supervision. But the particular form that it took and the alacrity with which it was accepted were due to other factors. Most important was the historic shift in the twenties and thirties from a social science to a psychological-psychiatric knowledge base for case work practice and the concomitant shift in practice from the prevailing socioenvironmental approach (now considered superficial and manipulative) to the psychotherapeutic "professional" approach. The new psychoanalytical gospel according to Freud and Rank was quickly made part of the curricula of schools of social work and the intellectual equipment of subsequent graduates. It was a mystery to former graduates, particularly to the large number of "semitrained" experienced workers whose education had been based on Amos Warner and Mary Richmond. The newly trained graduates, who increasingly filled supervisory positions, not only used this new knowledge to "case work" their supervisees but taught it to them. "When case work began to emerge from its sociological base, . . . supervisors became the brilliantly perceptive purveyors of the quickly developing psychological and psychoanalytic knowledge" (Rabinowitz, 1953, pp. 169–170).

Why were this knowledge and the new practice approach and skills related to it not taught to workers in classes and institutes? Why was it that the one-to-one tutorial relationship of supervisor and supervisee had to carry the educative function? In large part, it was due to the fact that the supervisors educated at the schools of social work often "supervised" students from these schools, an essentially educational process in which educational components appropriately were combined with but outweighed administrative components. This was the only kind of "supervision" which many supervisors had themselves experienced. The confusion of education and supervision was compounded by its rationalization in the literature and school of social work courses in supervision dating from the thirties. These were addressed without distinction to supervisors of students and workers. The assumption by supervisors, rather than other staff or outside specialists, of this educational function even in the larger, high-standard agencies is undoubtedly related to the fact that this development coincided with the Great Depression, requiring the conservation of agency resources and elimination of unessential personnel and programs—like the trainers and educational activities. The swiftness and success of this revolution in supervision was not only due to the previously noted need of supervisors for a role primarily dealing with professional rather than administrative matters. It was matched by the need of most supervisees, who had little or no training, to get a professional education.[29]

Because there were by now personnel of various ethnic and class backgrounds both among supervisors and supervisees, what does this change in the content of supervision have to do with the present discussion? Evidence indicates that the educational-administrative nature of social work supervision, which was functional for many workers during the thirties and forties, has been increasingly dysfunctional for them since then, particularly those of ethnic and class backgrounds different from that of their supervisors.

Although this new kind of supervision was generally welcomed by the untrained as a form of training, from its institution around 1930, growing dissatisfaction with it has been expressed by professionally trained workers. Criticism has increased as has the growing number of practitioners who have graduated from schools of social welfare. Since the mid-fifties, the literature has frequently questioned the soundness and even the necessity of such continuous supervision (Babcock, 1953; Henry, 1955). The crux of this criticism has been that supervision of trained social workers deprives them of the independence they should have in order to operate as professionals. A second major theme, emphasized more recently, is that the educational and administrative functions now carried by supervisors conflict.[30] But, more than the incompatibility of these functions is involved. The opposition of professionally trained workers to administrative oversight by professional peers is only aggravated by having to be instructed by them, both roles placing the supervisee in a dependent, subordinate position. If this position is resented by workers of the same ethnicity

[29] For social welfare as a whole, it is estimated that the approximately ten thousand paid workers in 1920 had more than doubled in number by 1930, reached forty-five thousand in 1940, and 91,533 in 1950. Very few of these were educated in schools of social work (Kidneigh, 1960, pp. 564, 568–569). The equation of supervision and professional education is indicated by the subtitle of Robinson's *Supervision in Social Work Case Work: A Problem in Professional Education.*

[30] For a summary of previous criticism and a similar position see Burns (1965), Miller (1971, p. 1495 n.), Bedford (1930), Lowry (1936).

and class as their supervisors, the impact upon those of another social identity can be surmised. Although explicit discussion of this issue has not yet appeared in the literature, it is unmistakably implied in writings by black professionals about the institutional racism in social agencies which places them in a "subordinate" position[31]—a major thesis in the chapter by Royster.

The great difficulty of providing social work supervision to untrained workers of different class and ethnicity than their supervisors has been most evident and abundantly documented in relation to indigenous workers in the federally funded community-based programs of the past decade (Pearl and Riessman, 1965, pp. 159–163, 202–206). Although it is too early for documentation, the increasing employment of untrained blacks, Chicanos, Puerto Ricans, and lower-status whites of various ethnic backgrounds in a wide range of other health, education and welfare programs, including those of traditional social agencies, indicates that resultant problems in supervising are multiplying.[32]

However, the full dimension of the issue of class and ethnicity in contemporary social work supervision is first apparent when it is realized that we have in the 1970s entered the era of the bachelor's degree professional. Unprecedented numbers of minority-group members and white ethnics of lower class origins than most present M.S.W.s will be social work practitioners with professional status resenting and resisting supervision on both sociocultural and professional grounds.

Conclusion

The lengthy historical experience of American social welfare institutions in employing and involving in supervision personnel of various class and ethnic backgrounds shows patterns of success and failure which can serve as guidelines.

Among the major conclusions that can be drawn from this ex-

[31] See the definition of white racism as "subordination" of blacks in Shannon (1970, p. 271).

[32] (Houston, 1970; Knoll, 1971, p. 284; Jones, cited in Weissman, 1969). While Mobilization for Youth is one of the new federally-funded programs referred to, Jones' discussion of its more or less traditional homemaker service demonstrates the feasibility of employing indigenous German and Italian-Americans as well as blacks and Puerto Ricans in traditional agency settings.

perience is that American welfare institutions have always tended to employ line workers of social identity similar to their administrative superiors. This pattern, which may seem questionable from the professional and liberal ideological perspectives, has generally been organizationally and sociologically sound. Consequently, a major method of dealing with the problematic relationship of supervisors and supervisees of various class and ethnic identities is to preclude it by enabling minority groups to have welfare institutions primarily employing their own members as workers and administrators in the traditional American way. Since, despite the black power, La Raza, and other such movements, equality of resources and opportunity is evidently not available to minority groups, another major conclusion which can be drawn from this discussion is particularly important: Workers of class and ethnic identity different from administrators have been successfully employed in social agencies. This has been most successful when they have been least supervised, as in the settlements. However, such workers have accepted and benefited from supervision when their supervisors have been not only organizationally, but actually, superior to them in knowledge and skill, particularly when supervisors and supervisees have had the social distance between them narrowed or eliminated by sharing a common occupational and professional orientation primarily as a result of training. However platitudinous it may appear, the principal conclusion of this analysis is that training is the key to coping with, if not solving, the problem under discussion. In our view, lack of training is the major reason that the Irish could not be employed by the WASP charity societies before about 1900 and the nonIrish by the Irish Catholic charities before about 1930. It is also why the "Russian" Jews employed by the "German" Jewish charities since about 1900 were generally not considered any more than agents to be supervised by board members and other volunteers until about 1930 when training finally became the norm in Jewish social service. Thus, historical as well as recent experience, sociological analysis, and practice wisdom support the position of those who advocate training as the major means of successfully employing indigenous workers.[33]

The historical data indicate that training of untrained or "semi-trained" workers facilitated their supervision. This thesis has been

[33] Pearl and Riessman, 1965, p. 156 and Ch. 8; Jones 1969, pp. 70, 72 et passim. For a more or less contrary view see Hardcastle (1971).

borne out by recent experience not only in social agencies, but in organizations in other fields. As an authority on administration states: "Training prepares the organization member to reach satisfactory decisions himself, without the need for the constant exercise of authority or advice. In this sense, training procedures are alternatives to the exercise of authority or advice as a means of control over the subordinate's decision. . . . It may often be possible to minimize, or even dispense with, certain review processes by giving subordinates training that enables them to perform their work with less supervision" (Simon, 1965, pp. 15–16).

This lessening of the quantity of supervision, of course, lessens the stresses and strains it must carry, so that the quality of supervision itself is changed. Whereas the in-service training of most workers in the charity societies, therefore, facilitated their supervision, it did not do so for the relatively few educated at the schools of social work. Fitting rather well into the role of supervisor, once it had become "professionalized" via the therapeutic and educational function, "fully trained," school of social work educated workers did not fit at all well into the role of supervisee. They had received training of a kind that enabled them to perform their work with a minimum of supervision or none at all. Despite the sacred tradition to the contrary, supervision is more or less dysfunctional for them. Because most social workers have until recently worked in private agencies of their own or a related ethnic grouping, sociocultural factors have not been much of a factor in their dissatisfaction with supervision. However, as the dysfunctional consequences of supervision on professionally trained supervisees are exacerbated by class-ethnic differences between them and their supervisors in the period we have now entered, the appropriateness of social work supervision of professionals is bound to be increasingly questioned. Hopefully, the profession will turn to its own history, including the long-neglected administrative counterculture of the settlement-group service field, for guidance in developing that collaborative and consultative mode of administration on the road towards which the supervision of professionals by professionals has been a long, necessary, but temporary phase.[34]

[34] The incompatibility of professionalism and supervision has been most cogently discussed by Etzioni (1964, Ch. 8).

CHAPTER 7

Group Supervision

Florence Whiteman Kaslow

Throughout the history of the social work profession in the United States, the standard supervisory practice model took the form of a one-to-one relationship between supervisor and supervisee. Protocol has dictated that each supervisee be seen in individual conferences—whether the agency has been serving individuals, families, groups, or communities. Group meetings of staff members have traditionally not had a supervisory focus; rather, they have been used for such purposes as: administrative-staff meetings to discuss general agency and client concerns, case conferences on dynamics and treatment of a particular client unit, or staff workshops on specific topics. Although all of these activities may be conducted as creative educational processes (Trecker, 1946, pp. 13–14), they differ in function, content, and structure from group supervisory sessions.

The literal meaning of supervision, according to the dictionary, is "to oversee": "to watch the work of another with responsibility for its quality" (World Book Dictionary, 1968). The role, thus defined, endows the supervisor with tremendous responsibility and control. Inherent is the supervisor's accountability to the agency director, board, community, and clientele for the type and quality of service rendered. He is expected to explain what the staff members are doing, how they are going about it, the cost of the endeavor, and what is being accomplished. His has traditionally been a mammoth, centralized task, and one wonders how the burden might be shared.

Rosemary Reynold's definition (1952) further illuminates what the prevailing ideal of supervision has been. She interprets it as a "disciplined tutorial process wherein principles are transformed into practicing skills." Tutorial implies that the one-to-one basis of the process is essential, an idea which has been challenged by increasing numbers of practitioners and educators in the past two decades and will be further challenged in this chapter. The second part of the definition, that of transforming principles into practice skills, remains a sound guide to what should occur in supervision, and it bridges the translation of theory into practice.

Traditionally, supervision has been depicted as serving educational and administrative purposes. Lucille Austin pointed out (1956, pp. 10–14) that the assignment of two such huge functions to one person leads to a concentration of power and to an overly complex assignment for the supervisor. In 1956, Austin recommended dividing these functions between two individuals, the main task of the supervisor becoming staff development and enabling workers to perform as responsible adults. Charlotte Towle emphasized (1954) enabling as a third function. A fourth component often emerges and deserves mention to complete the panoramic background against which controversies over supervision are played out. Many supervisors, particularly those rooted in casework practice, envisioned supervision as a quasi-therapeutic process. This approach is exemplified in Robinson's statement (1949, p. viii) in which she describes supervision as the most original and characteristic process that the field of casework has developed. She states that its use of relationship is rooted in deepest human sources and that its movement follows universal psychological laws. Its effectiveness in the production of personality change, essential for the achievement of skill in the helping process, is undeniable.

With all the inherent potential for personality change, perhaps because of it, supervision is perceived of as a dangerous tool. This position was amplified by Sidney Eisenberg in 1956. By then the role of the supervisor (which had been previously almost sacrosanct) was already being criticized in some quarters. Eisenberg (1956, p. 82) alluded to the "move to free workers from supervision when they reach an as yet undefined level of experience or skill." He asserted that the types of problems then being presented by clients at family service agencies were becoming increasingly severe. The emotional strain on workers dealing with very troubled clients was great, and the supervisor was expected to sustain the helper in her task through support, approval, encouragement and practical help. He describes supervision as the vehicle through which the worker herself "experiences the meaning of help" and continues to grow and develop as a helping person. He states that the guilt the worker carries "for having intervened in the life and problem of another is lightened because responsibility is shared by agency through the supervisor." He cast his lot with the urgency of continuing supervision for all workers and challenged the field not to become so immersed in the problems of supervision that its positive values would be overlooked.

In the same year that Eisenberg expressed these ideas, Austin (1956, p. 8) called for supplementing individual supervision with group supervision. Yet progress in this direction has been exceedingly slow, perhaps due to inertia as well as to the fact that many supervisors, particularly in "case work" agencies, have not felt adept or qualified in using group methods for staff development. The reliance on one-to-one supervision has flourished despite recognition that such supervision kept the worker's contacts with and access to other staff members limited and fostered dependence on and frequently resentment of the supervisor who maintained too great a modicum of control over those she supervised.

The rumblings alluded to above arose because the authority of the supervisor was being experienced by some workers as too total and often irrational. A 1960 *Study of Staff Losses* (William Tollen, 1960) analyzed reasons given for social workers leaving jobs. "Dissatisfaction with supervision was [listed] third in frequency" after "to accept offer of better job" and "moved from community." The data suggest that the major complaint was that supervision was overly close and pervasive and was not considered acceptable to or beneficial by many workers.

I will argue that when the supervisor risks herself enough to deal with several workers simultaneously, the authority she exercises is more rational and less pervasive than in individual conferences because it is open to group scrutiny. She will be less likely to exercise rigid, autocratic control, interpreting all difficulties as part of the "worker's problem" or the "worker's resistance."

In the past, the supervision structure in social agencies has had great value for inducting and training staff, providing continuity of service, and ensuring that the quality of service did not fall below a certain level. At the same time, intense, individual supervision has tended to obviate the right or ability of the worker to share his practice before and with his colleagues (Young, 1971, p. 4). Yet willingness to expose oneself to peer judgment and discussion is generally accepted as a hallmark of the professional in other disciplines.

The purposes of this chapter are to explore the rationale for and objectives of group supervision, to consider the manifold roles assumed by the supervisor in the group context and organizational framework, to analyze the structural and economic aspects of the group approach, and to add to the growing body of literature which validates the importance of group supervision as an additional and compatible approach to individual supervision in the effort to improve the quality of service being rendered. It is hypothesized that group supervision provides a broad approach which is contemporary, in keeping with social work values and principles and has a built-in flexibility.

Robert Vinter has stated (1959, p. 260) that supervision supplies a way of upgrading practice and validates the "profession's claims to technical competence." Harold Wilensky and Charles Lebeaux argue (1958, pp. 237–238) a far different view when they state that orthodox patterns of supervision (one-to-one conferences) hinder public acceptance of the claim to professional status and sometimes hamper effective interaction with members of other professions because the social worker is not esteemed as a qualified professional when he relies upon his supervisor for guidance and decisions. Social work was born and has flourished as an agency-directed rather than an individual worker self-directed profession. Historically, the need for community sanction of services fostered this development. But today it appears "antithetical to the proposed A.C.S.W. self-directed worker concept"[1] and to widely held ideals of the professional being responsible for exercising "self control over his own practice" (Barber, 1963, p. 79). This chapter is addressed to these dilemmas. I am convinced that group supervision constitutes an approach that is consistent with agency-based practice, carries out the societal mandate for service delivery by staff that is engaged in a continuous learning experience, and fosters worker autonomy and independence.

Objectives and Purposes

This section will be discussed within a Parsonian framework, viewing the aims of the supervisory process within the agency as a social system in his two dimensional model of instrumental goals and expressive goals.[2] In defining his typology of action orientations, he states (pp. 48–49):

> Action may be oriented to the achievement of a goal which is an anticipated future state of affairs, the attainment of which is felt to promise gratification: a state of affairs which will not come about without the intervention of the actor in the course of events. Such instrumental or goal orientation introduces an element of discipline, the renunciation of certain immediately potential gratifications, including that to be derived from passively "letting things slide" and awaiting the outcome. Such immediate gratifications are renounced in the interest of the prospectively larger gains to be derived from the attainment of the goal, . . . which is felt to be contingent on fulfillment of certain conditions at intermediate stages of the process . . .
>
> There is a corresponding type on the adjustive side which may be called expressive orientation. Here the primary orientation is not to the attainment of a goal anticipated for the future, but the organization of the "flow" of gratifications (and of course the warding off of threatened deprivations).

I have adapted this framework for the purpose at hand. Category I, instrumental goals, are those which are task oriented and therefore related to getting the job done. The following task-oriented goals

[1] See Young, 1971, p. 9. ACSW stands for the Academy of Certified Social Workers.

[2] See Parsons, 1951. The entire book analyzes social systems, their functioning, and their interdependence.

of group supervision seem to be paramount. (1) Establish shared learning goals. At the point where the common goals are linked to discussion of achieving individual goals, a "group contract" should be formulated (Abels, 1970, p. 307). (2) Clarify roles and functions of supervisor and each staff member as individuals and as members of the same supervisory unit to determine the nature of the relational system as a system of roles (Parsons, 1951, p. 80). (3) Utilize staff time in optimal way. (4) Enable members of supervisory group to benefit from pooling their knowledge and insights. (5) Identify special competencies of the workers and have them serve total staff as resource specialists in these areas. (6) Determine needs for additional training in specific practice areas and see that appropriate workshops or courses are provided. (7) Provide learning experiences geared to the level of competence of the members of the supervisory unit—in the areas of understanding of self and of theoretical base of practice. (8) Build loyalty to the agency and concern for the clientele. (9) Engage workers in group problem-solving efforts (Abels, p. 305). All of these subgoals contribute to the master goal which is to improve the quality of the services rendered.

Category II, expressive goals, are those with a feeling orientation. They center around supplying the emotional satisfactions to be derived from the work situation. Under this heading fall such aims as to: (1) Establish satisfying work relationships; (2) Augment self-awareness and deepen insight and acuity of perceptions; (3) Offer group support to staff members tackling difficult or controversial assignments; (4) Develop sense of belonging to a group embarked on a worthwhile, cooperative venture; (5) Enhance sense of mutuality and professional identity; (6) Provide positive feedback on each person's contribution; (7) Contribute to the pleasurable experience of mastery of new knowledge and skill; (8) Minimize sense of isolation or alienation; (9) Increase member self-esteem and confidence; (10) Foster worker's sense of autonomy, individuality, and responsibility. Maximize his ability to be self-directing.[3]

Parsons (1951, p. 80) highlights one problem likely to be encountered, "establishing the patterns of order both *within* the instru-

[3] In 1971, the National Association of Social Workers, in developing its examination for competence for the Academy of Certified Social Workers, used the concepts of "self-directed" and "autonomous" as criteria.

mental and the expressive complexes respectively, and *between* them, since every actor must have relationships of both types."

To the extent that group members can explicate both the instrumental and the expressive goals and utilize the supervisory meetings to facilitate moving toward continual realization of both sets of goals as an interrelated whole, the problem Parsons points up can become a challenge for all to meet together.

Paul Hare (1962, pp. 7–22) isolates six variables that affect the interactive process in groups. Brief consideration of these factors contributes to both a deeper understanding of the Parsonian framework utilized here and a deeper understanding of the variables that influence supervision within the small-group context. He defines interactive behavior as "the compromise between the needs of the individual and the demands of the situation." The key variables are: the task, the communication network, the leadership, the personality, the social characteristics, and the group size. Each of these variables will be elaborated upon briefly.

The ultimate task of the unit supervisor is to enhance the ability of the staff to provide service effectively. The subtasks that the group sets should bear a direct relationship to this overall objective. The communication network which evolves may be hierarchical in nature. If so, the supervisor will function primarily as the expert-teacher and administrator who possesses "the answers," sets standards and follows up on performance through evaluation (Austin, 1956, p. 8). In so doing, she may become the worker's externalized superego, thereby decreasing his sense of responsibility for his own behavior and practice and fostering dependency and conformity. In addition, workers are likely to react to the supervisor with fear and hostility. This syndrome is often repeated in traditional agencies utilizing individual supervisory conferences. However, if the process of peer-group supervision is allowed to flourish, a horizontal communication network is likely to evolve in which everyone learns from the interchange and also makes an input to his colleagues. In the latter case, individuality, creative thinking, maximum self-direction, and responsibility for one's own practice, consistent with agency policies, would be the prevailing values.

Leadership is closely tied in with the communication network. If the supervisor is authoritarian, the network will be hierarchical. If she believes in a laissez-faire philosophy, messages on expectations and issues will be unclear, and members will tend to respond with irritability and dissatisfaction. If she is democratic, a communication system will develop that allows everyone to contribute and raise questions.[4] Personality is so specific a trait that discussion of it would not illuminate the current analysis. Social characteristics (group composition) and size will be dealt with later in this chapter.

In their attempts to "solve problems in both task and social-emotional areas, groups face an equilibrium problem" (Hare, 1962, pp. 93–94). If they become too absorbed in their task, the needs of individual members are neglected; if they become overly preoccupied with group structure and member satisfaction, productivity declines. The most productive groups are those in which the rules are appropriate to the task at hand. Generally, "cooperation results in more individual motivation, . . . effective intermember communication, friendliness, and group productivity. When group members expect to cooperate, any behavior which reflects individual 'self oriented' needs tends to disrupt the group" (Hare, 1962, p. 271).

Much evidence indicates that when the amount of stress applied increases too much, groups, like individuals, are likely to react "by a lag, then overcompensation, and finally collapse." Heightened productivity is more apt to result from response to slight stress than to either extreme pressure or no pressure (Hare, 1962, p. 271).

Let us examine a program in which group supervision has been utilized in the light of the rationale and objectives explicated above and try to determine their validity and the feasibility of operationalizing them. Apaka, Hirach, and Kleidman (1967, pp. 54–60) describe how group supervision was introduced and became established in a hospital social work department. The department, lodged in a New York City veterans administration hospital, retooled itself from an individual supervisory training model to a group model. The department was comprised of fifteen professionals including twelve case workers, two supervisors, and the chief. When the new approach was initiated, a group therapy program already existed in the department. In the beginning, group supervision was only offered to the group-

[4] This typology of leaders is drawn from writings by K. Lewin and R. Lippitt, "An Experimental Approach to the Study of Autocracy and Democracy." (*Sociometry*, 1938, 1, 292–300.)

therapy leaders. After a two-year period, when evaluation showed that the experimental training had proven successful, it was decided to extend group supervision to the entire staff. At a meeting, all were told that the group method would supersede individual conferences in order to "enlarge the scope of learning to include learning from one's peers [and] increase the scope of the workers' independence and responsibility" (Apaka and others, p. 56). Underlying assumptions were that all staff would be able to "tolerate the give-and-take of group learning," take responsibility for sharing and listening in such a milieu, and that this approach would provide a road to greater maturity. Workers were divided into two groups; senior workers who had been unsupervised were included. The two persons who had been the individual supervisors became the group supervisors. Provision was made for emergency conferences and for one individual session per month in which areas such as job accountability, size of caseload, and evaluation could be handled in the traditional manner.

A review of some of the emotional responses evoked depicts the type of worker reactions that can be anticipated by anyone embarking on a similar venture. Some anxiety was obvious in everyone involved. Questions were raised as to what appropriately belonged in the group sessions and what in individual conferences. The format of the groups had to be decided upon as well as how to rotate presentations. Another issue was how "analytical" the group should become. Some workers felt deprived and frightened at being asked to operate more independently; they felt "cast adrift." Worker problems were compounded by the supervisor's uncertainties as to when to lead and when to allow the group to take the initiative. The experienced workers resented having to return to regular supervision. Each feared exposure to and attack from his peers. Some intense episodes occurred when the hostility and competitiveness among workers within the same group and between the two supervisory units flared into the open. The group process brought out previously concealed or unacknowledged subtleties of staff relationships.

Within several months, the group process was experienced as "freeing," and it did facilitate learning. The anxiety level was reduced as the supportive nature of the group structure was realized. Workers came to know that they "could concretely universalize . . . feelings by sharing them." The initial ventilation of negative affect was followed by the emergence of much positive feeling. The individual relationship with the supervisor, which some workers had difficulty relinquishing at first, soon fell into new perspective as an adjunct to group supervision. All staff accepted the group norm of increasing independence and individual decision making (Apaka and others, pp. 57–59).

Both instrumental and expressive goals came to the fore as the program got underway. Within a few months, progress was made and recognized toward the realization of these objectives. Whenever group supervision is employed, members of units expect preparation, clarity, risking, and honesty from the supervisor just as he demands it from them. These elements are essential in the shared learning experience and in the development of a sense of mutuality and trust.

Roles and Techniques

Historically, the supervisor was entrusted with two main functions: teaching and administration. In the 1950s a third task, "enabling," was added. Another role, that of quasitherapist, was identified and explicated above. Let me now present an overview of the techniques the group supervisor may use in fulfilling these functions and discuss the new role of consultant. (In this chapter, enabling is subsumed under teaching because it does not seem to be a separate role to me.)

A growing body of literature shows how urgently necessary it is to clearly delineate the roles and responsibilities of everyone involved in any work group. This delineation can be accomplished through articulation of goals and functions in the opening session, followed by the drawing up of a written agreement or contract.[5] The group's ability to follow through and realize these goals can only be ensured if the agency has developed a supportive structure that enhances the group's activities by giving them full sanction and provides for each unit to be linked into the total system in a reciprocal network.

It may be necessary to lodge responsibility for the major functions in more than one individual, that is, to designate a teaching supervisor, an administrative supervisor, and a staff trainer or consultant, not only because each job is in itself time consuming, but because the functions may have a degree of incompatibility and cause too much role conflict and confusion if delegated to a single individual.

[5] For data on contracts with groups see Berne (1966, pp. 15–16) or Bradford, in Bennis, Benne, and Chin (1961, p. 493).

No matter what functions are lodged in the supervisor, the supervisory process will evolve through certain stages.[6] The initial stage is preparatory; during this period, the supervisor thinks through his roles and how he can most effectively meet them while future group members have time to become oriented to the idea of a group supervisory process. Next is the beginning phase of becoming acquainted, exploring individual and group expectations, fears and anxieties, needs and objectives. At the end of this period, the contract should be formulated by all involved parties. Some initial trust in each other and a working relationship should come to fruition during this stage. In the next phase, which is perhaps the longest, the specific training or problem solving occurs. The group begins to try to meet its stated aims utilizing whatever teaching-learning approaches are best suited to its purposes. When one set of learning objectives is mastered, either the group as a learning unit can summarize its experiences and accomplishments and dissolve itself, or new goals can be set and the procedure for implementing them undertaken. When a group has developed in such a way that it operates productively together, it appears advisable to keep it going rather than to regroup too often. New staff members can be introduced into ongoing groups, providing these members have been oriented to the agency and to the concept of group supervision. Separate groups for new workers can also be added. When termination is desirable, the ending point should be jointly determined. In the final sessions, achievements and remaining gaps should be assessed.

There should be careful selection of students by schools of social work and of staff members (by agencies) who show promise of being capable of cognitive learning, of emotional growth and change and of the ability to translate knowledge and empathy into action or practice. Such qualities are imperative if learning is to occur and performance norms are to be established and met.

Educational Functions (The Pedagogue)

In an agency where group supervision already exists, individuals applying for jobs should be told of the approach. If they are

[6] The concept of stages appears in the literature on consultation. See, for instance, U.S. Department of Health, Education, and Welfare. This report deals with the San Mateo County Project. Also see Abels' article (1969) on supervision. The discussion here reflects an amalgamation of these sources with the author's observations and experiences.

unwilling to accept it, they will not undertake the position, and a self-selecting process for staff will be in effect. Individual orientation to the agency may be necessary if only one new worker is hired at a time; if several are added, then orientation should be joint. The agency, through the supervisor, training director, or in a manual should provide greatest clarity of job description, worker responsibility, clientele, and agency purpose. As soon as possible, the new worker should become part of a supervisory unit.

The position of director of staff training has become increasingly important as the idea of a career ladder has gained wide acceptance in community agencies. The utilization of paraprofessionals[7] and workers with associate or bachelor's degrees in addition to those with a master's poses new challenges to those charged with in-service training. The provision of educational resources, the creation of conditions under which learning can take place, maintaining focus on content to be mastered, and helping workers integrate learning experiences vital to their professional role are the major tasks Abels highlights (1970, p. 307) for the supervisor of the learning group. Possible impediments include: (1) a student's inability to consider his own or another's practice objectively; (2) the way in which he presents or interprets material; and (3) inability to tackle problems that have a "loaded" meaning. It is the students' responsibility, individually and collectively, to master the cognitive content and affective components of the learning.

The director of staff training must organize each program in light of the composition of the training unit, that is, the background and level of education and experience of the staff members and whether the group is homogeneous or heterogeneous.

By way of illustration, Atkeson relates (1967, pp. 81–82) that workers employed in Community Action Programs, which are by design temporary, express "anxiety about their insecure positions and lack of a foreseeable future." Training for neighborhood workers should be designed to: help them develop community organization and social action skills; foster awareness of common, shared problems and their underlying causes; and enable them to learn how to teach

[7] See Willard Richan's chapter for full discussion of the supervision of paraprofessionals.

problem solving and social action skills to neighborhood groups. The staff developer should help workers to: master techniques of organizing in low-income neighborhoods; understand the syndrome of poverty; serve as problem analysts, negotiators, and social action specialists and facilitators for developing "viable neighborhood and community leadership."

Evidence indicates that in many such programs professional workers are threatened by this transforming of potential clients into colleagues. However, if the position open to the "nonprofessional" is sharply defined, the areas of cooperation spelled out, and the feelings of each subgroup toward the other dealt with, then these "threats" can be minimized. Atkeson posits (1967, pp. 84–85) that training sessions which bring professional and nonprofessional staff together should be held to establish close relationships between both groups of workers. She also states that as the nonprofessional develops more job skills, the crossover into higher-level positions should be facilitated so that they can, with additional training, prepare for jobs as "case, welfare, legal, and teacher aides." However, only those nonprofessionals who voluntarily choose to receive training should.

Atkeson's position is diametrically opposed to that taken by Hardcastle (1971, pp. 56–64), who advocates placing paraprofessionals together in separate training and work units to keep them from becoming influenced or coopted by the professional culture. He believes that if the latter occurs, the benefits of the indigenous qualities for which the worker is hired are canceled. The dilemma is critical. To isolate the paraprofessional may keep him "pure" and uncontaminated, but it may also curtail his motivation and opportunity for upward career mobility and be perceived as a rationalized new form of de facto segregation.

The above exposition of the kinds of decisions the director of staff training has to make in regard to one category of workers, the paraprofessional, is illustrative of the issues faced in all training programs. The two chief concerns are: who is to be grouped together and what is the essential content of the training sessions. The type of grouping selected will necessarily influence the nature of group interaction, the substantive areas to be covered, the frequency and duration of meetings, and the definition of function of workers at various levels of the career ladder. A case can be made for both grouping models cited above, the homogeneous group or the heterogeneous group; the implications of each for staff training and staff morale should be carefully weighed before a training program is undertaken and should be reassessed periodically and modified when such alterations appear essential for improved learning to occur. A third possibility might be a combination, namely, supervisory units comprised of individuals with homogeneous backgrounds and skill levels plus larger staff-training sessions attended by workers with diversity of backgrounds and skills. Participants should be able to derive maximum benefit possible from each potential grouping.

The role of discussion leader and of lecturer are two approaches which are part of the group supervisor's armamentarium. A worker may be asked to present a troublesome case around which all members of the group can engage in a discussion which will lead to new interpretations and suggestions for handling. Or everyone may be asked to read about a particular issue or treatment modality and come prepared to discuss it. The skill with which the supervisor serves as discussion leader and encourages all to participate, her ability to be open and responsive to the group's cues, and her competence in enabling them to synthesize their learning will all contribute to how fruitful the sessions are. When a didactic lecture on a given subject is in order, the supervisor should make a well prepared presentation in an interesting fashion and allow time for questions and comments. The atmosphere she fosters will influence the type and amount of feedback. If other members of the group have expertise in a given area, they might also be asked to be a "presenter" or a resource specialist.

Arthur Leader has shown (1968, pp. 288–293) that joint participation in an interview by the supervisor and worker gives the junior staff member a "chance to see the consultant in action and to add to his own knowledge of approaches and techniques. . . . [It] permits the consultant to bring out key issues and feelings through demonstration, through emotional involvement while verbal and nonverbal reactions are taking place, rather than through filtered memories and intellectual discussions."

The supervisor's willingness to have his practice open to scrutiny conveys an attitude of receptivity to the ideas of others, of willingness to do himself what he expects of workers, and of willingness and ability to share in interviews as a cotherapist or coleader. The crisis of confidence a worker may experience in relation to his supervisor is reduced when he sees the supervisor's advanced practice skills. A worker's terror about others viewing his practice is substantially reduced when he observes his own supervisor and other staff members in direct practice. Observed interviews become normative in the agency and are experienced with less anxiety.

In the practice of family therapy, cotherapists are often used because the intensity of the emotional interaction and the complex network of communication in troubled families may be better understood and treated by two therapists working in unison than by a single one. In couples group therapy the treatment approach preferred may be to use a male-female cotherapy team. The cotherapy team present to the family a model of a more effective type of communication and the cotherapy model provides leeway in the kinds of therapeutic responses to be given (Framo, cited in Nagy and Framo, 1969, pp. 196–201). The student worker or staff member who has an opportunity to become engaged as a cotherapist or coleader of a group led by a seasoned professional can be exposed to intensive learning by direct observation of and participation with the supervisor. Such experiences can be exhilarating and highly productive.

Kohn (1971, p. 45) points up some cautions that should pertain to the use of joint interviews. The presence of the supervisor and the trainee's reaction to him will necessarily modify his "therapeutic approach." Also, because the primary treatment responsibility is likely to be carried by the senior staff person, the student may begin to "imitate him, rather than developing his own thinking and style."

Where such a coleader arrangement is not warranted, an alternative method for providing the learning opportunities inherent in the observer aspect of the role can be made available. Members of the supervisory unit can watch the supervisor's practice directly either through a one-way mirror or on video-tape. Discussion of what has transpired should occur as quickly as possible after the interview when questions and impressions are still fresh. The supervisor may find himself acquiring new insights into his own practice and characteristic behavior by addressing himself to the supervisees' responses; he can also utilize the live interview interaction as substantive material for illustrative purposes.

The same rationale applies when any member of the unit is

selected to have his practice observed. Watching a live interview between a caseworker and his client affords the supervisor first-hand knowledge of the total verbal and nonverbal interchange. Data acquired in this way lend themselves to more thorough analysis of the client's situation, the worker's actions, and their impact than do process recordings which, at best, entail worker selectivity. Although the worker's transactions may be influenced by the knowledge that he is being observed, the variation from his usual style will be less than if the supervisor is actually present; the fear that the client will sense the "superior skill" of the supervisor is diminished as is any "competitive element" (Kohn, 1971, p. 45).

When group supervision is the medium, the utilization of the observed interview can be extended. Everyone in the supervisory group can view the staff member in action. This observation allows consensual validation of perceptions (Sullivan, 1953, p. 29) and permits each member to bring his impressions to the next group meeting. The worker can utilize the feedback he receives from his colleagues to sharpen his own assessment of the clients, of their needs, of how he is relating to these needs, and of what alternative interventions he might explore. Anything salient that he has missed may be noted by someone else and a multidimensional view of what has transpired can be gained. When all members of a unit periodically have their practice observed and critiqued by one another, peer-group supervision thrives and hierarchical, authoritarian structures and policies become unnecessary. Mutual respect, trust, and freedom of interchange are fostered, and the workers serve as mirrors for each other (Apaka, Hirach, and Kleidman, 1967, p. 59).

When the supervisor in her teacher-trainer role utilizes such varied approaches as those described above, learning is made more vital and relevant to client needs than it is by rehashing process recordings in a routine series of individual conferences. Students and staff members truly learn by doing, by observing, and by thinking through problems individually and conjointly.

Administrative Functions

In most agencies, the supervisor is a member of the administrative staff.[8] He also maintains a close working relationship with prac-

[8] See Archie Hanlan's chapter for a full discussion of administrative supervision.

titioner staff. Because of his dual function, he is in a key position to help evolve sound connections between staff development and agency services (Austin, 1956, p. 5).

As an administrator, the supervisor carries a responsibility for helping paid and volunteer staff grow through individual and group activities and for developing initiative and learning from the consequences of their actions and decisions. Harleigh Trecker insists (1946, foreword) upon joint meetings of professionals and volunteers to "facilitate intermingling of minds" and places emphasis on coordinated, harmonized group participation in administration. He argues that the administrator must develop a social structure within which democratic interchange is possible. In his view, continuous mobilization of positive elements occurs through interaction of all persons concerned with the total agency. Such a process requires leadership with great insight into behavior, and skill in helping people relate to each other so that unity of purpose and effort is created.

In carrying administrative duties, the supervisor should be flexible in his procedures and capable of adjustment to meet changing conditions and needs. He is uniquely situated to be in touch with these shifts because of his continuing connections with direct services. He should see to it that policy making and operating phases of the agency are integrated so that policy flows out of operations and operations truly represent policy (Trecker, 1946, pp. 14–20).

Historically, the status of the supervisor was derived from his combination of prestige, power, longevity, and expertise. Knowledge and skill were the ingredients essential for his appointment. Lodged in this role have been decision-making authority, the right to bestow rewards, and the necessity of evaluating performance. Sources of problems for the administrator-supervisor were the disparity between "professional orientation and administrative requirements" and the need to place limits on worker initiative and autonomy, thereby invalidating the profession's claim of the self-directing nature of social work practice. Strains increased as workers gained greater competence, particularly in the frequent cases of the male worker with strong achievement and success aspirations working under a female supervisor (Vinter, 1959, pp. 261–262). Social work, which purports a nonauthoritarian ideology, contradicts itself when in practice great exercise of control and authority exists in the administrative context. In actuality, self-determination exists more for the client than for the workers.

The administrator-supervisor is expected to do many things. He is supposed to: (1) enlarge the channels of communication to promote full and continuous interchange of ideas between groups; (2) help groups know and carry their responsibilities and broaden their areas of competence; (3) organize the group's past experiences into a strong foundation for ongoing development; (4) define program aims so that immediate and long-range goals will be compatible and mutually supporting; (5) help each group define its own purposes and the relationship they bear to other groups; (6) promote an atmosphere and attitude of "harmonious interdependence" between groups—an atmosphere leading to agency unity; and (7) see that meetings are planned and conducted so as to "create and distribute satisfactions" among all members (Trecker, 1946, pp. 27–28). The first six charges are in the category of "instrumental" tasks; only the seventh pertains to the "expressive" task orientation. Some, but not all, of the responsibilities cited above overlap those that the supervisor carries in his teaching function.

Quasitherapy

Roy Lubove (1969, pp. 168–169) states that the theory of supervision in social work resulted from organizational pressure for efficiency. Professionalization through supervision became a means of assuring that the worker's performance did not fall below agency minimum requirements. Lubove indicates that during the 1920's, "a self-conscious awareness of *supervision as a kind of case work with psychiatric content emerged*—a helping process applied to the worker instead of the client. Just as the case worker labored to remove mental or emotional blocks which obstructed the client's social adjustment, the supervisor endeavored to eradicate or reshape personal attitudes and habits which detracted from the worker's professional effectiveness." This was the decade of the great psychiatric deluge.

Young has recently stated (1971, pp. 8, 11): "I think it is this image of supervision [as therapy] which most conflicts with the changing modes of today's practice as well as with the kinds of individuals who are electing social work as a career." She posits that some supervisors lost sight of the fact that "it is the worker's responsibility to change—not the supervisor's to treat."

Any new experience entails entering unknown arenas and therefore engenders a mixture of excitement, curiosity, and anxiety. New learning, particularly learning which undergirds clinical service to clients and therefore seems crucial to master so as not to cheat the client, is extremely tension laden. Add to this learning the necessity of enabling the worker to grasp the essence of the helping process, self-awareness leading to conscious use of self in the therapeutic or helping relationship, and you have the ingredients which have led many supervisors to conceive of supervision as a therapeutic process or relationship. Often, supervisors were, and still are, promoted from their positions as case workers and mold their new task from their prior one. Thus, they treat their supervisee to heighten his insight, reduce his resistances, and promote healthier personality integration rather than educating him to his tasks and how to best perform these. Because all education has growth and learning goals, therapeutic benefits may be derived from any learning experience; but therapy should not be a central goal of supervision. Supervision is geared to raising the worker's level of competence so that he can offer better service; in order to be able to do so, he should overcome emotional "blocks" to rendering such service. It is for this reason that it is so difficult to completely separate the therapeutic and educational aspects of supervision.

Clearly, in the atmosphere surrounding group training, the supervisor cannot fall into a therapeutic interaction with any given supervisee without the other members challenging the nature of the relationship and the purposes being served. Thus, group supervision offers a buffer against this danger and forces the supervisor to focus on less personal learning. In the event that a worker expresses the desire for personal therapy, she can be referred to the appropriate resource outside of her own agency.

Consultation

The increasing emphasis on autonomy for experienced workers has brought increased use of consultants. Each worker is free to seek consultation when he so desires and to accept or reject the ideas discussed. When several workers voluntarily come together for group consultation, they bear a major portion of the responsibility for agenda setting. The consultant's role is advisory and collaborative. Strain is minimized because the competence of each worker is recognized and accorded respect (Vinter, 1959, p. 263). Even though the consultant, when he is also a supervisor, may bear some administrative authority and perform evaluative functions as a regular staff member, prevailing practice has seen a shift to sharing power with high-level practitioners.

When the consultant is hired specifically as a consultant, he carries no line power of administrative authority for evaluation or promotion. Whenever a consultative model is used, accountability for practice rests with each individual practitioner; it is not a weighty burden on the shoulders of one person only. The consultant's authority is derived from his expertise in the area in which he has been called upon and his ability to "turn on" workers to deeper understandings and new interventive strategies.

Before this section on the roles and techniques of the group supervisor is drawn to a close, let me point out some possible pitfalls and provide some balance to a rather positive description. Norman Polansky (cited in Kahn, 1959, p. 315) has indicated that all staff members may turn against the parent authority figure, that is, the supervisor, and one can deduce that this possibility might be increased in the group configuration if competitive sibling-type rivalry becomes entrenched or if the supervisor attempts to create too much family feeling within the unit. As the role of the supervisor is modified to suit the demands of the group supervisory process, decision-making power inevitably becomes shared instead of centralized. Vinter (1959, p. 264) argues that as this process occurs, the authority of the supervisor is diminished and the existing structures are altered. An unanticipated consequence of these shifts may be that effective communication is impeded, unless someone assumes the responsibility for seeing that the flow of information from practice staff to administrative staff is ensured and that the work of the various units is coordinated. Another by-product may be that the prestige and gratification of the supervisor may be drastically reduced. Such a development may cause great discontent if the supervisor is not ready to "tolerate" such deprivation. Hopefully, new satisfactions will accrue that will more than offset these losses.

Despite these drawbacks to the group method of staff development, positive contributions for fulfilling the tasks of supervision appear to far outweigh the negative features.

Group Composition

It is folly to attempt to establish hard and fast rules for how large, how long, and how often group meetings should be held. But the factors which enter into the decision making can be highlighted and some guidelines suggested.

I consider the ideal group to include from four to six workers plus the supervisor. With this size group, splitting into subgroups is unlikely. The unit is small enough to afford everyone an opportunity to become an integral part of the group, yet at the same time it is large enough to provide a lively interchange of ideas. The group is comprised of enough people to share planning or executing tasks and to dilute the intensity that emerges with dyadic or triadic relationships. My view concurs with Hare's finding (1962, p. 245) that: "the optimum size for a small discussion group may be five members, since members are generally less satisfied with smaller or larger groups. In smaller groups, members may be forced to be too prominent and in larger groups they may not have the opportunity to speak. In the group of five, strict deadlocks can be avoided and members can shift roles swiftly." Hare indicates that subgroup formation is more likely when the group has an equal rather than an odd number of members.

Decisions as to frequency and length of meetings should be made after careful consideration of the level of academic and professional training and practice experience of staff members. In the past five years, increasing numbers of nonprofessionals have been hired "because they . . . add something to the service delivery in their own right." It is believed that "the nonprofessional's indigenous characteristics will allow him to serve as a bridge between the community and the agency" (Hardcastle, 1971, p. 57).

The goal of supervision, with the nonprofessional as with the professional, is to upgrade the quality and effectiveness of service being delivered. However, if, as Hardcastle states, the indigenous worker is valuable to the agency specifically because of his "ability to communicate and maintain a natural rapport with the client population unencumbered by professionalism," then the supervisory process should not seek to inculcate professional ethics, standards, or treatment approaches. Rather, it should focus on helping the new worker understand what he does that is beneficial for the client and how to do it better while encouraging him to retain the ability to spontaneously empathize with clients and to relate to them candidly on an equalitarian basis.

Hardcastle (1971, pp. 59–61) posits that paraprofessionals will be less likely to be subtly pressured into adopting professional values if they are supervised in a group of their own peers than if each is involved in a one-to-one supervisory relationship. In group sessions, the strength felt in a common purpose and orientation can be sufficient to enable each to withstand the process of cooptation. Hardcastle calls separating of indigenous workers into their own unit "compartmentalization" and states that this should "shield the nonprofessional from the dysfunctional influences of the agency and reenforce the functional influences of his peers."

If Hardcastle's model of compartmentalization of workers is followed, certain implications present themselves. Because peer group support is deemed important in enabling the indigenous worker to learn and execute his task, group supervisory meetings should be frequent, weekly if possible. Hour-and-a-half sessions should be long enough for group interaction and deliberation to occur in meaningful depth, yet not so long that restlessness and diminishing interest will set in.

A different picture emerges as we move to the opposite end of the spectrum: individuals with five or more years of practice experience after their master's degree. These workers should be able and willing to assume almost total responsibility for their own practice. The 1962 NASW Delegate Assembly established a standard of five years of full-time agency practice under a skilled supervisor as the minimum for private practice (National Association of Social Workers, 1967, p. 5); similarly this period should mark the point in the agency staff member's development when he can operate independently while still carrying out his service in accordance with agency assignments and policies. Thus, the mature, skilled practitioner should have the freedom to seek consultation from a valued colleague when he comes up against a perplexing practice problem. In addition, group supervisory meetings held, for instance, on a monthly basis would provide the opportunity for a mutual exchange of concerns, a sharing of new insights and approaches, challenges to rigid stances, discussion of current literature and research findings, and a pooling of the worker's knowledge of client needs. At group meetings workers can also be encouraged to express their own desires for change. Such a built-in avenue for expression and interchange of ideas for advanced, highly qualified personnel should add interest to the job, serve as a recognition of different levels of competence, and foster self-directed, autonomous practice. Perhaps those best able to appraise how long meetings should be are the staff members who will be participating.

Between the paraprofessional worker and the highly trained, experienced staff member with an M.S.W., there are several other categories of workers, each functioning at a different rung of competence. I will explore one more group to further illustrate the idea that the size, frequency, and duration of meetings should be adapted to worker needs, interests, and abilities. (My whole argument is predicated on grouping together workers with similar amounts of education and work experience.)

Austin has suggested (1956, p. 7) that for the first two or three years of practice after conferral of the M.S.W., the worker be considered an intern or resident in the agency. This period roughly coincides with the time required to be eligible to apply for ACSW (certified social worker) status. During these early years of professional practice, the worker has a chance to test what she has learned in graduate school, to modify it in light of what she learns from practice and from her continued readings and observations, and to immerse herself in perfecting her clinical practice skills based on an increasingly firm theoretical foundation. Group supervisory meetings held weekly for perhaps one and a half hours would be advantageous for this type of integration. By the time staff members pass their qualifying examinations for the ACSW, they have been adjudged capable of independent practice and unit meetings could decrease in frequency to twice a month. This changing structure provides recognition for the climbing of steps in the career ladder.

Individual Supervision

Abels (1969, p. 305) states that "supportive teaching opportunities such as individual evaluations . . . and conferences" are essential in addition to the group supervision. Apaka, Hirach, and Kleidman (1967, p. 59) reached the same conclusion from their study on the utilization of group supervision. Generally, I concur, but I would exempt the highly trained worker from individual supervision in favor of a consultative arrangement.

In agencies in which both individual and group supervision are part of the educational set-up, two arrangements are possible. The group supervisor can also be responsible for seeing all members of his unit in separate conferences when such is warranted for purposes of evaluation or for discussing anything which either party prefers to keep private. Either the worker or the supervisor should be free to request an individual conference, or these conferences can be scheduled on a periodic basis for all staff members. The other structure is having the group supervisor handling only the group meetings and having the members also assigned to an individual supervisor. In the latter case, it would be necessary for the two supervisors to work in close consort to prevent the worker from either "getting caught" between them or playing one off against the other. On a more positive note, having one supervisor for both parts of the educational experience lends itself to integration rather than fragmentation.

Economic Considerations

The high cost of administering social services is often decried. Community-planning committees, welfare funds and councils, and agency directors must continually seek to pare budgets without curtailing services. How can the quality of service be upgraded, effectiveness augmented, and the monetary costs decreased or kept constant?

Group supervision merits serious consideration as an economic measure. In order to obtain some current data as a basis for formulating a valid set of figures, I did a content analysis of the salaries listed in advertisements for supervisors (also coordinators and directors who are charged with supervisory functions), utilizing the July 1971 NASW Personnel Information Bulletin.

Twenty supervisory positions appeared; these were geographically distributed throughout the United States and Canada and were situated in large and small, public and private agencies. Where a salary range rather than one figure was given, the lowest figure was used for the purpose of categorizing. The spread was from $8,556 to a possible $18,000. No salary range started higher than $14,500. The breakdown according to salaries offered appears in Table 2.

Both the median and mean salaries fall in the $10,500 to $12,499 category. For purposes of computation, the midpoint of $11,500 will be used as an assumed average annual salary for social work supervisors. This average annual salary converts to a weekly salary of $221. Given an agency work week of thirty-five hours, our typical supervisor's time is compensated at the low rate of $6.31 per hour.

Table 2. Salary Range of Supervisory Positions Listed In NASW Personnel Information Bulletin; July 1971

Salary Range	Number of Positions
$ 8,500 to $10,499	4
$10,500 to $12,499	8
$12,500 to $14,499	5
$14,500 to $16,499	3
	20

The following figures are based on hypothetical averages. Six individuals supervising in diverse Philadelphia-area agencies were contacted and queried. Their time spent in supervisory conferences fluctuated between four and eight hours per week. The median figure of six hours will be used for analytic purposes. At a salary cost of $6.31 per hour, the weekly tab for individual supervision of six workers comes to $37.86. On a yearly basis, the cost for supervising six workers amounts to $1968.72.

If the same six workers were supervised in a small group which met weekly for one and a half hours, the weekly cost would be reduced to $9.47; the yearly cost would add up to $492.44. Thus, by instituting weekly group-supervision sessions to replace individual conferences, $1476.28 is saved in one year. Where large staffs are involved, this figure would multiply to a sizeable amount.

The ideal combination recommended earlier in this chapter—group supervision supplemented by individual conferences—would cost between the $492.44 for group supervision only and the $1968.72 for strictly individual sessions, depending on the package plan deemed most feasible for a given agency at a given time. Here, factors such as years of experience, level of competence of workers, pressure of service duties, and agency budget should be considered. Obviously, the economic argument for group supervision is convincing but has not often received the attention it warrants.

Summary

In this chapter, some of the criticisms and limitations of individual conferences as the only approach utilized for supervision have been discussed. Representative literature on group supervision has been considered and appears to bear out my original hypothesis, namely, that the group method provides a broad approach to supervision. The method is contemporary, consistent with social work principles and values, and has built-in flexibility. It simultaneously fosters continuous learning in the areas of conscious use of self, client needs and problems, and policy issues and theoretical knowledge. Also, the amount and variety of interchange is increased by virtue of the group participation factor. The dilemma of how to continually upgrade the level of practice to remain consistent with the "professions' claims to technical competence" without violating either the individual worker's right to be self-directing and responsible for his own performance or the agency's purpose and mandate appears to be resolved when a soundly conceived group-supervision program is implemented. Each worker then assumes responsibility for her own learning and practice, and the authority of the supervisor flows fully from his real knowledge and skill and is therefore rational. Decision making becomes a shared process and the problems confronting staff members with clients or with each other can be aired and resolved. The supervisor's energy is freed to teach, demonstrate, stimulate and synthesize rather than to control and to dominate.

I used a Parsonian framework to analyze the instrumental or task-oriented and expressive or affective goals that should be met through supervision. Here too, the use of unit meetings seemed particularly well suited for realizing individual, group, and agency objectives.

In reviewing the traditional functions of the supervisor, the two functions that are always acknowledged, administration and teaching, were viewed in terms of how these are carried out in the group context. We identified an exciting diversity of approaches. The infrequently cited role of the supervisor as quasitherapist was considered within the group framework and its intensity appeared to be diminished. The new role of the supervisor as consultant was also highlighted.

Decisions as to group size and composition, frequency, and duration of meetings need to be predicated upon a knowledge of the workers' educational and experiential backgrounds and whether the principle of homogeneity or heterogeneity of worker background and skill is used in forming groups. Increasing levels of competence should be recognized by decreasing frequency of supervisory meetings and increasing opportunities for self-directed practice.

Group supervision is much more economical than individual supervision. A "package plan" lies somewhere in between the two. To cost-minded agency executives and boards of directors, such a saving should be attractive, particularly when it can be accomplished without decreasing or diluting service. In fact, overall efficiency and the effectiveness of service will probably improve.

In conclusion, the case for adding group supervision to individual supervision is strong. The question is why the challenge to do so, which was first presented almost twenty years ago, has received so little attention. Only recently has some momentum gathered. Initiating group-supervision and staff-development programs requires courage, a sense of freedom, a willingness to risk making mistakes, a belief in the efficacy of the group process, and an eagerness to expand one's horizons and approaches. The next few years will show if we can rise to the challenge.

CHAPTER 8

Laboratory In-Service Training

Matti Gershenfeld

Professional group work was once the province of social group workers. Social workers were among the first to recognize the importance of peer norms and goals of self-directed-leadership. Yet in recent decades, social workers have shown little recognition or utilization of new theoretical knowledge and experiential techniques for working with groups. There has been little laboratory training or organization development training in social work education or welfare agencies. This may be attributable to lack of awareness of this new body of knowledge or to general fear of being unable to predict behavioral outcomes evoked by laboratory training if it were to be used.

In this chapter, I attempt to explain human relations and laboratory training so that even the reluctant may perceive it as an exciting educational advance, hopefully to be considered in their supervision and training endeavors. This approach adds yet another possible avenue for staff development to the many group-training methods discussed in the chapter by Florence Kaslow.

To mention human-relations training is to lift the lid of a Pandora's box. Human relations training has its zealots who report a workshop as having produced more effective problem solving and interpersonal growth than anything that has ever happened in their organization. Yet human-relations training also has its cynics who refer to it as a "touchy-feely" bunch of games which are not only ineffective but harmful. Some leaders are referred to as astute behavioral scientists who are cognizant of the latest psychological theories; other leaders are referred to as charismatic charlatans, out for a quick buck. It is not surprising that human relations today has its advocates and its adversaries, its supporters and critics. During the past twenty-five years, laboratory training has grown from its beginnings, when psychologists and social workers collaborated in the summer of 1946 in a training-research workshop, to what can be described as the phenomena of our times—with groups developed for everything, whether it be understanding modes of meditation, curing drug addicts, or creating organizational change in mammoth bureaucracies. The *New York Times* (Jan. 3, 1971) referred to the 60s as "the decade of the group."

There has been a fantastic outpouring of professional and popular books and articles on sensitivity or human-relations training. This period has seen the emergence of a plethora of in-plant training courses, a burgeoning number of training laboratories and seminars, the creation of new departments of psychoeducational processes or group dynamics at universities and a galaxy of meetings centered on such topics as: "What is Sensitivity Training?" "Is Human-Relations Training Effective?" "Laboratory Training or Titillating Therapy?" Little wonder that when the heat of debate is diminished and there is a brief pause, a neophyte asks: Can you tell me about human-relations training?

It is interesting to read some of the replies given when such questions were first raised and to find that the answers have not changed greatly. In 1950, John McConnell (1950, p. 549) answered: "Facetiously, someone has remarked that human relations are whatever those interested in human relations study. If one may judge by the divergent approaches of a number of research groups, no single definition is at present possible." Not only have the approaches of researchers diverged, but so have the usages made by psychologists, behavioral scientists, teachers, writers, social work practitioners, and lay people. Often, the key source of difficulty is semantic—people refer to encounter groups, sensitivity groups, marathons, laboratories, group-dynamics courses, and T-groups as if they were synonymous. Certainly, the term human relations or laboratory training means various things to various people. If the term is to continue being used, it must be defined more precisely. Four principal usages of "human relations" have developed during recent decades (Tannenbaum, Weschler, and Massarik, 1961, pp. 1–21). The term has been used to refer to:

(1) *Inter-and intrapersonal phenomena.* Interpersonal phenomena include any relationship between two people, between members of a group, between groups, and between organizations. Less frequently, the term is employed to refer to intrapersonal phenomena, the increasing of self-awareness. Although the focus of some human-relations training may not be primarily directed toward increased intrapersonal learning, it frequently occurs as additional and sometimes the most beneficial learning derived.

(2) *Techniques.* In order to find ways to increase and deepen the participation of individuals in groups with regard to inter- and intrapersonal relations, practitioners (trainers and consultants) developed a large number of innovative approaches. Techniques were developed or exercises were designed to enhance specific learnings—to afford the participants greater awareness and insight. The techniques have become so successful that some view human relations as a "bag of tricks," a field of techniques, a bunch of gimmicks.[1] Role-playing, T-grouping, trust walks, consensus testing, nonverbal games, and

[1] *Role-playing* is a technique whereby a situation which presents a conflict or aspect of behavior is identified, participants are cast in roles that that situation requires, and the action begins. Once a decision is reached or it is evident there will be no decision, the action is stopped. Participants debrief,

brainstorming are techniques which have become the basis for courses, seminars, and programs offered by industrial organizations.

Some are so enthralled by the tricks that they use them as parlor games. They also use them as a basis of "instant expertise." Unfortunately, many an "instant expert" has found that the "tricks" which were so meaningful when used by the conference leader are a "dud" when he uses them. For him, human relations is a great field so long as the technique works and a "bag of tricks" when it does not.

(3) *Ethical orientations.* Human relations has also been perceived as a set of values. If one learns to use the "proper" techniques, one will develop good human relations, as these evolve from considerate behavior. A "spirit of cooperation and understanding among individuals and groups at all levels of the organization" is promoted. In this usage, human relations is both a guide to behavior and the desirable end to be sought.

(4) *Scientific discipline.* Finally, the term "human relations" is used to denote a field of scientific inquiry—one that cuts across the traditional lines of psychology, sociology, and social work, and attempts to examine human problems in holistic, rather than narrowly defined traditional disciplines. Popular designations for this emerging interdisciplinary research oriented field are "the behavioral sciences" or more recently, "psychoeducational processes." Teaching,

---

observers report, others examine the behavior enacted for better understanding and gaining skill in empathy or conflict resolution or negotiation—whatever the goal of that particular role play is. *T-grouping* is a form of laboratory education described later in this chapter, but is basically a group which meets regularly with a professional facilitator to examine "here and now" behavior; special emphasis is placed on feelings rather than on a product or task. A *trust walk* is an often-used technique in which groups are divided into dyads; one member is blindfolded. The seeing member becomes the leader and guides the blind member. After a fixed time interval, the partners may reverse. Members then discuss their feelings about leading, being led, and the quality of the experience (typically of great closeness) to their partner. *Consensus-testing* is a method of determining whether a perception stated by one member is similar to that of other members. *Nonverbal games* are designed to use senses other than speech (touch, smell, taste, body movement) to enhance awareness of self or sensitivity to the environment. *Brainstorming* is a technique for eliciting many ideas, some practical, and some to be discarded, in a given area. It has as its goal the production of additional, more creative solutions to problems. For a fuller description of these techniques and when they can appropriately be used, see Napier and Gershenfeld (1972).

research, and applied practice are all easily discernible components of this interdisciplinary trend.

In considering replies to questions which arise most frequently, it is important to remember the diversity of meanings attached to the phrase *human relations*. Criticisms aimed at one aspect of human relations tend to be perceived as being critical of the entire field. Often questions are raised about one type of intrapersonal or interpersonal group ("Is a T-group experience a form of therapy?") and the reply is generalized to apply to all human-relations training. Sometimes, the discussion centers on a particular technique, for instance, a charge that "game playing is a waste of time," rather than an understanding of the appropriateness of the particular game to accomplish the goals of the training. Sometimes discussion centers on bizarre or flamboyant behavior by the leader, as if he characterized all group leaders; little attention is paid to the fact that the particular leader may have inadequate training, know little of scientific discipline, and nothing about the phenomena on which the discipline focuses. There seems to be limited realization that human-relations training, which is substantially different from both T-groups and encounter groups, is backed by scientific theory and research findings, albeit still evolving, and is a scientific discipline, not just an emotive experience.

Is Human-Relations Training a Fad?

The rise in the number of groups, especially human-potential and personal-growth groups, and the variability of the quality of many groups' experiences, has led some to refer to the group phenomena as the "current cult," the phase of groupies, or our mania for alternatives to alienation. To some persons, human-relations training is a passing fancy. Some of the techniques which are powerful when appropriately and competently used are meaningless gimmicks when ineptly inserted into a string of techniques. Brainstorming, perception checks, and role reversals,[2] for instance, can be highly productive when used appropri-

[2] A *perception check* is a technique whereby one checks that his perception of what is happening is shared by others; it is used to determine whether a perception is unique to the relationship of two people, or whether the given perception is a reality shared by a number in the group. *Role reversal* is a frequently used technique to allow one person to feel what it is like to be "in the shoes of another." In a supervisor-trainee conflict, it might be suggested that the

ately. Because of this success, zealots return from the group experience to the "outer world" to convince others that the technique is the way to "solve our problems." The techniques are oversold; frequently, like last year's "in thing," they are discarded for this year's "in thing."

Another fad is the use of T-grouping or sensitivity training as laboratory training. The belief that T-grouping solves all problems or is the way to increase the effectiveness of a group was a fad, and, unfortunately, still is for organizations which did not adequately understand laboratory training. Laboratory training may or may not utilize T-groups as part of its design.

The cult doing the "in thing," of going to personal-growth weekends or joining personal-growth groups will undoubtedly diminish for those seeking novelty as an end in itself or searching for intimacy among strangers as an ersatz substitute for friendships.[3]

However, when human relations training is viewed and treated as a scientific discipline, there is little reason to doubt that it is here to stay. In fact in this framework it is viewed as only in its infancy; the full impact and application of human relations training has yet to be felt. Although this evolving discipline is still young and immature, it increasingly offers insights into the problems of the individual and the organization and better ways of dealing with these problems in a constantly changing society than do traditional problem-solving methods.

Social and Organizational Milieu

Laboratory training is difficult to describe because of the variety, intensity, and complexity of the human experience generated by it. Perhaps the term *action painting* with its connotations of motion, involvement, and building on feelings and understandings of the present conveys the concept. Laboratory training is experience-based learning. It does not fit into conventional categories of education or therapy. It contains elements of both, and it is far from being understood either in terms of processes or outcomes. Its popularity is based on the singular appropriateness of this educational strategy for dealing with some of the core crises facing contemporary society. One of the newest direc-

---

supervisor act as if he were the trainee and the trainee act as if he were the supervisor. For a fuller discussion of these techniques, refer to Napier and Gershenfeld (1972).

[3] For a breezy account of a year in groups, see Howard (1970).

tions of laboratory training is known as organizational development (Bennis, 1969, iii), an educational strategy designed for bringing about planned organizational change.

Core crises exist at an individual as well as organizational level. They emerge from the increased reliance on science and technology for the solution to men's problems. They are coupled with increased bureaucratization and mechanization of communication systems and increased rates of mobility accompanied by a reduction of influence of the family and community. Man frequently is alienated, lonely, desperately seeking purpose and identity. At work he is expected to perform more and more complicated roles. It is not enough that he be a competent technician, or specialist, or business man, or administrator. He is expected to develop interpersonal competence, to work well with those on his level as well as with those above and below him in the hierarchy. He is expected to be aware of the social and political forces within which his work is imbedded and is expected to carry out his functions in a constantly changing environment in which employee turnover necessitates the development of new relationships with peers or supervisors. He may be transferred or the field of work may change and he may find himself working in a different area than the one in which he had previously developed skills. For instance, the case worker is now in community organization, and the community-organization neighborhood worker is now conducting groups in a community mental-health center. The individual's success and self-esteem may be dependent upon his interpersonal competence, adaptability, and capability of developing new skills.

The problems of organization are even more massive. During the industrial revolution, a social-institutional structure evolved which coordinates the business of almost every existing organization—bureaucracy. Bureaucracy was perfected at the time of the industrial revolution (last quarter of the nineteenth century) and was appropriate to that era. Bureaucracy seems to consist of the following components: (1) a well-defined chain of command; (2) a system of procedures and rules for dealing with all contingencies relating to work activities; (3) a division of labor based on specialization; (4) promotion and selection based on technical competence; (5) impersonality in human relations.

This model, typically viewed as the hierarchical table of organization, developed as a reaction against subjugation, nepotism, willfulness, and subjective actions that passed for management practices during the Victorian period. Bureaucracy was well suited to the values and demands of that time. Today there are four major threats to bureaucracy. First, there is rapid and unexpected change. The strength of bureaucracy lies in its ability to manage efficiently that which is routine and predictable in human affairs. The knowledge explosion, the quest for freedom and self determination, and the reordering of structures and priorities make bureaucracy, with its defined chain of command, its rules and procedural rigidities, ill-adapted for providing the kind of change the environment now demands.

Second, contemporary organizations are undergoing radical changes in size. Growth in size often creates more levels of hierarchy and increased communication difficulty. The element of complexity accompanies great size.

Providing flexibility and adaptation to the needs of a particular portion of the structure is increasingly difficult in an organization where the rules "apply to everyone." Sometimes, the traditional client of the organization either no longer exists or has moved, and the organization is faced with a need for reexamining its purposes and reordering its priorities.

Within the complex, modern organization, integration between activities and persons of diverse, highly specialized competence is required. Increasingly, specialization is not viewed as within a department but may cut across departments; promotions may not be based on technical competence alone but also on the ability to work cooperatively with others. Thus, interpersonal competence is essential in coping with changing rules, various associates, and possibly a different job than the one previously carried.

Finally, a change in preferred managerial behavior is underway. The previous trends are readily discernible: this last trend is shadowy. Yet, a changing philosophy of man seems to be emerging. It sees man as having shifting and complex needs; this concept replaces a simplified, "pushbutton" view of man (McGregor, 1960). A new concept of power based on collaboration and reason seems to be replacing power based on coercion and threat (Marrow, Bowers, Seashore, 1967). A concept of organizational values seems to be emerging (Argyris, 1964a). Organizations are opening themselves to self-inquiry and self-analysis (McGregor, 1967).

If the four threats to bureaucracy are compared with the components of bureaucracy, it becomes apparent that the hierarchical pyramid is crumbling. Whereas once bureaucracy was the standard form of organization, both individuals and organizations are faced with reexamination of this institutional form in a changing society. A series of problems exist; some involve the integration of individual needs with organizational goals; others revolve around managing and resolving conflicts. Another issue involves power and its distribution. The autonomy of any organization is changing. Increasingly, economic developments influence an organization and the individual; the government is and will be more frequently involved; there must be a maximizing of cooperation between organizations rather than competition, especially when their fates may be intertwined. Like adolescents, organizations are going through their identity crises; they are experiencing a vague uncertainty about who they are or where they are going. A changing population, emerging social needs, and concommitant changes in funding may distort previous simple goals.

These problems of integration, distribution of power, collaboration, adaptation, identity, and revitalization will generate some of the major crises with which organizations will be faced. How they manage these problems will undoubtedly determine the viability of the organization.

If we believe that every age develops an institutional form and life style most appropriate to the genre of that age, then the bureaucratic form based on an environment thought to be predictable and uncomplicated and in which man was assumed to be simple and predictable is highly questionable. It can be assumed that the bureaucratic form, and organizations based on these assumptions, will fail.

Laboratory training comes at a time when turbulence is increasing. It is an educational strategy which aims at bringing about improved human communication and collaboration and to produce improved mechanisms for coping with externally induced stress and change.

By itself, laboratory training is not capable of solving these problems, but it is one tangible and vital method which can be applied in examining and diagnosing them. At most, it provides a basis for improved mechanisms of choice and processes for solving the problems. At the least, it may help organizations and individuals to develop sensitivity to foreseeable problems.

Any educational mechanism contains a value system and a normative structure—the series of "oughts," "shoulds," and "hopes" that guide action. The basic value, the one laboratory training depends on, is "that of inquiry, examination, diagnosis, and experimentation as opposed to action, procedure, strategy, operation, and deed" (Schein and Bennis, 1965, p. 7). Specific laboratories vary greatly in goals, delegate populations, length, and setting of the laboratory as well as training design. Also, laboratories attempt to create a total and integrated learning experience, which makes it difficult to capture the feeling of the whole of the program by explaining the parts.

Laboratories attempt to provide a learning experience which is based on emotional as well as intellectual learnings; thus, each laboratory evolves in its own unique way as it expresses the personality of the participants.

Basic Premises

Action based on collected and analyzed data. A prime assumption developed by Kurt Lewin (1951), the brilliant psychologist and founder of group dynamics, is that action is to be based on carefully collected and analyzed data. The central idea of this process, called action-research, is that action should be based on as much reliable, scientifically validated data as available. Continual checks should be made on the results of the action and these data should be evaluated before further action steps are taken. In laboratory training, whenever possible, data having a here-and-now focus, and data that can be verified by those present are used to influence action. Here-and-now learning is based on experiences which are shared, immediate, direct, first-hand, and self-acknowledged. "Here and now" provides a reference point for reality, that is, concrete behavior to which concepts, words, and ideas can be related and compared.

Laboratory training based on intervention. Lewin (1951) said: "If you want to understand how something really works, try changing it." Training is directed toward intervention and change. Intervention occurs in "feedback," a process that describes messages about deviations from a desired goal. Popularity of laboratory training today may betray an important flaw in our society, the lack of an adequate and trustworthy mechanism of feedback built into our social institutions. Bosses do not level with their employees, nor do employees level with their bosses. Husbands do not level with their wives, nor do parents and children communicate candidly with each other. Feedback can be used to establish valid realities. There may be a "force-field analysis" as a means of problem solving. There may be a gathering of data for direct experiencing of conditions and an action-research procedure formulated for selecting among alternatives for action. That changes in behavior, in an approach to a problem, in reformulation of goals based on current data can occur are assumptions underlying training.

Laboratory training attempting to influence social roles. In traditional education, learning is evaluated by the teacher; results of laboratory training are evaluated in terms of the participant's increased competence and accuracy in the social and external worlds of the individual and in his contribution to the increased effectiveness of the organization.

Based upon these assumptions, laboratory training has as its goals development of self-insight or objectives related to increased self-knowledge; understanding the conditions which inhibit or facilitate group functioning; understanding interpersonal operations in groups; and finally, developing skills for diagnosing individual, group, and organizational behavior. A particular laboratory may have as its aims any of the above. For example, a trainer may design a program stressing personal learnings or create one which focuses primarily on organizational diagnosis and problem solving.

Stages

However, there is a general agreement about how attitude change and behavioral change take place. These ideas are also based on the work of Lewin, especially with regard to change theory (1951, pp. 188–237).

Briefly, change takes place in three stages. The first, unfreezing, is a graceless term which implies a period of unlearning or of being "shook up." This process can be observed in almost any enterprise in which new behaviors are required and have to be internalized—from the training period in a new job to the honeymoon in marriage. Goals may be unclear, and the reward system is nonexistent or not readily visible. There may be disconfirmation in that people hear and receive cues about their own behavior which may not be consistent with their usual perceptions about themselves. The goal of this unfreezing is a heightened desire to learn. However, ambiguity and disconfirming information may increase anxiety so that an individual is immobilized and impervious to new outputs. To create an atmosphere in which positive norms for learning, exploring, and being open to information are facilitated, a climate of psychological safety must be created. A person can behave in a "cultural island" (Lewin's term for a place away from routine pressures and responsibilities), among a group of strangers and take risks that would be terrifying to him in terms of possible repercussions on the job or with his own clients. At an organizational level, the unfreezing may take place in gathering data among the members and then sharing it. The unfreezing process can introduce a way of understanding the familiar differently.

The second stage is change, movement toward the desired behavior. A laboratory consists of skill sessions, communications techniques, simulations, experiencing of alternatives—all toward creating movement based on first-hand, direct experience with some of the desired changes. Efforts are directed toward transferability of these insights, skills, and understandings to produce increased effectiveness in social or organizational roles.

The third phase, what Lewin calls refreezing, is even more difficult than the second. It consists of stabilization of change. Often, the change that has occurred in a person after a laboratory is significant to those with whom he is in contact. He returns changed from a weekend laboratory, bringing new skills and sensitivity—at least until the next Sunday—and then he may revert back. We have learned from bitter experience that stabilizing of change, perhaps not at the level that exists upon immediate return from the infusion of the laboratory, but at a level above that of original entry, requires either reenforcement or a follow-up in training to work through difficulties encountered in attempting to maintain initial change.

These three steps, unfreezing, change, and refreezing or stabilization of change are components in creating an appropriate training laboratory for change.

Description

There are several ways to experience laboratory training. One is that an individual or an organization may decide that it is important that members increase their personal learnings. A company may send a supervisor or a team from the organization to an outside laboratory. The National Training Laboratories conducts a variety of laboratories, ranging from some in personal growth or human interaction to others in specific skill areas like conflict resolution or organizational development. The organization pays the tuition for its delegates, but it will not set the dates nor determine the consultant, the staff, or the design of the laboratory. The educators and community-specialist labs have been particularly effective in introducing the variety of perspectives which are derived from professionals in a common area but who come with a multiplicity of experiences from all parts of the country and frequently of the world. One kind of laboratory training occurs as those designated for training are delegates to an appropriate training experience. It is hoped that their learnings will be transferred to the job and will be of direct benefit to the organization through an increase in their personal or group effectiveness.

Another kind of laboratory training occurs when an organization is faced with a specific problem and desires help in its diagnosis and subsequent possibilities for action. With this approach, often a consultant is selected who is not on the organization staff, typically a behavioral scientist skilled in group training and organizational development. The consultant will meet with the "client" to determine what is viewed as the problem. Frequently the representatives of the organization are also unaware of the problem. They may speak in terms of symptoms or a general malaise. For example, one school principal spoke of the reluctance of faculty to assume any other than direct classroom assignments. They would not be sponsors of clubs, nor be class sponsors, nor take monitoring duty in the halls. These were symptoms of what?

At other times, there will be a specific task for which the organization desires the consultant. For example, an agency which specializes in work with drug addicts had received a grant to conduct a two-week training program for sixty teachers.[4] The goal of the training was to develop teams of teachers in schools within these school districts to conduct "drug" programs: programs which would reduce the need for drugs in their students. The client, the consultation and education staff contacted me to (1) develop a model program for laboratory training which with revisions could be applicable to future teacher institutes; (2) train staff in how to design, conduct, and evaluate such a program; (3) be responsible for the first two-week institute; (4) increase their team effectiveness; (5) increase their trainer skills before and after the teachers' institute. A laboratory-training experience had to be developed uniquely around the problem the client presented. Part of the training occurred on a weekly basis in the offices of the staff, part took place in a two-week residential laboratory at a nearby college. The follow-up sections of the training took place in a two-day program in each of the three school districts.

When an outside consultant is utilized, the organization pays the fees for the training program. The fee is part of the consultation contract. Effectiveness is based on the talent of the consultant, the willingness and ability of the client system to be committed to the plan of approach, and the relationship between the consultant and the organization. Training can occur at a residential site where the daily problems of family and job do not intrude. Or the setting may be nonresidential and consist of a day of training in the place of business. It may also be only several hours of training per unit extended over a period of time. There are advantages of each model although for unfreezing to take place, the residential setting has obvious advantages.

For many kinds of organizational change to occur, at least at the beginning, the consultant must be outside the organization. An outside consultant has access to influencing the power structure to an extent unlikely by a lower ranking member of the organization. There is also psychological safety in the recommendations the consultant makes. As a result of these, he can lose the consultation contract, but that has limited impact compared with the in-house consultant who can lose his job. Finally, the outside consultant can view the organization, its needs, resources, and problems with greater objectivity based

[4] Eagleville Hospital in Eagleville, Pennsylvania: Summer, 1971.

on experience with many organizations as well as lack of involvement in the relationships and norms of any one specific organization. When training has these implications, an outside consultant is most likely to induce the changes needed.

Another kind of laboratory training may be developed by the training staff of an organization, typically known as "inside consultants." In some large corporations, like Union Carbide, RCA, and Gulf, there are behavioral scientists trained to conduct laboratory training for new employees, for first-line supervisors, and for divisions. When training involves diagnosis of the organization or reexamination of goals and priorities, an outside consultant will be called in to work with the regular training staff for reasons mentioned above. In some cases, as with the U.S. Civil Service, the training staff hires consultants to conduct workshops as needed by various departments.[5]

Elements

The initial steps have been highlighted. To summarize, it is necessary to establish the goals of the desired laboratory training, obtain a suitable place, make arrangements with a trainer or consultant, formalize a contract, and arrange for release-time schedules for participants.

Next, it is important to develop a training design. This phrase refers to the schedule of the training program, which is predicated upon the previously developed laboratory assumptions, understandings of change theory, and, specifically, the expressed objectives of any given training program in the time schedule agreed upon.

The trend is toward shorter laboratories, a weekend or five days. Sometimes, the design will consist of a basic human-relations lab, a lab in which the goals are personal learning and "learning to learn" through the laboratory method, followed by working toward developing more specific skills needed by the organization. Frequently, the training will be limited to a weekend with a specific focus, followed by other weekends for additional training. In a nonresidential setting, the design will be spaced over a designated time period.

[5] The Philadelphia region of the U.S. Civil Service conducted a series of training laboratories focused on women in management. They used consultants who were expert in this area during 1970–1971. The Philadelphia region staff contacted and hired the consultants. They designed the program based on expressed management needs.

Laboratories generally are made up of the following components as appropriate to that training.

T-groups. These may be the basic-learning group which continues to meet throughout the course of the laboratory. It usually consists of about ten people who meet with one or two staff members. Sessions are usually unstructured and the staff provides a minimum of formal leadership. All training programs do not necessarily have T-groups, particularly organizations working on team building as units, or working as task forces on a problem, or where the prime goal is not personal learning.

Information or theory sessions. Laboratory training is not anti-intellectual. Rather, it is opposed to teaching which only takes the form of didactic or intellectual approaches. There may be a general session for the entire group in which a staff member gives a demonstration, imparts knowledge of research, or explains a concept. This is usually done informally and is based on integrating experience with cognitive knowledge.

Focused exercises. Exercises are generally introduced and conducted by the staff member who at the end of the session leads a discussion on the implications or learnings derived as related to the goals of the laboratory. For example, if increased communication skills are one of the goals of the laboratory, then people should begin to hear each other and talk to each other. Thus, listening skills can be the basis for a focused exercise. The staff member will ask that the participants divide themselves into groups of three. He will ask that one be the observer, that is, observe behavior of the other two, feed it back to them, and also monitor them to make sure they adhere to the rules. He will ask the dyads to have a conversation on an agreed upon subject. One will begin the conversation and express his point of view. The other, prior to responding with his opinion, must paraphrase to the first person's satisfaction what has just been said. If the first person indicates that the paraphrasing is incorrect, the second person modifies his statement or may ask for clarification and rephrase. Once approval is attained, person two continues the discussion with his own new input and the rules reverse. This continues for about ten minutes. Afterwards, the facilitator will ask how people felt in this exercise. Some will report that it required a great deal of concentration and that they were tired. The implication develops that if we are tired after listening for ten minutes, how much do we really listen? One participant commented that it felt strange because he became aware that he does not listen. He picks up a few cues, formulates his reply and simply waits for an opening to insert his opinion. Another person said that she realized that she changes what the person says to disagree with her so that there can be an argument. She never realized how much she did this until it became apparent she seldom paraphrased correctly.[6] Hopefully, these vignettes provide enough to explain how focused exercises are utilized to enhance skills and understandings appropriate to the laboratory goals.

Diagnosis of organization: problem-solving. Participants may learn a model for diagnosing their organization or dealing with a problem by gathering data on it, and presenting the findings for critiquing. Other times, it may be a genuine analysis leading toward a design which has as its goals organizational diagnosis, selecting among alternatives for a plan of action, considering steps, and evaluation of the actions. Sometimes, the diagnosis is developed at the laboratory, areas of alternatives brainstormed, but the follow-up work is done subsequent to the laboratory, where task forces can gather data beyond the laboratory and formulate recommendations for later presentation.

Informal contact and grouping. Except in a very short laboratory in which too much is planned, segments of time are purposely left unplanned. This affords an opportunity for each delegate to meet with whoever may have generated an idea in him, an opportunity to clarify a misunderstanding, a time to informally discuss with others feelings about the structured learnings. Because a great amount of emotional energy is generated with little physical outlet, this becomes a time to physically release tension in touch football or a lethal game of basketball or simply to talk and reflect.

Anything else. Laboratory training is flexible in its design. Participants may make suggestions for alteration of the design for any reason, for instance, a "kooky spontaneous idea" that "one way to develop team relationships is to create a contest." Other ideas pre-

[6] These comments were expressed at a communications workshop for Presidents of B'nai Brith chapters which I conducted in Atlantic City in the Spring of 1971.

sented included one to start everything an hour later and go an hour later so that all could have more morning sleep. If we are committed to a spirit of openness of communication and flexibility and one of the goals is joint responsibility, why not? Sometimes, the design is changed because an issue has developed which diverts the group from its prime goals and unless this issue can be settled there will be little effort expended in the planned direction. Like an action plan, a design is a first approximation of a goal. It may be modified after the first step is taken and from that vantage point its appropriateness for continuance is surmised.

Evaluation. The last portion of a laboratory will be devoted to evaluation. It may be a simple feedback device to obtain the participants' responses to the training with simple questions like: On a scale of one to ten, how would you rate this laboratory? The ratings may be followed by asking: What did you find most helpful? What did you find least helpful? What would you need to build on the learnings here? This may be tabulated after the laboratory; however, it is most effective to share on the spot, to reinforce the concept of sharing and learning from data. It also allows the appropriate follow-up or future training.

Another form of evaluation is to divide people into small groups and ask them to discuss their learnings and how they might utilize them in their "home environment," on the job. They may be asked to consider what resistances will be encountered and how these can be overcome. The members take turns responding to the question and sharing both their hopes and anticipated frustrations. Others in the group serve as both a support to sharing problems as well as consultants for examining possible approaches for reducing the constraining forces. The effect is to allow participants to bridge from the training to the back home situation and recognize that transferability of learning is to be considered thoughtfully.

Follow-up training. The stabilization of change produced by the laboratory is of short duration; regression to the former position or a slight modification occurs with discouraging frequency. A follow-up training experience is increasingly built into the training design for two prime reasons. First, the knowledge of the follow-up acts as a motivating force to each person to attempt to practice and hopefully report favorably on the utilization of his new skills. In addition, he develops a subconscious sense of a group involved with him. Whatever happens, he feels he will share it with others, they will understand, and he will know at a deeper level the difficulties and the support needed by the others.

A training laboratory will be constructed from the components described. Depending upon the goals, those components most applicable will be incorporated. It is a seductive trap to present a design for one training laboratory as an example. The seduction takes place as the reader takes the design "in toto" and uses it in his program, and the first rule of laboratory training is abhorrently violated, namely, that a laboratory is designed for a specific population, to meet their needs, and recognize the environment in which they work and the objectives of that training program (Miles, 1959; Golembiewski and Blumberg, 1970).

Organization Development

There is a specific form of laboratory training evolving known as organization development which seems to be the future of laboratory education. It is an educational strategy specifically "intended to change the beliefs, attitudes, values, and structure of organizations so that they can better adapt to new technologies, markets, and challenges and the dizzying rate of speed itself" (Bennis, 1969, p. 2). It is based on the principles of laboratory education previously described except that its focus is organizational change, specifically the people (rather than technology or structure) aspect of an organization. It includes (1) problems of the future—identity, change, revitalization; (2) problems of interpersonal relationships and human satisfaction; and (3) problems of organizational effectiveness (Bennis, 1969, p. 13).

Organization development occurs much like the consultant-client relationship previously described. There is an outside consultant who meets with the authorized planning group or executive of the organization to discuss the exigency with which that organization is attempting to cope. A point of entry or procedure for beginning is based on a variety of criteria, and an organization development program (educational strategy) is designed. Data are generated with regard to the exigency; there is feedback to the people and groups who would be affected by these data, and an action plan is formulated based upon the results of steps one and two. The difference in organization development is that a consultant continues to work with an organization over a period of time not only designing, training, and developing programs but also possibly consulting with the head of the organization, gathering data through interviewing, using a variety of approaches toward helping his client, namely, the organization.

It might be helpful to cite some examples of laboratory training from my consulting experience to offer a full picture of the subject, rather than to leave the reader with only abstract concepts.

Example 1: Board Training. A large, prestigious, venerable, community recreational agency was faced with a dilemma.[7] In the past it had been relatively easy to obtain funds for the organization. A board, made up of members who passed both their allegiance and seats onto members of their family, had been willing to sit and discuss and then rubber stamp professional staff decisions. The board was faced with the fact that there would have to be a sizable expansion program or the agency would continue to slip in the performance of its services. The new staff required a working board to sit on committees, and arouse community interest. The board in the past had poor attendance and had disdained actual involvement in working with the clientele of the agency; it had been passive.

Some of the more active members of the board, as members of a study committee, recommended that new members be appointed who were representative of the community, representative of a variety of skills and professions, and willing to become involved in the future development of the agency. In attempting to fulfill these criteria, 40 per cent new board members were elected.

The problems to be confronted were: that the board not become polarized into new and old groups; that information be transmitted to new board members on relationships to other organizations and on funding; that there be created an atmosphere of revitalization; and that new, more positive norms be created.

Since board members donate their services, and funding was not available for a residential training experience, it was decided to begin the changes with a training meeting for the total board. It was held as a dinner meeting, and the importance of attendance was

[7] The agency described is a Jewish community center in Philadelphia; the training occurred in 1970.

stressed. Members of the executive committee greeted people at the door, introduced them, and seated members at tables for six. Old and new board members were heterogeneously grouped. After the sociability and beginning of communication, the formal session began. The design was ostensibly simple. By tables, groups were asked: What information do you need to be an effective board member? List your questions on newsprint (large sheets of paper frequently used to gather and share data). This afforded members a chance to raise questions and in some cases have them answered by old board members who no longer felt threatened because they felt rather like teachers. In situations where a question was asked to which old board members did not know the answer, they initiated "getting an answer to that." The questions gave legitimacy to surfacing hidden agenda questions which a person would have been embarrassed to ask. The board immediately got into an active role.

The questions were festooned on the walls. Then resource people answered the questions. A check was made that the question was answered to that group's satisfaction. Then a second question was asked: Given this information and an understanding of the present and future of the agency, what do you see as the functions of board members? Discuss them and list them. Board members could privately confront their own roles and examine them in light of the newly understood needs of the agency. As a group, they were faced with defining their role on the board in their own terms. The identified conflict lay between a nonpressured attitude toward attendance and involvement versus the commitment of time and energy required to implement agency objectives. There was also the facing of the question: Is board membership a prestigious listing on a letterhead, or is it more? Although half an hour was allotted, it was insufficient. Discussion was animated. Functions were eventually listed, posted, and shared. There was unanimity that a board membership meant an active, working role.

The third question posed was: "How can the board carry out these functions? What recommendations do you make?" Post these. The data on functions was visible to all and had been agreed upon. The third question was viewed as a logical extension of the previous one. Participants worked seriously in discussing problems, dealing with potential constraining forces, and exploring possibilities for approaches.

The newsprint listing, now familiarly posted and eagerly awaited, cited recommendations. The recommendations stated that each board member is to be active on at least two committees; each is expected to attend at least one activity a month; meetings would be held monthly, with one hour devoted to business and the second to training so that members become familiar with the community and the agency.

In the two years since that initial training meeting, there has been a significant change in the agency in the direction desired. The recommendations were adhered to because the group developed and made a public commitment to the functions to be served as well as how they would be carried out. The active process, the shared data, the utilizing of each others' resources, and being accountable for decisions made were in embryonic form that evening. However, they developed into powerful norms in the revitalization of that agency.

Example 2: Team Development. A professional staff of a recently opened community mental health center was deluged with difficulties of rivalry, suspicion, confusion as to rules, and ambiguity as to role.[8] Staff meetings were stormy and frustrating. People who had only worked for the center for a few weeks were putting out feelers for other jobs. Client services were often in a state of confusion as to responsibilities, especially with regard to additional duties, coverage on holidays, even answering the phone when the receptionist was out. A strategy was developed with the director of the center which was a variation of one created by McGregor (1967, pp. 171–172). A meeting of the staff was called, and I was officially introduced. They had previously voted to hire me and entertained high level fantasies about the potential for change I might accomplish. After a brief talk in which I explained that they would be gathering and sharing data and making recommendations toward development of an "effective management group," I suggested that we might begin gathering data. After some initial reluctance (I think they expected me to advise them on what they were "doing wrong") we began. The McGregor Team-Development Scale was to be the instrument for helping the group understand the dimensions of becoming a team, reporting their feelings, and sharing in discussing common concerns. After the scale was

[8] A community mental health center in Philadelphia encountered the situation described in the Fall of 1969.

introduced and each variable was discussed, the members were instructed to fill out a form anonymously, rating their personal view of the group on each dimension. The data was collected and the tallies were recorded with the median high and low scores marked. All of this was posted on newsprint and immediately available to the group. On the basis of the data, the group discussed how the "lows" felt, how the "highs" saw it, and how most people saw it. This was done for each variable and, based on the discussion, the group decided which dimension to begin to work on. The training continues with the ranking of areas to be worked on in future training sessions.

The rating scale (Table 3), as varied, might be helpful for understanding how a simple instrument can be the vehicle for the process of laboratory education and building an effective team.

This exercise allows members to validate their feelings about the group and begin to analyze how the group can become effective. Because, on the illustration cited, the data were theirs, the usual hostility toward or negation of data did not occur. There was high confirmation for what each member perceived himself as feeling privately but did not believe was shared. It was a surprise that there was so much agreement about the "state of the team." The results led to an immediate change in the communication as perhaps for the first time members began to "level" with each other.

Hopefully, these two illustrations serve as reminders that laboratory training involves entry based on exigencies or problems of the organization, involves gathering and sharing of data, requires giving and receiving feedback from others as the "people component" is viewed as of high priority, and is based on experienced data.

Conclusions

Laboratory education is a relatively new educational strategy aimed at enhancing the range and validity of alternatives to improve the process of choice. It does this by promoting conditions in which experiential data can be the basis for increased understanding of self, relations to others, and organizational roles. It attempts to create an attitude of inquiry and openness to human phenomena (Klein, 1968).

Laboratory training is not a panacea (Krafft and Howe, 1971). It can be ineffective, frustrating, and even dangerous. In planning that it become a boon to a staff development or training program in any social or welfare agency or organization, consider the following:

(1) What are the problems being faced? What are the short- and long-range goals? What are the methods available for meeting

Table 3. TEAM-DEVELOPMENT SCALE

(1.) Team objectives:

1	2	3	4	5	6	7
Not understood					Clearly understood	

(2.) Degree of mutual trust:

1	2	3	4	5	6	7
High suspicion					High trust	

(3.) Communications:

1	2	3	4	5	6	7
Guarded					Open, free	

(4.) Degree of mutual support:

1	2	3	4	5	6	7
Each takes care of himself					Shared responsibility	

(5.) Handling conflicts within team:

1	2	3	4	5	6	7
Avoidance					Working through conflicts	

(6.) Degree of influence on other team members:

1	2	3	4	5	6	7
None					A great deal	

(7.) Organizational environment:

1	2	3	4	5	6	7
Restrictive: no room for deviation					Supportive: respective of individual differences	

Adopted from McGregor (1967).

these objectives? Utilize resources of those who have skills in this area to minimize risk of a new strategy.

(2) Limit the objectives. When one has unrealistic expectations, disappointment and disillusionment are inevitable. Most organizations have problems and difficulties which cannot be resolved with two weeks of training.

(3) Transfer of learning should be the primary concern in every training intervention. The protected environment of the training program needs to be enhanced with role-plays, follow-up sessions at work, or simulations. These "transfer" sessions give the person an opportunity to reexamine his goals and design alternative strategies based on the tests of personal and organizational realities.

(4) Training in one part of an organization will not solve human problems in other parts unless parallel and complementary changes are made there. Training a board to take a more active role in an agency is of limited value if the professional staff prefers to operate in privacy and secrecy.

(5) Find and use competent resource personnel. Choose someone who openly states his own values: someone who can be trusted to do whatever he can to accomplish what he sets out to do. His goals should be consistent with the defined goals of the organization. Seek someone who has a broad range of intervention experiences rather than just sensitivity training. Select a person committed to an organized but flexible problem-solving approach; avoid someone who seems to have all the answers prior to, or even after, thorough diagnosis. Be wary of someone who has a packaged set of techniques applicable to a broad spectrum of objectives; the package is only appropriate if it meets a specific need which has been carefully diagnosed. A consultant should be able to define specific objectives and describe why certain objectives are more appropriate than others.

Laboratory training is a relatively new approach capable of coping with the unparalleled changes ahead. In its spirit of inquiry, in its stress on learning to learn, in its continued openness to human phenomena, it may provide a potent model for continued self- and organizational renewal.

Hopefully, as social welfare agencies and institutions examine their roles for the future, they will venture toward new kinds of relationships utilizing laboratory training and organization development in their striving to become effective, adaptive, and congruent with the needs of the times. Laboratory training can be considered in training new staff, in supervising those at a lower level, in creating peer teams. Organization development can be an effective means of diagnosis of an organization and examining areas of stress. It can become the basis of problem-solving and subsequent action plans. It is an educational strategy worthy of serious consideration.

CHAPTER 9

Student Training in a Geriatric Center

Ruth Cohen

In an earlier chapter, Florence Kaslow discussed the rationale for and approaches to group supervision and staff development. I will amplify the idea of training, focusing on a small unit of workers who constitute a peer group. All have a similar level of education and experience. This chapter evolved out of a specific practice situation and validates the proposition that a staff-training unit composed of from four to six members meeting weekly can be an effective learning vehicle and provide an atmosphere

I wish to gratefully acknowledge my students' permission to quote freely from conference material, unit meetings, and their papers. I also wish to express my appreciation to the Philadelphia Geriatric Center and particularly to the social service staff. Their warmth, enthusiasm, and cooperation facilitated the creation of the Student Training Unit and helped expedite its operation.

conducive to mutual support, stimulation, and deepening understandings necessary for effective practice. Although the unit was composed solely of graduate social work students and their supervisor, it is posited that similar training would be beneficial to beginning graduate workers in this or a comparable setting for the aged. The training, in addition to sharpening practice skills, encompassed familiarizing the workers with the agency, its functions and purposes, its community environment and the fields of gerontology and thanatology.

The University of Pennsylvania and the Philadelphia Geriatric Center jointly instituted a training program in the field of aging for students of the university's graduate School of Social Work in September 1969 (Cohen, 1971). This pilot project was made feasible for a five year period by a grant received by the university from the National Institute of Mental Health. This program represented a pioneering effort in broad scale cooperation between a school of social work and an institution for the aged. It was aimed at providing social work students with a well rounded understanding of the problems of the aged individual and the members of his family. This chapter analyzes and summarizes the essence of the student-training unit for the two-year period from September 1969 through May 1971. It should be possible for the reader to extend its applicability to a variety of practice settings.

Agency Setting

The Philadelphia Geriatric Center is composed of four constituents: the Home for the Jewish Aged; the York Houses, which are apartment-type residences; a hospital accredited by the Joint Commission on Accreditation; and the Gerontological Research Institute. The entire population includes men and women whose ages range from 62 to 101. They come from diverse socioeconomic backgrounds and represent several generations of elderly people. The heterogeneity of the residents served within the Home is reflected in the facilities in which they reside. The facilities are set up to allow for movement of the individual along the continuum of care, matching each person's changing needs with appropriate services essential at that point in time.

In addition to the elderly groups who actually live at the Center, a number of other groups are served. These reside in the outside community. Applicants to the Home comprise one of these groups.

Requests for admission are frequently made at a point of crisis and may be precipitated by problems for which institutional care may or may not be an adequate solution. The service is therefore viewed as family counseling rather than a screening or referral process.

Those on waiting lists comprise a second group. The social work staff maintains contact with persons awaiting admission in order to assist with interim planning, refer them to supportive services, and be "tuned in" to warning signals of crisis. In addition, there is a special "deferred status" list consisting of aged persons who prefer to remain in the community as long as possible but who want a link with the institution as a protection for possible future usage.

A third group consists of those in intermediate housing. The Center owns several small houses on an adjacent street. These have been renovated to accommodate three women in each house. Although some services such as heavy cleaning, distribution of frozen dinners, social work, and recreational services are provided by the Center staff as needed, these women are viewed as essentially independent.

The Philadelphia Geriatric Center has played an innovative and leading role in the field of treatment of the aged. It has attracted an outstanding staff, which includes many knowledgeable professionals who have earned recognition in their particular disciplines of geriatrics, gerontological research, and social work. Thus, the level of sophistication of the staff and the wide spectrum of facilities and services of the Center combined to make it a unique and fine setting for this undertaking in graduate-student training in the field of the aged.

Program Focus and Content

In planning the students' caseloads and other assignments, my focus as field-work instructor was on making field-work placement stimulating, enriching, and challenging.[1] With principles of generic social work as the theoretical base, one of the aims of the unit was to provide the type of educational experience that would enable the students to master a body of knowledge and to test out the theoretical material content through a practical application of beginning skills. Integrated experiential learning was the goal sought. Having super-

[1] During the first two years of the project, I was a lecturer in social work and the field-work instructor of the training unit for the School of Social Work, University of Pennsylvania.

vised many graduate students entering the field of the aged during the past eighteen years, I was cognizant of the pessimism and negativism that students can bring to field-work placement in this area of specialization. Our students are a product of our youth-oriented culture and begin their field-work training with many stereotypical ideas regarding the aged (Blank, 1970). Therefore, the students' beginning case assignments were carefully picked and included persons who were reasonably well and those who were most intact and capable of establishing relationships.

The student's clients were selected from: (1) persons in the application process; (2) residents in the Home; and (3) those on the waiting list (active and deferred). Such a composite caseload provided a wide range of experiences in that their clientele included people of both sexes, people with a diversity of status and family composition, and people with some degree of mental or physical impairment or both. As the year progressed, older persons with severe disabilities were added to their caseloads so that by the end of the year each student had become experienced with the aged ranging from persons reasonably well to the severely impaired. Throughout both years, the complexity of the assignments was increased. Many cases involved not only working with the older person himself but with his relatives, including adult children, nieces and nephews, siblings, and interested friends. Implicit in the selection of cases, too, was involvement with other community-health and welfare agencies, either on a cooperative or collaborative basis, thus providing the student with firsthand knowledge of the community network of resources.

The fledgling staff members also received an exposure to gerontological research in a very alive, dynamic way in that they learned how much of the research undertaken at the Center was applied research and became integrated into practice, thus enabling staff to provide effective service to clients.

During the students' first month, they became involved in an orientation program consisting of ten sessions. These sessions provided them with an opportunity to meet with the administrative heads, chiefs of services, and directors of departments, to learn about each one's particular area of competence, and to become familiar with the various programs and services within the Center. This orientation helped to lay the foundation for a meaningful, ongoing relationship with professionals from other departments. Throughout the year, the students attended many interdisciplinary conferences, occasionally as observers, more frequently as participants. These conferences afforded excellent training. Each student presented her own cases, and in needing to "work up" the case, began to learn how to formulate diagnoses and to determine treatment goals.

The students were also given the invaluable opportunity of working directly with staff representing other disciplines within the Center. They collaborated with physicians, nurses, occupational therapists, psychologists, and volunteers. These cooperative efforts helped expose students to the mutual respect and the exercise of self-discipline essential for an effective multidisciplinary team approach. Although their major concern was always the individual resident, their client, they began to take hold of the concept of the resident as part of a larger field with the institution representing and replacing the community in which the elderly person had formerly lived. This piece of knowledge helped to extend the student's perception of her own role as advocate and helper and of the role of the agency as the "change agent" in the broader spectrum of social welfare services.

From its initiation, the student-training unit was an integral part of the Social Service Department. The students were included in the weekly staff meetings of the department, carried the responsibility for taking minutes, presenting problem cases, and preparing abstracts of current articles in the literature on the field of the aged. They were expected to fulfill responsibilities similar to those carried by the regular staff. The students were encouraged to raise questions and express their ideas. Their presence stimulated a provocative exchange of viewpoints and fostered consideration of many crucial issues. The Center staff felt strongly the responsibility to make available its many resources for educational programs to students in all disciplines (medical students, social work students, and nurses), and the prevailing climate was one of acceptance and receptivity to the neophytes. Most important, the students were given the feeling that they were vital and helpful and that their contributions augmented service to the clientele group of the Center. The spirit of warmth, cooperation and helpfulness that prevailed within the agency, and particularly within the Social Service Department, was a heartwarming barometer of the quality of collaboration that existed as the student training unit moved ahead to become a live, viable, creative unit within the Center operation.[2] In the second year orientation period, students from the Center were invited to the other agencies to become familiar with that agency's program and operation. This cross-fertilization contributed to a broad understanding of the aged and how their needs could best be met.

Students

During the first year of its operation, the student-training unit consisted of four graduate students (three first-year and one second-year),[3] a field-work instructor, and a secretary. The students knew little about the field of gerontology and had little, if any, professional experience with older persons. Being a product of today's society, they all harbored many stereotyped impressions and myths about older persons. They were oriented toward children, youth, and young families, and displayed negative attitudes toward the elderly.

Each student had been to the geriatric Center for an interview prior to her decision and the school's to place her in this unit. When the placement began, she had already had some contact with the aged residents. However, I am certain that the students' decision to come was more related to their excitement at being admitted to graduate training, to the generous size of the stipend, and to the quality of the setting than to a strong interest in the field of the aged. The staff and the residents regarded these attractive, bright-eyed, mini-skirted young women as a breath of fresh air. Their spontaneity, so characteristic of today's student, was refreshing in this milieu. Their questioning was challenging, albeit ofttimes exhausting. The girls' common denomi-

[2] The students in the unit helped to lighten the burden of an already overworked and dedicated staff. For example, after the first six weeks of the first year, by which time they had become familiar with agency operations, the students carried responsibility one day a week for the telephone inquiries and walk-in receptions, totalling 93. During the 8½-month year (1969–1970), the students carried 74 cases, held 384 interviews with residents or interested members of their families, and had 170 interviews with applicants of which 126 were home visits.

[3] Three were in their early or middle twenties, one was several years older. Two were married, and one had a daughter nine years old. Two went into graduate school immediately following graduation from an undergraduate college, and the other two had some prior experience in social work. They were all females, and one student was black.

nator was their deep sense of caring about people and their growing commitment to learning.

Again in the second year, the unit was composed of four students; this time two second-year students and two first-year students. In addition, two other students in the field of aging, one placed at the Philadelphia YMHA Jewish Centers and one at the Jewish Family Service, participated in some of the unit's meetings. They also joined the unit on our field visits. The visits included a trip to a private sectarian family agency which had a specialized department for services to the aged, the county home for the aged, a home for the black aged, a high-rise low-cost apartment building for the elderly, and a community center with a division of services to senior citizens. These additions broadened the input and enabled the group to gain an expanded view of the gamut of services to older persons and of the problems and concerns with which the practitioner needs to deal, whether the older person is reasonably well and living in the community or is physically or mentally impaired and a resident of the Home or a nursing home.

Components of the Training Process

Individual supervisory conferences were held weekly for an average of one and a half hours. These conferences were supplemented by on-the-spot conferences as needed with colleagues, coworkers, other personnel, and their field-work instructor. In addition, there were biweekly student training-unit meetings which gave the group as a whole opportunities to discuss basic concepts of working with older persons, common concerns pertinent to their cases, and broader and general issues. All of this made for harmonious working relationships and contributed to open communication and a healthy flow of ideas and suggestions.

The students' initial impact on their clients was surprisingly positive. The students were favorably impressed with their clients' vitality, strengths, and will to live. As one of the students said to me in an early conference and subsequently in one of our group meetings: "I was *surprised* to find myself liking and admiring Mrs. N." I can still remember the student telling me, in a rather starry-eyed fashion and with a tear in her eye and in her voice of that first encounter with Mrs. N. in her home. Mrs. N. was a physically impaired woman of seventy-eight, confined to the use of a walker. Her husband was in the hospital after having suffered a severe stroke. Her adult son was mentally retarded. Yet, here was Mrs. N. still interested in living and wanting to remain in her own home. But she had to ask for placement of her husband in the Home for Jewish Aged because she could no longer care for him. This woman's courage made a powerful impression on the student and contributed to her beginning understanding of the strengths that elderly persons possess. Conversely, her first visit to an applicant in a proprietary nursing home almost shattered her. She reacted with: "What a horrible way to live. What are we doing about it? If that is what old age is for some people, then it's horrible! Horrible!"

No one should underestimate the amount of mutual support and the strengthening component that the sharing of feelings and reactions provides in the student-unit pattern of field instruction (Saul, 1970). Vividly, I can remember the day that the first client in the unit case load died. The death was a devastating experience for the student. She rushed into my office, tears streaming down her face, sobbing, "Mrs. H. died and I wasn't there and didn't know anything about it." Intuitively, the other three students came out of their offices and the four of them sat with me for the next hour as we talked about their own feelings about dying and death and how they needed to find a way of coming to grips with death in working with any age group, particularly when engaged with the aged. Real comfort was derived for each of them and for me, too, as in a very poignant manner we lent support to each other. The next death of a client which occurred in the unit case load about six weeks later was met with greater balance and equanimity, although still with tremendous feelings.

The reverse side of the coin of mutual support, however, can be one student's negativism or pessimism feeding into others'. During a student-unit meeting around the middle of November, one student began with: "If this is what it's like to grow old, who wants it. It's terrible!" Whereupon each student began to share the depressed, upset, gloomy feelings that had been accumulating following the earlier weeks of excitement. Indeed, "the honeymoon was over." They were expressing thoughts such as: "How can it ever be better? Society has done them in!" The flood gates opened and there sputtered out a deluge of negativism, plunging them into a morass of despair. All were experiencing the frustrations and aggravations that many of us who have been in the field for many years still experience. The students had become starkly aware of the inadequate incomes, the lack of facilities for the ailing aged, and the lack of interest or concern on the part of city and state officials in the needs of the elderly. They had witnessed the loneliness and emptiness of their clients' lives.

At unit meetings, much consideration was given to relevant material in the field of aging which is not taught at the university and which is essential to the practitioner (Blank, 1970). Although some content in the field of aging has been incorporated into the school curriculum, there are practical limitations to the amount that can be included. For example, in the first-year course, "Dynamics of Process: Individual and Social," given in the human-growth and social-environment sequence at the graduate school of social work at the University of Pennsylvania, aging is taught very late in the year because the course follows the life cycle, beginning with birth and proceeding sequentially through death. This, therefore, means that consideration of the final phase of life is not reached until late spring, and some classes never reach this topic because they dwell on earlier periods of life which are of greater interest to many of the students.

A first-year student working with the aged cannot wait until this late date to learn material that is fundamental to understanding his clients and to offering effective services to them. Similarly, a course in "Illness and Disability" is not offered until the second term. This material, too, comes too late for the student in a placement with aged clients. The answer to the seemingly eternal question of social work educators engaged in curriculum planning, "What that is generic, what that is specific should be taught and when during the two years of graduate study?" determines the nature of the knowledge that the student brings with him to his agency assignment. The field-work supervisor has to help identify learning deficits—learning that either is not available in the school curriculum or is needed at an earlier point in time than it is taught—and then teach that material essential for providing competent service (Brody, 1968). For this reason, pertinent material became the subject matter of many of our unit meetings. Assignments were made for reading relevant articles, chapters in books, and research studies. These publications were made available in the agency office, and reading was regarded as part of field-placement activity. Other necessary information, such as the needs of the aged and the contributions of other related fields, such as medicine, were part of the content both of our unit meetings and of the general department staff meetings.

Placement in a setting such as the Philadelphia Geriatric Center offers the students a rich opportunity to study and to become acquainted with the whole person. Because the older person is the product of all that occurred in his previous seventy or eighty years, he should be understood in terms of what took place at his various developmental stages which prepared him to reach this final phase. The worker should ascertain the answers to the following kinds of questions: What was his family background? What were his coping capacities and mechanisms? Where did he succeed? Where did he fail? How did he fulfill his various life roles as child, sibling, spouse, parent, worker, and member of the community? What were the strengths and the weaknesses of this older person and how can I, as his social worker, enable him to make the fullest possible use of himself in his remaining years?

In this milieu, too, the student needed to learn to use herself flexibly, for the informality of the setting lends itself to modification of the individualized professional approach. Gradually, the students learned the value and validity of establishing informal contacts with the residents between formal scheduled interviews. They realized there was inestimable meaning to stopping by in the morning to say "Hello, how are you?" to a client or dropping in after lunch to find out if she were feeling better. A great deal of supportive help was offered to the residents through brief and frequent contacts. These not only contributed to the development of a continuity of each relationship but lent support to help a client work through a critical situation. Happenings such as adjustment during the early weeks of admission to the Home, a change of room, introduction of a new roommate, or loss of a close member of the family are some of the kinds of crucial events occurring in the client's life space. As the student became increasingly aware of the changing needs of her individual clients, she learned that frequent contact and expression of interest were important preventive aspects of service.

There were myriad opportunities for the student to use herself creatively at the Center and also to draw upon other resources within the Home collaboratively in order to foster motivation and to further treatment goals. For example, one of the first-year students was active with a resident, Mr. M., a former druggist and a depressed, embittered, negatively oriented man of seventy-nine. He had much in his situation about which to be bitter—he had lost his wife and his daughter, become estranged from his sister and other relatives, suffered a stroke, had a leg amputated as a result of diabetes, and finally retreated from the world into a bed in the permanent hospital wing of the Home. He had been there for several years. When the student was assigned to Mr. M., she related to him in an "I dare you to get out of your cocoon" manner. Mr. M. gradually responded to this warm, yet at times biting (positively so) concerned interest and challenge from the student. A journalism group in the Home was responsible for putting out the monthly newspaper. The student was able to interest Mr. M. in dictating his memoirs to her and allowing her to transcribe them. When, with his permission, the story of his life appeared in several installments in the Home's newspaper, other residents who had ignored Mr. M. became interested in him as a person. This caring enabled Mr. M. to begin to relate a little more positively to the world around him. The gains might have appeared minimal but were "giant steps" for Mr. M.

Fortunately, we were able to provide the students with occasional opportunities not only to "work up" an application but to see the procedure culminate in an actual admission. This opportunity gave the student the additional experience of helping the older person through the admission process and his beginning adjustment in the Home. This service was also extended to relatives, particularly the adult children.

Throughout the second year of the project, the members of the student unit took an active part in the community life of the senior citizens. From the latter part of October 1970, into the beginning of November, the students became involved in the political process in connection with the election of the state's governor. They planned a political rally for the residents of the Center, putting considerable effort into securing the speakers, publicizing the platforms of both parties (particularly about the elderly), and making posters and talking with the residents with regard to exercising their right to vote. The emphasis was to give the older person a feeling of "senior power" and a sense that, whether he was ambulatory and well or in a wheelchair, his vote counted, and he had a right to exercise that vote. The students, with the help of the Center staff and volunteers, arranged for residents of the Home who needed assistance to be brought to the auditorium for the rally. The students from other agencies affiliated through the unit also were actively engaged in this project. The York House residents (the nearby apartment-house dwellings) as well as all staff and members of the residents' families were invited to attend. The resulting audience had more than 250 persons. Following the presentation of each party platform, there was an active question-and-answer period, making the rally alive and stimulating. On election day, the students assisted in transporting many of the elderly to the voting booths, and, because a number were in wheelchairs, they were nicknamed the wheelchair brigade. This whole experience helped to revitalize the older person's sense of usefulness and self-worth and gave him a feeling of connection with the world outside of the Home. This activity was a first in the Center's operation and both the students and the elderly residents derived tremendous benefit from this experience.

During the latter half of this second year, the students became concerned about the lack of participation, particularly on the part of the male residents, in the group activities of the Home. They decided to conduct a research survey which included a structured interview with a sampling of the male resident population in order to determine their interests. The objective of the survey was to collect data that would, hopefully, provide a basis for the development of a group-activities program more closely geared to these interests. The students also suggested a lounge just for the men where they could congregate and just gab or play cards, chess, checkers, dominoes, and other games. Possibly, one of the small dining rooms at the Home will now be used several hours a day for this purpose because the majority of the male residents looked upon this suggestion with avid interest. Based on the information yielded from the survey, numerous suggestions have been made to the Home for an activities program for the male residents. This practice-oriented research activity on the part of the students was another vital learning experience. It gave them an opportunity to experience how they can function in an additional important aspect of their social work role, namely, trying to effect change in improving services to older people while affording their clients an opportunity to participate in and to facilitate such change.

This activity also helped to strengthen the male residents' own sense of self-worth, and they are now looking forward to developing additional group activities in which they have a voice.

I have previously alluded to the stereotypes about the aged that younger people have and that the students brought with them as they began to work in this area of specialization (Farrar and Bloom, 1967). In our last few unit meetings prior to the ending of the term, we re-examined their feelings about working with the aged. Quoting directly: "It's not so bad to be old." "You can always connect with old people." "If you're really interested in them, they know it." "What frustrates all of us is the amount of prejudice and ignorance about the aged that exists among the public." They agreed that one of the most salient facts they had learned about old people is that they are people—friendly, likeable, and capable of change and wanting to live. "You discover this only after you overcome your misconceptions and prejudices," they all agreed. "This experience has aroused my interest in the aged, and beyond that it has given me insight into all kinds of people." "No matter where I may work in the future, I'll do a better job because of what I learned here!" Said our black student: "America's big problem is not primarily racism but what our society does to the weak. Anyone who lacks political or economic or physical strength gets a bad deal. The condition of the aged is a conspicuous example. If a country as wealthy as this one cannot provide decently for its old people, it is pretty disgusting. I'm glad I was able to make their lives more bearable."

Feedback to the University

Let us now consider how this training program fed back into the School of Social Work. A few comments about the role of the field-work instructor in this particular educational setting are essential as a basis for understanding what transpired. Briefly, the involvement of the field-work instructor in the educational life of the school gave stimulus both to the program and to the school. My chief efforts in the first year of the project were essentially focused on the development of the unit with its multifaceted concerns (Cohen, 1971). However, despite time and energy limitations that were heightened by my dual involvement with school and agency, I attempted to update bibliographies, add current articles and books to the library, and introduce new and pertinent data into course content through participation on committees and at faculty meetings. The major feedback came through the students. The students, in their written papers, in their classroom discussions, and in their case presentations, provided meaningful content regarding this final phase of the life cycle and shared their impressions on how to effectively help the aged client. Their positive feelings about their agency experience offset many of the negative stereotypes that many of their classmates held. I would like to think that they helped to dispel many of these, but this impression was not scientifically tested. When I spoke to various faculty members, each mentioned the valuable contribution that the students made in their courses. These contributions helped to enlighten and deepen the students' understanding of the aged and their problems. Perhaps as important as the interchanges in the formal classrooms were the informal discussions that took place between students at lunch, in the lounge, at coffee breaks, in whispered tones at the library, or whenever these four students were challenged by their peers: "How come you're working with older people?" "How can you bear to work with the old?" "Isn't it pretty dull and unchallenging?" Perhaps a more dramatic way of conveying how these students answered their peers is to present excerpts from their papers.

> Working with the aged has been an incredibly painful, though I can now say, invaluable experience. It has greatly expanded my understanding about man's growth potential until the very end of the life cycle. Unsuccessful aging is tragic, but to do so successfully, with integrity, is very beautiful. Those who do so invariably have past strengths upon which to draw, past successes to remember, and sense a self-worth which sometimes seems miraculous in the face of the low value which our society assigns to the elderly.
>
> My clients taught me a great deal. Previously, I had hardly thought about aging and when I did it was with generalized, stereotyped disdain and dread. However, I am no longer afraid to grow old; I really perceive it as a natural part of life. At the same time, I also believe I now know what I must try to do so that I won't regret reaching that stage.

Another student wrote:

> I have suddenly realized (or perhaps have allowed myself to do so) and perhaps due to my "ending," that my experience in

> working with the aged has afforded me a perspective about myself, personally and professionally and about people generally, which I might never have acquired had I not had the "freak" opportunity to work with the aged. They truly do have much to teach us if we only free ourselves from our fears and anxiety sufficiently to "listen."

Still another wrote:

> I think I have learned from old people to have more patience, to "count" success as a smile, or a hello, or even the throwing of a pitcher across the room in anger and complaints about the food. I no longer "lump" them all together; they are all quite different and are not like children nor should they be treated as such because to do so is to negate their humanity. I no longer view old age and death as something repulsive—the thought and sight of which is to be avoided at all costs. I don't think I'm afraid to grow old and at the same time, there is something magnificent about successful aging; yet it is so difficult to help a person make optimum use of the time he has left if he hasn't reached the point of feeling that he got through the rest with reasonable success or if he lacks self-esteem.
>
> I feel the need to add something which I recently observed about the faces of old people. I think they are the most interesting faces of all. A younger person's face, in repose, has no wrinkles. An older person's face in repose can reveal so much—how prominent are the smile lines, frown lines, worry lines?—What have those eyes seen, the heart felt, the mind thought?—Integrity? Fear? Resignation?
>
> This experience has been invaluable and will probably take on greater significance as time goes on. Yes, I feel somewhat guilty about leaving. But they, the aged, aren't invisible any more and I am a more complete person for having known some of them.

Summary

Briefly then (Cohen, 1971), what were the gains for the students in these initial two years? (1) A broad exposure to the field of gerontology and a "live," meaningful connection with experts in the fields of geriatrics and gerontology. (2) Enrichment of their educational experience by their contact with a variety of research activity basic to the Center's purpose and program. (3) Increased understanding of the multidimensional aspects of work with the aged. The multidisciplinary team approach and the interdisciplinary activity involved the students in an intensive collaborative enterprise with many others on the Center staff. (4) Becoming related to every aspect of the Center's comprehensive social service program. This contact provided them with an opportunity to handle a variety of cases. It helped them to achieve a greater depth in their experiential learning. (5) A marked change in the students' attitudes toward the aged: from despair, hopelessness, and negativism to an appreciation that life for the older person can have meaning, value, and hope. Social work goals, if realistic, are attainable (Wittman, 1968).

In terms of the feasibility of the supervision and training design devised, everyone concerned agreed that the weekly unit meetings for discussion of shared concerns, feelings, and frustrations as well as for exposure to theoretical material related to understanding of and working with the aged proved satisfying and productive. Asking the students to read specific books and articles and to come prepared to discuss them insured that they were being exposed to the expanding literature of the field and were gradually able to incorporate it into their own body of working knowledge. The students formed a mutually supportive group and this stabilized and strengthened them during times of crisis, such as when a patient died. The unit meetings, combined with individual conferences for the purpose of evaluation and working through special, personal areas of concern, maximized the benefits derived both from individual supervision and from group training. Generally, the students' relationships with the supervisor embodied mutual respect, trust, and affection.

In addition to the above training components, students had a wide exposure to other agencies working with the aged through field trips and through attendance at meetings of related agencies. The ongoing effort to maintain a close tie-in between the student's learning in his field placement and the classroom at the School of Social Work heightened the possibilities for a totally integrated learning experience.

I believe that this pilot project utilized generic principles of practice and techniques of staff training that are transferable in adapted form to many kinds of private and public agencies. The open nature of the communication system for all participants within the unit, between the unit and the social service department, between the unit and staff members in other collaborative disciplines, and with cooperating agencies produced a flexible approach to direct practice, collaboration, supervision, and overall learning. Ultimately, the clients derived the benefit from the coordinated-team approach.

CHAPTER 10

Supervision of Juvenile-Court Probation Officers

John Main

It is not possible to discuss the function of a supervisor in the probation department of a juvenile court without first clarifying the function of the probation officer, for supervisors are, or have been, first and foremost, probation officers themselves.[1] Conflict, dilemma, and confusion about the probation officer's role have long pervaded the field of juvenile corrections.

1 Because the function of probation and parole officers is essentially the same, for the sake of brevity and clarity, only that of the probation officer will be discussed here. Parole does differ from probation, however, in one essential aspect. The child on parole is returned to the community after a significant absence from it; the child on probation is not removed from his home environment. By "function" I mean those activities performed by a social worker in carrying out the purpose of his agency.

Supervisors have not been immune from these difficulties. Indeed, because they have often risen through the ranks, they have been exposed to the difficulties and, in many instances, have helped perpetuate them. A review of the problems involved, therefore, is essential to the explication of the function of the supervisor. Unless the supervisor has a clear and cohesive concept of the probation officer's function, he will be hazy and fragmented in regard to his own.

Gault Decision

Prior to the Supreme Court decision of 1967, *In Re Gault,* the primary thrust of the juvenile court was the removal of the child from the jurisdiction of the criminal court so that he could receive a more personalized justice that emphasized the protection and treatment of the child. The Gault decision reestablished a less personalized and more legalistic relation to the child by affording him the right to due process; this condition was brought about by granting him the right to counsel, to confrontation and cross-examination, to a transcript of the proceedings, and privilege against self-incrimination.

One of the positive side effects of the Gault decision has been to bring sharply to the foreground the already existing conflicts in regard to the probation officer's function.[2] With the introduction of defense attorneys and, in some cases, prosecuting attorneys as obligatory participants in the juvenile-court process, the need to reformulate the probation officer's function has been forced upon many juvenile-court officials who previously saw it as closely allied to that of one or the other of the attorneys. Because the defense attorney serves as an advocate for the child, the probation officer's role as an advocate is perceived as being reduced with this change. With the consequent assumption that the probation officer may no longer be seen as a friend of the child, the systematic introduction of a prosecuting attorney has been recommended to strike a balance[3] and to represent the probation officer's authoritative aspect, a role historically difficult for most social workers to assume.

[2] For details of the impact of the Gault decision and various anticipations of change and suggestions about how to meet them see Fant (1969, pp. 14–18); Berg (1966, pp. 93–97); Cayton (1970, pp. 8–13); Stansky (1967, pp. 1204–1218).

[3] This is not Cayton's recommendation (1970, p. 12), but that of probation officers who were members of a study conducted in California.

Janet Stansky, who believes that the probation officer carries a prosecuting function because he sometimes presents allegations which support a finding of delinquency to the judge, regards the lawyer as the child's natural ally and advocate.[4] She sees the social worker, apparently divorced from his probationary function, as participating on the pure treatment end of the scale. Therefore, the social worker as therapist could serve on a committee with psychiatrists; such a committee might replace the judge in making the dispositional decision (Stansky, 1967, p. 1218). Paulsen (cited in Fant, 1969, p. 15) of the University of Virginia Law School also sees the Gault decision as relieving the probation officer of a number of duties which are essentially prosecutory in nature.

Not infrequently in certain juvenile courts, probation officers have considered themselves as prosecutor first and then as overseer;[5] others have found themselves, willingly or reluctantly, performing a quasijudicial role (Berg, 1966, p. 95). Conversely, other probation officers have viewed themselves primarily as the ally of the child. In the latter instance, the officer's role is diminished and threatened by the introduction of defense attorneys. Those social-worker–probation-officers who see their function as primarily therapeutic and who believe that treatment and authority are antagonistic no doubt hail the introduction of due process and a more legalistic court as a means of purifying their role and relieving them of a number of uncomfortable duties. However, whether the probation officer has seen himself as prosecutor, overseer, advocate, or dispenser of treatment, the Gault decision must force him to change his outlook if his view has been exclusive. "The more the court becomes a court and the judge, a judge, the greater will be the demand on the social worker to define and clarify his responsibilities within the court setting" (Berg, 1966, p. 95).

As the defense attorney struggles to clarify his own role between the two extremes of advocate and rehabilitator, he infringes on the

[4] Stansky (1967, pp. 1212–1213) assumes that a lawyer *representing the child* (italics mine) will present a more unbiased picture of the facts than a probation officer who has a recommendation in mind!

[5] Attendance at any regional meeting of the National Conference on Crime and Delinquency will give ample evidence of this.

role traditionally held by some probation officers (Cayton, 1970, pp. 10, 12). Ironically, as Charles Cayton notes, he moves closer to the combination the Supreme Court found so distasteful in Gault. As the juvenile-court judge's traditional role of *parens patriae*[6] becomes ever more constricted to a judicial and legalistic function, and as the police and the prosecuting attorney take a greater part in the adjudication process, the probation officer who has formerly emphasized the prosecutory and overseer aspects of his role may find himself in the peculiar position of being replaced by others. He may also find himself in the position of the villain in clearly opposing the lawyer and the child. In addition, he may feel restricted and baffled by rules of evidence and procedure. The probation officer who has allied himself exclusively with treatment will find that he can no longer disavow his connection with authority. For as the court becomes more legalistic, its authority becomes more apparent. "It will no longer be possible to deny that the court *is* authoritative and that social workers must take this reality into account if they are to attain maximum effectiveness" (Berg, 1966, p. 95).

Although the confusion and ambiguity in the probation function may seem new, in reality it has its origins in an age-old dilemma. This dilemma, which has been brought into greater relief by the effects of the Gault decision, lies in the unresolved issues of control versus change, of authority versus treatment.

The fundamental conflict between control and change or authority and treatment is inextricably involved in any definition of the probation officer's function. The officer must continue his ongoing contacts with the offender, and he must assess the probationer's readiness for discharge. The nature of his contacts and the basis on which he forms his judgment will, of course, be influenced by his position regarding this conflict.

It will be necessary, then, in attempting to define an appropriate function for the probation officer, and consequently for his

[6] The common-law concept of *parens patriae* (father of his country) derives from England. According to this doctrine, the king was the protector of all incompetents including minors, and, as such, had inherent powers to care for their best interests. In court usage, the judge as the state's representative replaces the king as protector of children.

supervisor, to explore first the ideas of some authorities in the fields of criminology, delinquency, and social work in regard to this conflict.

Control Versus Change

John Conrad (1967, p. 14), in his penetrating report of an international survey of correctional apparatuses, attitudes, and practices, states: "The dilemma between control and change is at the bottom of the correctional muddle." (See also Czajkoski, 1965, pp. 24–28.) Conrad notes that in standard practice, the resolution of the conflict between control and change is "in favor of control—control through surveillance by the field agency, and control through the traditional limiting characteristics of the total institution in both juvenile and adult institutions" (Conrad, 1967, p. 55).

Arthur Miles' self-image study of forty-eight probation and parole officers in Wisconsin revealed that their basic dilemma was "the protection of society versus the social treatment of the individual offender." Like Conrad, Miles found that both trained and untrained officers tended to resolve their conflict by accepting "a point of view which emphasizes that the basic function of probation and parole is the protection of society, with the rehabilitation of offenders as an important secondary function." A significant part of this resolution was the rejection by experienced officers of psychoanalytic case work and interpretations of behavior. Instead, they attempted to accommodate to the realities of probation and parole by rationalizing "the psychoanalytic theory of case work with the structure of surveillance and the protection of society." They also had to "rationalize the assumption of 'sickness' of offenders with the belief in the 'wrongness' of offenders as enunciated by criminal law" (Miles, 1965, pp. 21–22).

Although some trained social workers may resolve their dilemma by emphasizing control as their chief task, the literature indicates that there are many other social workers in probation and parole who swing to the other extreme and minimize or reject the authoritative aspect of their duties, seeing it as antagonistic to treatment.[7] As Berg states (1966, p. 95): "Although social workers have accepted the view that authority can be used constructively, they have by no means embraced the idea fully."

[7] See Silverman (1960, p. 263); Meeker (1960, p. 28); and Fisher (1960, pp. 78–79).

Thus, it is no surprise that social workers face a dilemma between the usual assumptions of case work and the realities of probation and parole and tend to minimize or negate one aspect of the conflict. Although intellectually social workers posit that authority can be used constructively, historically the dual concepts that authority interferes with treatment and that treatment can only occur in an aura of permissiveness, acceptance, support, and self-determination pervade the thinking of some social work practitioners. (See Austin, 1937, p. 283.) They feel that case work cannot be effectively offered in an authoritative agency and propose that counseling services be supplied by a nonauthoritative agency and that the child be referred for such services by the probation officer. Richard Chappell, in discussing this view (1964, p. 359), states: "The prime argument against the use of case work in an authoritarian relationship is that case work is a unique personal relationship that can be useful only if the client seeks help voluntarily and is entirely free at all times to choose between continuation and termination of the relationship."

Ironically, although this view holds that probationers should be referred to nonauthoritative agencies for counsel, support, and help, the staff of such agencies are reluctant to accept them and are usually unable to use authority when it should be invoked.[8] These factors render this view ineffective. Voluntary agencies that support the philosophy of an individual's right to seek help only if he is willing to and the freedom to choose between termination and continuation of the relationship use this same argument to reject court referral. Elliot Studt (1954, pp. 231–238) and Dale Hardman (1957, pp. 215–221) also attest to the reluctance of social workers to employ authority in their casework and to their tendency to deny it in their practice or to refer the exercise of the authority to someone else.

Thoughtful writers on the dilemma of control versus change, of authority versus treatment (for instance, Conrad, 1967, pp. 172–175; Berg, 1966, pp. 95–96; Fink, 1961, pp. 34–40; Studt, 1959, pp. 20–21) have urged practitioners to combine the use of control and authority with efforts toward change, rehabilitation, or social restoration.

[8] See Treger (1965, pp. 23–28). Treger no doubt has had the same experience as this writer. See also Berg (1966, p. 96).

> It [alternation of emphasis on control to provide for the objective of optimal social restoration] does not imply the abandonment or even the relaxation of control. No utopia of education, therapy, loving-kindness, or magic is in sight for the offender or his keeper. For the foreseeable future, correctional clients will need external control. This control will be certainly coercive, and no attempt can be made to disguise the fact from the client, the staff, or the public. For our goal is not to release our motley collection of thieves and cutthroats from coercion. Rather, one must accommodate what coercion is necessary to a rationally conceived plan for making as good purses as we can out of the sow's ears we have to work with. This is quite different from contributing as good a plan as we can in accommodation of a system of control which has been conceived without reference to what a client may need before he can safely be returned to society [Conrad, 1967, pp. 174–175].

Conrad points out that, in its "incessant attention to the statistics of recidivism," the community itself obviously wants the offender to change "to a person who can function within the limits of public tolerance." Conversely, in a statement instructive to those who would emphasize treatment and avoid invoking control, he stresses (1967, pp. 173, 177) that not even juvenile courts can disregard the demands of retributive justice and that the "very act of making a finding and a disposition implies retribution." Of primary importance in the above quotation is the use of authority and control to *facilitate* treatment and social restoration, which would seem to me to be the first step in combining what appear to be conflicting functions.

Regardless of how the worker resolves the seeming disparity between control and change, most thoughtful analysts see the problem of the trained social worker, who is hopefully oriented toward change, as centering in his own relation to authority. Bad past experiences with authoritative figures, the need or desire to be liked, the association of authority with punishment, the wish to be loving, and guilt for being withholding are all elements which may enter into a social worker's use or misuse of authority (Hardman, 1957, pp. 215–216). Conversely, lack of emotional maturity, satisfaction in a position of power, and fear of hostility are cited as contributing to an exclusive emphasis on control and authority (Carter, 1961, pp. 52–56).

It is possible to isolate three basic steps in the integration of control and change. The first step is the social worker's continuing development of self-awareness and his coming to terms with his own feelings about authority and authority figures.[9] One of the chief tasks of the supervisor is to help him to accomplish this. A clear understanding of the officer's function and the degree to which the supervisor has settled his own relation to authority and synthesized the control and treatment aspects of his responsibilities are of central importance in helping the worker arrive at this level of self-knowledge.

Many social workers, in assuming that authority interferes with the voluntary and self-determining nature of treatment, forget that social work in any setting is based upon sanctions and the use of authority. Contrary to Miles' conclusion (1965, p. 23) that the probation officer's dilemma is caused by "the inherent conflicts between certain assumptions as taught in social case work and the realities of probation and parole," it appears that some trained social workers choose, because of their problems in relating to authority, to make their own assumptions and to forget their authoritative connections.

All social work is *authorized* by the community out of its concern about certain social problems. All social work "inherently involves not only the sufferance but the conscious, deliberate utilization of a fixed framework of limiting conditions with opportunities for free choice and judgment within those fixed limits"—as does probation and parole (Chappell, 1964, p. 361). Every social agency is authorized by the community, which in turn has control over the types and direction of service, the clientele served, the standard of service, and the expenditure of funds as mandated in legislation and by governmental bodies, boards, and fund-raising agencies. Because of its accountability to these controlling bodies, each agency must operate within a set of policies and rules which limit both client and worker (Hardman, 1957, p. 217). The worker, as the direct agency representative, is expected to hold his client to these rules and procedures.[10]

This brings us to the second basic step in an integration of con-

[9] See Berg (1966, p. 96); Treger (1965, p. 24); Carter (1961, pp. 53, 56); Keve (1967, p. 20); Hardman (1960).

[10] Functional social work makes use of agency policy and procedure for therapeutic help to the client in the empirical knowledge that valid and appropriate voluntary and self-determining movement on the part of the client can only be made within the reality of his own limitations and of the limits created by the policies and procedures connected with the institutionalized and organized giving of help.

trol and change: the social worker's internalization of the fact that all social work is rooted in the authority vested in a particular service by the community and is limited and focused by existing policies and procedures established for the dispensing of the service.

In addition to the power granted by the community, the social work relationship is based upon the authority of knowledge. The recognition of this authority on the part of the client leads to a psychological relationship between the client and the worker. Studt cogently elaborates (1954, p. 233):

> Every casework relationship starts with a formal authority relationship. The caseworker is unknown to the client, but is brought together with him by reason of the caseworker's position in an agency to which has been delegated the community's power to help . . . the formal authority relationship must become a relationship of psychological authority if the client is to be helped . . . whenever the psychological aspects of the authority relationship develop strongly, the formal, social authority aspects, although still present and effective, become secondary; and the casework process emerges as a particular, highly skilled form of the exercise of influence.

Thus we deduce the third basic step in an integration of control and change: the recognition that all helping relationships are based in the authority of knowledge vested in the helper by the one being assisted.

Improved Probation Practice

What has proved to be good probation practices coincides with what is considered valid social work practice. "In actual practice, the effectiveness and success of probation is closely related to the extent to which principles of casework are applied. There must be respect for the individual, understanding of the motivation for his behavior, and a recognition that all forms of behavior which may be encountered are human responses to a given set of circumstances and have some meaning and relationship to the individual's total personality structure" (Chappell, 1964, p. 233). The following social work principles are inherent in good probation practice: (1) helping the client within the framework of an agency's function, procedures, and policy, not in spite of them; (2) recognizing the individuality of the client and his need for treatment specifically geared to his uniqueness; (3) understanding and using the client's limits as an essential element in growth and change; (4) helping the client to make responsible decisions in the light of the reality of his situation, limits, and capacity; (5) confronting the client with his share of responsibility for what he is and does; (6) helping the client to analyze the appropriateness of his actions and to come to terms with their consequences; (7) addressing efforts to the client's positive ego strengths rather than to his "sickness" or weaknesses; (8) involving the client in participating in plans that affect him and having him initiate and follow through with such plans where possible; (9) setting flexible and realistic goals and expectations appropriate to the client's demonstrated potential; (10) maximizing the client's self-determination and self-control; (11) helping the client to face and deal with the reality of the present in regard to his feelings, attitudes, situation, and behavior. Basic to all of these is (12) the honesty of the worker in regard to the purpose of the helping situation and to his own responses, attitudes, and feelings about the client and his situation.[11]

If the social worker has come to terms with his own reactions to authority, and if he has fully recognized the authoritative base of all social work practice, the principles explicated above can form the basis for a further integration of the control and treatment aspects of the probation officer's function. In like manner, the probation officer can only help the client through the framework of the court and the probation department, with all their myriad procedures and regulations. To minimize this framework and to pretend that the court is a treatment center is to be unrealistic. To attempt to make the court what it is not is to give the probationer a phantom instead of something real to which he can relate. Social work principles of honesty about purpose and of helping the client to face and deal with his life reality would be violated as well.

Any attempt to deny the true nature of the client-worker relationship is detrimental to the reality of the probationer's situation, to his choices, and to his ability to face and deal with that situation. Such avoidance will probably contribute to the probationer's anxiety and suspicion and to his problems in relating to authority.[12]

[11] The principles enumerated above are based on the work of Chappell (1964); Conrad (1967); Fink (1961); Keve (1967).

[12] Conrad (1967, p. 229) reports on the use of the reality of the re-

The worker's reality includes the cold facts that every offender indulges in rationalizations and excuses to evade responsibility for his offenses, (Keve, 1967, pp. 33–34; Fink, 1961, p. 35) and that often the offender has had negative experiences with authority and consequently feels angry, hostile, and resentful toward the court and the probation officer (Fink, 1961, p. 35; Hardman, 1960, p. 250; Hardman, 1957, p. 217). To ignore this aspect of the relationship is to ignore the possibility of helping the probationer to come to terms with his present reality. The worker who sees himself solely as a friend of the client is only fooling himself; he is certainly not deceiving the probationer.

The client, superficially at least, is unwilling (Carter, 1961, p. 55). Elliot Studt notes (1954, p. 235), however, that often such clients have the ability to damage their lives by producing emergencies, warring with authority, and alternating between "acted-out expressions of hostility and dependency." She also notes that "for a large number of these persons, the provision of a supervisory individual in their lives seems to be a particularly appropriate response to the needs they are expressing." Perceptive social workers have realized that delinquency is often a "cry for help" with problems the juvenile has been unable to solve alone. The control vested in the probation officer's function can "hold the client within a relationship from which he cannot legally withdraw and within which the problems leading to delinquent behavior can be identified and tackled" (Studt, 1954, p. 235; Conrad, 1967, pp. 174–175; Fink, 1961, pp. 36–38; Treger, 1965, pp. 25–26).

The legal obligation which forces the probationer to sustain the relationship and which exerts the community's expectations on him represents another aspect of his reality situation and of the consequences of his behavior, which he must digest and come to terms with. The delinquent's reaction to control should be used as an essential therapeutic dynamic in helping him to find a new relationship to authority and to society (Hardman, 1960, p. 250; Carter, 1961, p. 55; Fink, 1961, pp. 35–39). The community, through the court, has, be-

---

lationship and its authority to facilitate change at the Institution for Psychopaths at Heistednester, Denmark. See also Keve (1967, pp. 14, 29), on the bad effects of unreal reassurances and Hardman (1957, pp. 218–219).

cause of the probationer's disruptive behavior, imposed certain controls and expectations on him. It insists that he conform to certain regulations, that he report on all his activities, and that he resolve whatever problems may be related to his antisocial behavior. As he struggles to relate to these controls and expectations, he can be helped to make decisions in the light of his reality situation, to become involved in thinking, planning, and doing for himself. Positive ego strengths rather than "sickness" or "weakness" can be nourished by the worker as he helps the probationer relate to the reality of his situation and the consequent areas of control, and as he challenges him to live up to the community's expectations.[13]

It is important to emphasize that the authority held by the probation officer is not personal authority. Rather, he represents a "personalized version of community authority" (Carter, 1961). The officer and the client are subject to the same laws in the community, and both are limited by the same controls in the court. A dishonest, unfeeling, dogmatic, punitive, or capricious use of authority only further alienates the probationer from law and society. A weak, vacillating underuse of authority serves the same purpose. All such uses of authority constitute abuses and reduce the effectiveness of treatment. The probation officer's use of authority must be impersonal and must reflect the requirements of the community through the court and the consequences of the probationer's acts and situation.

Reality Is the Key

The word *reality* appears frequently in the above discussion—reality in relation to: the institution in which the probationer is placed; the relationship between the probationer and the probation officer; the community's response to the probationer's behavior and its consequences; and the stigma and the resultant expectations of the community in regard to the probationer.

One other aspect of the adjudicated youngster's reality merits comment. Shaping the probation officer's use of both authority and

[13] Keve reports here (1967, p. 9) on the success untrained probation officers had with probationers who, because of their lack of professional knowledge, searched for and addressed themselves to the probationer's ego strengths rather than to the causes of his malfunctioning of which they had no understanding. These were '"hopeless" cases, assigned to untrained workers, rather than "taking the time" of professional staff.

treatment is the inescapable fact that probation is, in itself, *punishment*. "Whenever correctional practice has emerged from the age of legitimated sadism, this axiom has been accepted as self-evident. Whether the commitment is to prison or probation, the punishment takes place in the court room where new conditions of existence are assigned. The aphorism of Sanford Bates that offenders are sent to prison *as* punishment, is basic doctrine" (Conrad, 1967, p. 12). The act of making a finding and a disposition implies retribution (Conrad, 1967, p. 177). Any staff member who would like to believe that probation comes as a welcome opportunity for help to the probationer is fantasizing. He does not understand the true nature of this experience for the person being sentenced, nor the probationer's feelings about the experience. The imposition of strict accountability, the limitation of movement and associations, and the expectation for change (even when desired) are coercive and therefore abrasive. Still, there is no need or room for a condemning punitive or personal use of authority by the probation officer; the judgment has been made, the punishment has already been inflicted. Treatment and authority come together in the probation officer's understanding of the punishment inherent in this experience for the probationer, in his individual emotional, attitudinal, and behavioral responses to the stigma, in quietly but firmly holding the probationer to a coming to grips with the imposed limitations and expectations. They merge when he aids the probationer to consciously live through the probationary experience in all that it means in terms of the community's attitude toward his past behavior, its expectations of his present and future behavior, and the choices he can make about it. Thus, "reality" emerges as the key concept essential for delineating the direction, focus, and core of the probation officer's function.

Officer's Functions

The probation officer's function is not, and never should have been, exclusively that of advocate or adversary, overseer, or rehabilitator. Rather, his function is to represent and reflect the reality of the situation in which the juvenile and his family find themselves as a consequence of the juvenile's behavior. The officer's authority lies in the community's power, reflected in him, to hold the youth and his parents to the limits and expectations imposed until they can be lifted and shifted to become internal constraints. The officer has no personal authority. But he has the knowledge of further consequences if the youth chooses not to adhere to expectations, and he carries the responsibility to report any violations or further offenses to those institutions empowered to apprehend the probationer and to enforce the probation regulations—the police and the courts.

The role of overseer has no place in such a design. Surveillance and arrest should be the exclusive prerogatives of the police, for it is they who have been charged with this responsibility by the community and who have the special skill and training for it. The probation officer's control resides in the rules and conditions of the youth's probation and in his assumption that they be adhered to voluntarily, because the juvenile and his parents have supposedly demonstrated their ability to use probation and have expressed their desire to do so. The probation officer who spies or checks up on his probationer loses the position essential to his function as a reflector of reality and to his ability to help. He also makes a lie of the concept and purposes of probation. Probation is supposedly an opportunity given the child to demonstrate that he can abide by the laws of society so that he may remain in the community. Checking and spying by another remove behavioral responsibility from the youth and his parents; spying also indicates that the court has no trust in their ability to take such responsibility and that there was no real expectation that they would. The client's agreement to the disposition, his prior demonstration of ability to use probation, combined with the officer's faith that he will take responsibility for using this opportunity appropriately are the chief dynamics afforded the officer for treatment.

If the officer performs his task as a reflection of the reality of the youth's situation, the youth must be free to relate to that reality as he chooses. The youth and his parents must be accountable for their choices and for the degree to which the youth complies with what is expected of him. They must carry the guilt for whatever lack of honesty or betrayal of trust is involved as well as the task of communicating such to the probation officer or must suffer the consequences if any transgression is discovered. The officer's authority resides in the fact that he carries the community's expectation that the youth will make restitution to it through a time-limited testing period in which a constructive relation to society is demonstrated by his improved behavior and actions taken toward the resolution of whatever problems in the past led to antisocial solutions.

The treatment aspect of the probation officer's function lies in his skill in helping his clients face and consciously live through the community's disapproval, the punishment meted out, the meaning of their feelings, attitudes, and behavior as they struggle with the reality of the consequences of the youth's delinquency, and the narrow choices open to them. There are possibilities for treatment and growth as offender and parents are made aware of their own patterns of response in relation to: stress, authority, limits, responsibility, integrity, expectations, and problem-solving. The offender is confronted with the consideration of the acceptability and appropriateness of his patterns, the desirability of their consequences, and the alternatives available. An opportunity to change undesirable patterns is made available as they test out old behaviors against expectations imposed by the community and as they see the results of their efforts reflected in the response and interpretation of the probation officer.

Supervisor's Function

We are not concerned here with the general techniques and skills of supervision, but rather with the supervisor's specific focus and his primary areas of attention within the court setting. The specific supervisory focus in probation, as in any field of social work practice, is on the officer's use of self. However, the specificity of the probation officer's functional role requires a somewhat different use of self from what would ordinarily be required. As we can see from the foregoing reformulation of the probation officer's function, the officer's use of self is of central importance in three areas: (1) his relation to authority and authority figures; (2) his willingness and ability to embody social work principles in his functional role; and (3) how he handles the limits of his function and authority.

The supervisor has many opportunities to encounter the officer's relation to authority figures as it is revealed in relation to himself. The officer's willingness and ability to relate appropriately to the authority inherent in the supervisor's position is indicative of his relation to authority figures in general. The officer's willingness to meet such expectations as being on time for conferences; his ability to share his work, his progress, and raise questions regarding his caseload in the form of case material and agendas for discussion; and his willingness to submit those decisions designated for supervisory clearance reveal his orientation and response to authority. The quality and frequency of the officer's use of consultation between conferences, and the kind of responsibility he is willing to carry in regard to the management of his caseload are also significant as are how he integrates the supervisor's suggestions with his own ideas and how he follows through on direct instruction in retrospective evaluation. His expressed attitudes and actual behaviors are significant indicators for locating an officer between the extremes of complete capitulation to authority and complete disregard for it. The worker's responses and actions become the data the supervisor draws upon to help the officer develop self-awareness and to work on his pattern in regard to authority.

The officer's use of shared court facilities reveals his relation to authority in regard to the formal or informal procedures for usage and affords further content for supervision. Is he willing to use the sign-in, sign-out sheet so that, in case of emergency, his whereabouts are known? Is he willing to abide by the procedures established for the use of secretarial help, dictaphones, and agency cars, or does he attempt to evade, manipulate, or disregard such procedures? Is he able to make valid changes in the procedure if the need arises, and is he able to be flexible himself in order to accommodate another officer or emergency court needs? Such examples may seem petty, but they are cues to workers' attitudes, and they provide the supervisor with concrete and dynamic instances for engagement.

Let us now turn to the officer's functional use of social work principles. Court policies and procedures in regard to intake, detention, or release of a child; criteria for recommended dispositions, social studies, and evaluations; requirement and duration of probation and parole; and criteria for discharge are specific directives guiding and limiting both officer and client. They are the bridge which connects the officer's relation to and use of authority and his functional use of social work principles. The officer's ability to hold himself and his client to policy and procedures and also to make alterations through appropriate court channels when the situation demands it, provide data about his ability to maintain a balanced relation to authority. The officer's ability to utilize policies and procedures appropriately and to help his client find a constructive way to relate to them will be revealed in court summaries, case material, and written and verbal communications to the supervisor and court. The wisdom of the officer's recommendations and judgments, the management of his caseload in regard to scheduling appointments, the duration of probation, and the appropriate use of the court's authority all provide the supervisor with ample opportunities to gauge the officer's ability to utilize social work principles effectively. The refinement and finesse with which the officer is able to integrate and implement these principles functionally depends on his training and skill.

In general, however, the supervisor must help the officer to maintain the reality of the relationship and to avoid the temptation to soften it by pretending to himself and to his client that it is something other than what it is. In response to the defenses and the negative feelings aroused by the circumstances and the involuntary nature of the situation, the probation officer may be tempted to smooth over discomforts by avoiding any discussion about the offense itself, its consequences, or the response of the juvenile and his parents. He may attempt to minimize the elements of control by not holding his charges to an adherence to probation regulations and by not expecting change in the youth's behavior and situation. Conversely, the officer may attempt to close off his client's negative responses by showing blindly positive feelings. He may attempt to side with his client or help him justify his behavior by either agreeing with his excuses and projections or not challenging them. The adoption of an unfeeling, disinterested, routine, or dictatorial approach by the officer may also effectively foreclose engagement with the problematic aspects of the situation. The officer must be enabled to see that tension, defense, and negative feelings are a part of any helping relationship.

Negative feelings and the need to defend, justify, blame, deny, resist, and criticize the officer or the court can become intensified because of the nature of the situation in which the youth and his parents find themselves. A strong tendency in the opposite direction is equally possible and might be evidenced in an inability to express any negative feelings, questions, or doubts and in the need to be enthusiastic and positive about every aspect of the experience—the need to be a good child. Both client and worker can be tempted toward either extreme in order to avoid facing the harsh realities created by the youth's behavior.

The worker can help his client to engage with the reality of his situation if he can become aware of similar tendencies in himself, and if he can be assisted in gaining insight into the responses that ordinarily are aroused by involuntary association with a juvenile court. Parents often come to court with deep feelings of guilt, shame, humiliation, failure, and panic. Public exposure of wrongdoing often arouses feelings of defiance, fear or deep-seated anger in youth. Extremes of resistive or overly compliant behavior are often means of coping—by fight or by flight (Maas, 1958, pp. 66–72)—with turbulent feelings, narrow choices, and harsh realities.

Resistance to imposed regulations and the involuntary nature of the probationary process is not unusual. Neither is the tendency to escape by psychically seducing, manipulating, or deceiving the probation officer. No one likes to be closely regulated. That is why probation is punishment! The probation officer will need support from his supervisor in holding firmly to the regulations and expectations of the court while helping his client to discover or rediscover that *limits can be a valuable support for self-organization while more constructive ways to respond to stress and problem situations are found.*

The court setting and its policies and procedures; the officer-client relationship with its element of authority, expectation, and control; and a knowledge of the client's mixed feelings and coping mechanisms are the framework for a functional integration of social work principles. These areas all involve tangible, concrete, observable instances which give evidence of the officer's use of self and afford the supervisor excellent opportunities for helping the officer unify theory with practice—thinking with doing.

If it is accepted that the core of the officer's function is to help his client meet and constructively live through the reality of the total court process, then the limitations of the officer's function and authority become clear. If he is neither advocate,[14] adversary, nor overseer, then he can cease building up defenses, proving delinquency, or playing detective and leave such matters to those who have the skill and the professional and community authorization for them. When

[14] This does not mean that the social worker should abdicate his advocacy responsibilities for protection of children's rights and for the alleviation of adverse conditions or requirements in the court, in institutions, or in the community.

and if such tendencies become evident, they should be directly pointed out by the supervisor, and the officer should be made aware of whose needs he may be serving. The officer's own relation to authority or his difficulty in assuming his functional role may account for his actions.

The officer has a responsibility to the child, the parents, and the court for compiling as true and unbiased a social history as he can. His recommendation to the court for the child's disposition and rehabilitation must be equally factual and free from bias and must depict as accurate a rendition of the child's social situation as his knowledge and insight will allow. Any tendency to defend or convict may distort the picture and must be checked by the supervisor. Such accuracy is in the child's best interest and does not eliminate feeling and concern for the child or his parents.

The officer's personality and biases will be reflected in his ongoing work with the child and the parents. Sometimes, the officer may have a legitimate reason for checking. Such reasons emerge from the plan for rehabilitation and involve collaboration by the worker with others involved in helping the child. Institutions or agencies such as child-guidance clinics, child-welfare agencies, school social workers or guidance teachers, special instructors, hospitals or clinics, or private psychotherapists are all examples of such collaborative contacts. Communication between all concerned is vital for the youth's progress. The youth and his parents have the right to know that failure to cooperate with any of these individuals will be reported to the officer. However, the officer's central purpose is to keep lines of communication open and to help the family in trouble to relate constructively to the reality of their situation.

The youth's conduct in the home, including his relation to parental authority, his relations to siblings, and his family duties should be left to the parents, with the expectation that difficulties in these matters will be brought to the attention of the officer. Adherence to probation regulations—such as keeping specified hours, choosing friends and recreation, operating a motor vehicle—although taking place partly in the community, involve parental exercise of authority. Responsibility for reporting difficulties with or infractions of regulations imposed by the court must be carried by the youth, his parents, and the police. The worker's authority is limited to a use of his own discretion with regard to infractions and his ability—and sometimes the requirement—to report such matters before an official court hearing.

As with the original offense and adjudication, interviews in regard to alleged new offenses must be conducted with a lawyer present to represent the youth, and the youth must be officially adjudicated a delinquent by the court before the officer can handle this next alleged offense with the youth and his parents. Even though the youth may be found not guilty of the charge, the fact that he was suspected is a harsh reality of probation that will need to be faced.

The supervisor can help the officer not only to operate more appropriately within the limitations of his authority but also to make therapeutic use of such authority. The officer's development of treatment skill can be facilitated if he can be helped to relate his use of authority to the responsibility the youth and his parents are expected to carry. In terms of the officer's function as formulated here, it is not always of paramount importance to know whether the youth or his parents are telling the truth at any particular moment. It is certainly not so urgent that it should reduce the officer to accusations out of suspicion, to intense or tricky probing, or to physical surveillance. It is more essential for him to know the difficulties in relating to the abrasive elements of probation. Knowledge of the way an individual client has responded to stress in the past and during the court and probation process; of the individual's temperament and attitudes; and of the way he relates to the officer and other professionals will give the officer an array of responses to specific situations. The supervisor can help the officer become sensitive to this knowledge and can encourage him to reflect it back to his client. He should be supported in containing any need on his part to probe in any other fashion. The authority he does carry, combined with the expectation of responsibility which is placed on the youth and his parents, exerts a powerful psychological dynamic. The officer's willingness to accept what his client relates to him, yet his perceptive understanding of possible difficulties involved and his ability to speak of these and to offer his client an opportunity to talk about them creates an atmosphere in which his client can be freed to share the difficulties and to work toward their solution. If, on the other hand, the client is unable to find a constructive way to relate to the officer's authority (in a sense, to internalize that authority), then a situation is created in which the client must struggle between his conscience, the responsibility he is expected to bear, and the knowledge of the officer's authority. He must grapple with his own denial, the reality of the situation, and the knowledge of the possible consequences if he betrays the trust and responsibility placed in him. The officer's ability to point up the possible difficulties in the specific situation intensifies this struggle, usually to a point of crisis in which, one way or another, the truth is revealed and a way is opened for constructive work to begin.

Summary

The supervisor must have a clear understanding of the probation officer's turbulent function and of the specific manners in which each officer has synthesized its control and treatment aspects before he can help the officer to make his integration. I propose that, because of relatively new developments in the juvenile court and because of long-standing unresolved issues, a reformulation and clarification of that function was necessary. I posit that the conflicting issues concerning the officer's role as advocate, adversary, overseer, or rehabilitator can become transformed and integrated and can find a more appropriate individualized emphasis *if the probation officer's function is defined as the reflector of the reality of the client's present and ongoing situation.* I proposed that the authority and treatment aspects (control and change) of the officer's function would thereby coalesce in a dynamic way for helping the probationer and his parents. A realistic acknowledgment of the nature of the client-worker relationship, the limits of the worker's authority, the true nature of the probationary experience for the probationer, and the officer's own relation to authority must be made before this function can be constructively mastered.

The supervisor, who is also a probation officer, must be fully cognizant and accepting of the probation officer's function before he will be able to help the office to integrate all aspects of his role. He must be sensitively attuned to the various ramifications of reality of both officer and client in order to help the officer make focused use of the dynamics of helping.

The primary and most immediate means of helping the officer develop a constructive use of authority is through joint analysis of his relationship to the supervisor, as the latter is an authority figure. Provided that the supervisor has knowledge and skill in the use of social work methods, he can utilize his expertise for imparting his knowledge and skills to the officers. He also is charged with responsibility for bringing the policies and procedures which serve as guidelines for all staff to the officer's attention as a basis for daily practice. These guidelines become the framework for the functional use of social work principles and the officer's use of self, and they determine the particular configuration of his role. The supervisor can help the worker to make therapeutic use of his authority if he himself is clear about the dynamics for helping which are involved in the tensions created by the placing of trust, expectations, and responsibility on the client. The way the supervisor carries his own authority with the officer can be an experience which can aid the officer in his understanding of these dynamics and can be extended in his work with his clientele.

CHAPTER 11

Supervision in a Large Federal Agency: Psychiatric Setting

Eugene Cohen

Throughout the years, there have been various ideas about the purpose and nature of social work supervision.[1] The changing theoretical base and supervisory patterns have been amply illustrated in previous chapters. But some of the crucial aspects and enduring values of individual supervision not already

[1] Subsequently referred to simply as supervision.

The opinions expressed and conclusions drawn are those of the author and in no way are to be construed as those of the Veterans Administration, Department of Medicine and Surgery, Social Work Service, or any element thereof. (See Epilogue.)

considered in this book merit exploration from the specific-practice vantage point. I will try to portray distortions as well as facts about supervision using a large federal agency as the prototype.

The history of supervision is replete with instances of fuzziness about outcomes and the techniques for reaching them. There have been many reasons for this fuzziness, not the least of which has been poor supervision due to the specific supervisor's[2] own lack of knowledge or understanding, lack of clarity or skill, incompetence, or even his own personal needs and problems. Bad practice is bad practice, at any level, in any field. Frequently, unskilled practice in social work gives rise and credence to the myths about supervision. And unfortunately, good practice often goes unheralded and little analysis is done of what is successful.

As has been shown earlier in the book, there is a marked trend away from the basic one-to-one supervisory method. In the past decade, great emphasis has been placed upon group supervision and staff development, administrative supervision and decision making, and program-planning functions. Indeed, these functions are vital as part of a total supervisory package within any given agency. However, the individual worker still has many areas of concern which are best dealt with in the privacy of the individual conference, and certain kinds of learning flourish best in an atmosphere and relationship that offers continuity, time, and opportunity to focus on the conscious use of self in behalf of the client. This chapter depicts some of the difficulties and benefits emanating from the use of individual supervision in the contemporary agency.

Some perceive a major purpose of supervision as being to restrict and control the social worker[3] and her practice.[4] Such require-

[2] Subsequently referred to in the male gender for clarity.

[3] Subsequently referred to in the female gender for clarity; also referred to as worker.

[4] For purposes of clarity, terms which have ambiguous usages are defined below to indicate how they are used in the context of this chapter.

Practice—fulfilling professional responsibilities in keeping with one's position by using one's knowledge and skills.

Structure—organized specific parts which assist in fulfilling the purpose of the whole (for instance, agency).

Function—the specific responsibility or tasks consistent with the purpose of the agency.

Process—the continous progression leading from the beginning to the reaching of a specific goal.

ments as regularly scheduled conferences, review of case interview material, process reports, tape recordings, narrative and statistical reports, and need for authorization from the supervisor to take or expedite various actions all can seem to the worker an attempt to control her. Being held to utilizing structure, function, and process often seems to be an obstacle to rendering the service which she wants to offer and which is the reason for the agency's existence.

There is an increasingly prevalent attitude that supervision is unnecessary because other professionals, upon achievement of their required degrees, do not receive anything comparable to supervision. There is also the charge that supervision *by its very nature* fosters dependence. To some, this means that supervision exists to meet the supervisor's needs, including his need to perpetuate his own job. The supervisory position in this view is seen as parasitic, taking much but giving nothing of value in return, and perhaps even as being harmful.

In reality, the primary purpose of supervision is to assure and facilitate the best possible service to the greatest number of clients most expeditiously and economically. A secondary purpose, which is also a means of accomplishing the primary one, is to contribute to the worker's professional growth and skill and enable her to provide service more effectively. Helping a worker to think clearly, to make her own decisions based on valid criteria, to take responsibility for them, and to learn from her mistakes and successes are all means for facilitating the realization of the above-stated goals.

To accomplish these, a supervisor must have a thorough knowledge and understanding of: (1) the agency, its operations, and service; (2) the administrative process; (3) the worker's self, which includes both the personal self and the professional self,[5] the level of his capabilities, and the extent and nature of his education and experience; (4) social work practice, which includes competence in the methods constituting the agency's service plus familiarity with other methods which possibly can be applied; and (5) the dynamics of

[5] *Self*—the totality of the individual which includes his view of and feeling about that totality.

Personal Self—the self minus the professional self.

Professional Self—the part of self, superimposed on the remainder of the self, specifically related to one's professional responsibilities and ethics. The separation of the self into personal and professional is arbitrary and only for the purpose of our discussion.

learning and teaching. This position is in accordance with that of Arthur Abrahamson (1959, pp. 22–23), who states that supervisory and staff-development programs have as their primary goal mature professional development. The "fulfillment of self" becomes a secondary goal. There has been much confusion about relegating personal growth to a secondary rank. Where this has been ambiguous, supervisors have offered casework, group work, or other modified therapeutic service to workers and students.

There is considerable difference of opinion about whether supervision's rightful province includes the worker's personal self. However, when considered within a practice context, the answer is not so much in dispute. Is it possible to help a worker gain an understanding of her practice in order to increase her skill and competence without looking at the core of her practice—her personal self? Obviously not. Whatever our profession or vocation, each of us is first a human being, a person. All of our life-roles are based on the same essential core of the self, regardless of the nature and extent of change which occur and alter one's personality. Therefore, the personal self is the basis of the professional self.

How far the worker wishes to grow is up to her, *but* she must have a real opportunity to make that decision. Otherwise she loses by default. In order to have that chance, she must understand what is involved, the various alternatives with their "hows" and their probable consequences. Unless these factors are known and taken into consideration, she has insufficient data on which to base a logical and rational decision. The tenet of social work which holds that freedom of choice exists only when sufficient information is known on which a valid decision can be made has long been utilized in sound practice with clients.

Essential Elements of a Federal Bureaucracy

An integral part of rendering service is the context within which that service is given, namely the agency. Agencies vary from one-man agencies to those employing hundreds of thousands of people, professional and nonprofessional, but all for the same purpose—ministering to the particular clientele that the agency is mandated to serve. Whether private, quasigovernmental, or governmental, agencies all have their own unique as well as similar aspects. Some workers are better suited to a small rather than medium-sized or large agency. Many work better in a private rather than in a public agency. The characteristics of a specific agency are as significant to worker satisfaction and performance as are the field of service and the social work methods utilized. It follows that each person should select the work situation in which she can most nearly approach her potential and achieve her professional goals.

A federal agency frequently is pictured as a large, cold, nonresponsive, self-serving, philosophically backward organization, employing innumerable "drones" who simply shift papers from desk to desk and cause interminable delays. Purportedly, it is staffed by many individuals who could not obtain similar positions in private industry because of their limited ability, intelligence, initiative, and caring. The service provided by these individuals is thought to be of low quality, sporadic, and inexcusably slow. Emphasis is on paperwork, red tape, and ways to avoid doing necessary work. Coffee breaks and lunch periods rate high in the hierarchy of values.

Admittedly, few people hold all of the views to the extent described here. However, these opinions are entertained in varying degrees by a portion of the public, including some of the clients of the various federal agencies. If this image is projected, the question as to why must be raised. We will discuss this question later in this chapter.

In actuality, what is a large federal agency? In what respects does it merit any of the criticisms mentioned above? Which of these criticisms? Why? First, let us look at the purpose of federal agencies. These agencies have been established by mandate of Congress to perform a constitutionally valid and usually socially accepted function of government. The size of the agency depends on the amount of work to be done which in turn is based on the nature and extent of the need for that specific service. With few exceptions, the need for the service is recognized only after a long period of time during which the service was nonexistent and the deficit became acute. Thus, by the time an agency is created and begins to fulfill its mandate, it is backlogged with clients who have long required unprovided services and now need and demand immediate attention. Such crises can be prevented by assessing needs on an ongoing basis and planning ahead instead of acting after the fact.

Next, let us look at the people employed in a federal agency. Aside from a few legislatively specified exemptions, federal employees are deemed qualified for specific positions by, and appointed to them through, the United States Civil Service Commission on the basis of a qualifying competitive examination. The commission was established by Congress in 1883 to avoid patronage in staffing governmental agencies and the inevitable resultant problems which emerge from such a system.

Many employees are sincerely dedicated and interested in offering high-quality service, in returning equal value for every dollar of salary, and in improving the operations and functioning of the agency. They take pride in their efforts and accomplishments. As in any large organization, others believe and function differently. To some, the work is merely a job which is a means of earning a living; their duties seem to them unrelated to the purpose for the agency's existence; their day-to-day tasks are monotonous or become an end in themselves; and their own needs are not being or cannot be met in their current position. Low morale and poor performance are the inevitable results of such circumstances and attitudes.

Administrative and supervisory responsibilities relate to all of these problems. A crucial part of the first-line supervisor's job is to know his staff well enough to be aware of their needs, aspirations and goals as well as their abilities, and whether their jobs and duties are consonant with workers' interests and capabilities. Frequently, the supervisor can help his workers clarify these for themselves, thus freeing the workers to act on them. Changes within the position as well as transfers to other positions (and sometimes even to another agency) are partly contingent upon the supervisor's understanding, imagination and ingenuity. The contribution which such shifts can make to optimal manpower utilization and high staff morale is significant.

A large federal agency is different from other types of agencies. One of the more obvious differences between a large federal agency and a small private agency is the layers of authority which constitute each office and agency in the nationwide network. Hierarchical structures exist outside the agency itself, for example, in the United States Civil Service Commission, United States Congress, and even the President of the United States, and influence the agency directly or indirectly. The local offices of federal agencies are generally under the jurisdiction of regional offices which, in turn, are accountable to the central office, which usually is in Washington, D.C. Although function, policies, procedures and line of authority all are clearly defined and delegated in manuals of organization and regulations, in the operationalizing of these, considerable flexibility occurs. Lack of clarity can arise from different interpretations, causing variations in practice. Nonetheless, ultimate discretion rests in Washington, D.C., and even there the agency has various levels and lines of authority, intertwined horizontally as well as vertically. The size of the agency, the mountains of work, and the necessarily large number of policies, rules, and procedures all combine to require the best in and of an employee for her to be able to perform effectively and creatively. The amount of paperwork is considerable.

To function in such a setting with satisfaction, to feel that she is accomplishing something worthwhile and can strive to improve her performance and the delivery of service, requires a person who can see the valid integral connections between the vast amount of paperwork, rules, and structures and the quality, quantity, and effectiveness of the service rendered. It also requires a person who believes in the service to be given.

Among the values supported by the social work profession are: the importance of each individual, his essential dignity, and his right to have the opportunity to meet his basic needs and to earn the means to satisfy his wants. Yet, in a large agency serving up to ten million clients, a personal relationship with the consumer through direct contact is difficult and sometimes impossible. Much of the service is carried out by correspondence and by telephone. There is danger of depersonalizing clients into "cases." Even where the service is rendered face to face, many factors may obstruct warm person-to-person interaction.

These practice realities seem to contradict the philosophic base of social work which includes operating in a warm, accepting, individualized, in-person relationship. Yet in spite of the limitations imposed by agency size, many times service *is* individualized and a positive connection *is* made with the client. Furthermore, the federal agency *is* there to meet the needs of its clientele, a purpose which is consistent with social work values. The worker who cares, who is dedicated, and who wants to perform her job well, generally does have the opportunity to do so and is helped to do so. A supervisor provides one such link and serves as an aide to accomplishing this. Social workers are particularly aware of the human element and are especially geared toward the delivery of service. They are sensitive to its meaning to the consumer. However, social workers do not have a monopoly on insight, skill or dedication. Indeed, many times professionals in federal agencies learn from devoted non-social workers and nonprofessional employees who express their caring by doing.

Qualifications and Role of the Supervisor

One requirement for appointment to a supervisory position is that the applicant have a minimum of three years of practice experience subsequent to obtaining a Master of Social Work degree. Often, many more years of social work experience are necessary before a person demonstrates the high level of competence in practice commensurate with the demands of supervisory responsibilities. He must also show evidence of his potential to perform the administrative and teaching functions. For example, the Veterans Administration *Program Guide, Social Work Service* (1957, p. 8) states:

> The case supervisor supports the chief social worker in planning, developing, and advancing the program, its scope, coverage, and quality; in evolving policies and procedures and in directing and controlling their application. He develops the program within his supervisory unit in collaboration with the chiefs of the service or program concerned, and coordinates the work of the various social workers supervised. The case supervisor knows and insures the quantity and quality of services provided patients and members toward whom he has responsibility, bringing recommendations to the Chief, Social Work Service, for changes in policies, procedures, staffing, and so on, that would improve the social work program.
>
> Through case supervision also, professional guidance is given the clinical social worker and students in the casework process and in work with groups. Such guidance is provided to deepen the professional knowledge and skill of staff and facilitate their accomplishment of the work expected of them. Methods in case supervision are taught beginning supervisors.

Although this guide was published in 1957, it still describes succinctly the essence of supervision. Minimal change is necessary to keep the description of the process current and dynamic. This clarification of function explicated many years ago provides a key to, and is but one manifestation of, the leadership role in social work played by the Veterans Administration, the nation's largest single employer of professional social workers.

Today, in addition to caseworkers, group workers and research social workers are recruited and employed by the Veterans Administration to help provide additional types of treatment and to build in evaluation of ongoing services. How to implement the supervisor's multifaceted, extensive role is a perpetual challenge. The chief social worker of each Veterans Administration (VA) station plays an important part as an enabler in its accomplishment.

Authority and Control

Each of us is affected by the authority vested in and exercised by others. Authority crops up in every facet of our lives from the moment we are born until the day we die. Situations requiring reaction to and use of authority are ever present—professionally, personally, and familially.

Learning to handle authority appropriately, constructively, and dynamically is in itself a major accomplishment. In today's society, authority is frequently viewed with suspicion, resistance and hostility, and many people never come to terms with it.

Supervisory or administrative authority in government agencies is likely to be conceived as "too establishment," "antiservice," and "antipeople." These misconceptions are heightened because of the various levels of authority and the necessity for approval through a chain of command. However, many matters can be and are decided upon, established, and implemented at the first or second levels of decision making.

One advantage of working in a federal agency is that each employee receives a written job description which specifies the responsibilities and the accompanying delegated authority. Policies and regulations also are in writing. In many private agencies, such clarification is absent.

In a large psychiatric setting, the authority issue is clouded by interdisciplinary collaborative relationships. Although the department of social work service has its own lines of authority and responsibility, these are interrelated with those of the medical, psychiatric, psychological, nursing, and administrative staffs. The domino effect[6] applies here. Relatively little can be done by one service or department which does not affect other departments. A knowledge of the system's framework and the interlocking nature of the parts is helpful in understanding the complex, gigantic public agency (see Loomis, 1960).

Closely related to authority is control. Some people immediately react negatively even to the word *control.* To them it connotes restrictiveness and loss of independence. To others, control implies a valid, essential mastery of and accountability for the various facets of the job in order to enable one to fulfill her responsibilities more effectively. Whether control is negative or positive depends on how it is used; intrinsically it is neither. An individual's need for excessive control or lack of any control is indicative of and results in serious difficulties. Abuse or abdication of legitimate, reasonable control evinces and evokes problem. The nature, purpose, and degree of control used largely determines its effect. The motivation of the person exercising control is a crucial factor in how it is perceived by others and thus in the results obtained.

A supervisor who uses control to meet his own needs, positive or negative, is abusing a constructive tool and converting a potential asset into a liability. Controls designed and utilized by a supervisor to assure and contribute to staff carrying out the agency's mission is more likely to fulfill its positive potential.

Control emanates from the authority inherent in or delegated to the supervisory position and from the personal qualities of the incumbent. A supervisor who has demonstrated considerable knowledge and skill or charisma is in a good position to have his staff view and respond positively to his legitimate constructive controls.

Identity

Basic to all that we are, all that we think, feel, and do is the concept of self. This concept is based on one's total life experience in relation to others and on his own accomplishments and failures, real

[6] The domino effect is a chain reaction named for the effect of the first domino in a long row of standing dominoes being knocked over so that it hits the second one knocking it down which in turn hits the third one which it knocks down, and so on.

and imagined. In addition to this personal self, there is also a professional self: for social workers, how we view ourselves in terms of our social work values and ethics, our goals and efforts, and our successes and failures as evidenced by the results. A social worker's professional identity and self-concept in a psychiatric setting are influenced but not determined by her relationship with the other members of the psychiatric and extended teams. The place in the hierarchy occupied by social workers, how the specific social worker is accepted by her colleagues and coworkers, the nature of her job responsibilities, and the kind and extent of the authority which she possesses and exercises in fulfilling her delegated responsibilities all contribute to her professional self. The degree to which the social worker identifies with her profession's values, ethics, goals, knowledge base, problem-solving approaches, and their place in contributing to the improvement of individuals and society all influence how comfortable she is in doing her job and how proficiently she does it.

How identified an individual worker is with her agency depends in large part upon how realistically or unrealistically she sees it. Does she accept the myths, particularly the negative ones? Can she see the realities, positive and negative? How well does she understand the purpose of the agency? When practice interferes with purpose, does she feel able and willing to exert effort toward change? Is the agency engaged in a constructive attempt to meet some of the needs of people? Can she recognize and work within the limitation that no agency in existence is set up to meet *all* needs and that there are realistic restrictions to its flexibility? Or does she see the agency as an irrelevant conglomeration of unfit drones whose primary concern is their salary and other self-interests such as self-aggrandizement? If the latter is the case, her anger and discontent will be so pervasive that it will interfere with her ability to deliver meaningful service to her clients.

How we work with others is an important measure of our self-concept and the degree of identification with our professional role. The degree to which team members operate in complementary harmony will determine the quality and integration of service clients receive. Interpersonal relationships occur either in formal networks, informal networks, or a combination of both. Formal networks are established by necessity in order for jobs to be performed. They are made up of coworkers, professional and nonprofessional, who are required to communicate in order that the tasks be accomplished. The prescribed relationships may be comfortable and satisfying and even have a degree of sociability, but they will differ markedly from those relationships which are formed largely, if not entirely, out of one's preference for certain individuals. These latter relationships frequently are an invaluable aid to doing one's job effectively and expeditiously. Relationships formed as a result of one's own personal preference have an added dimension of cordiality that cannot be established by mandate.

Formal and informal networks operate simultaneously. When these networks support and complement each other, their combined strength increases their effectiveness in producing the desired results—sound collaboration leading to better service.

However, there are occasions when formal and informal networks conflict and even when informal networks are used to sabotage formal ones. When the latter occurs, the worker who has been influenced adversely is often unaware of what is happening. For example, a staff member who has a poor relationship with her supervisor may convince a new worker, directly or subtly, that the supervisor is unreasonable or incompetent. Aside from the injustice to the supervisor, there is a significant disservice to the new worker who now has eliminated the opportunity for, or at least has a formidable obstacle to, using her supervisor constructively and as fully as might otherwise be possible, thus shortchanging the client. This "game" is also played by members of some teams and with other staff members, professional and nonprofessional. A contributory factor is the lack of clear, critical thinking with which to examine the merits of the arguments and to judge for oneself the supervisor, team member, or other staff member who has been disparaged as well as the worker who is doing the disparaging. Helping a worker deal with this problem is a difficult and potentially explosive task, but it is nonetheless an important supervisory responsibility.[7]

Collaboration

Collaboration is one specific kind of structured interpersonal relationship. In any large or multidisciplinary setting, collaborative

[7] See Berne (1964), for a discussion of hooking others into repetitive games.

performance is an integral part of the job. The effectiveness with which collaboration is carried out plays an important role in how well the assigned tasks are performed. Complexities increase in proportion to the number of people involved, particularly in a large federal agency. Complexity also characterizes the psychiatric agency.

Ideally, collaboration and cooperation should flow from the job to be done, the merit of the goals, the methods for accomplishing them, and from the specific competence of the individuals involved, rather than from personal feelings. The reality, however, is that frequently greatest cooperation is attained because of strong personal relationships (Broom and Selznick, 1963, p. 153). This sometimes fosters resentment due to the fact that one's profession and what that discipline has to offer are not recognized and valued. Such is the case when social workers are treated as second-class professionals on the team. The prestige accorded to the various professions enters into the kind of collaborative interchange established. One of the potential dangers is the leader's feeling that he is sufficient unto himself in treating the patient and that he does not need a team approach with staff members of other disciplines. When this is the case, the patient is shortchanged. The feelings and behaviors which this attitude sets off have wide repercussions. Annoyance and hostility to the team leader frequently persist for long periods, sometimes without even being recognized for what they are. However, when team members focus on the patient and the service to be given, the above problem does not arise.

Among potential problem areas in a large federal psychiatric setting, collaboration ranks high in frequency, intensity, and ramifications. Much supervisory time and effort are spent in helping workers cope with and develop in this area. Often, the real nature of the problem goes unrecognized by the worker, and the supervisor must help her become aware of it and identify the dynamics operating, their bases, and the possible consequences. Rationalizations, projections, and realities need to be understood for what they are as does their impact on the worker's self-esteem.

One of the best-known collaborative concepts is that of the team. In a team, the relationships of the individual members determine the likelihood of the team's serving its real purpose. Yet competence, not discipline of training, should be the decisive factor. Teams in which the leader directly or subtly ignores the other members' opinions and recommendations are a travesty of the entire concept and intent. Teams which simply go through the motions are at best a waste of time which might have been spent on important duties. The team which focuses on its real purpose, that is, reaching accurate evaluations and valid conclusions for the benefit of the patient and his family, does so by valuing and using the ideas and recommendations of staff members according to their merit and regardless of their source. Confidence in one another should be founded on competence and not on such traditional bases for status as which specific degrees a person holds.

Supervisory Responsibilities

Throughout this chapter I have spoken about the job and agency situation in which the worker finds herself, for in order to understand a supervisory job, it is necessary to have a picture of the milieu in which the supervisor operates. Because I have referred comparatively little to the responsibilities of the supervisor, let me focus on this topic now.

> Case supervision is a major educative resource provided for the clinical social worker. It systematically advances the individual social worker's capacity to perceive predominant social factors with their emotional complications, and to discern their causation and their relationship to illness and health. Case supervision expands the social worker's grasp of the full implication of these problems, their causes, and their effects. Through case supervision, the staff social worker sharpens his judgment, foresight, skill, and confidence in selecting and using the most appropriate social treatment measures, whether related to strengthening the inner or the external resources of the disabled person.
>
> The case-supervision process also affords opportunity for the social worker to test the objectivity of his thinking. The social worker is helped to develop capacity for analysis of the successes or failures growing out of the use of various methods and techniques, including the quality of the working relationships established by the social worker with disabled persons and with interprofessional, interstation, and interagency colleagues. Case supervision gives the social worker practice in learning to gain the full benefit from his experiences, so absorbing their meaning that it becomes part of his future thinking and work when similar circumstances are later encountered. *In summary, case supervision provides the climate in which the in-*

quiring creative mind can grow [Veterans Administration, 1957, p. 32].

Aside from the obvious role of a supervisor (the variegated individual and group-training and teaching functions and the administrative duties spelled out in previous chapters), there are the daily obstacles, frustrations, misunderstandings, resentments, hostilities, and competition which are part of the vocational sphere of life with which the supervisor must help workers cope. Several examples follow.

One of the most difficult facts for workers to comprehend and fully appreciate is that colleagues are human beings. Generally, workers are able to empathize sufficiently with their clients so as to be able to accept much of their undesirable and provocative behavior. However, all too frequently, similar understanding in relation to colleagues is absent. Often within a psychiatric setting even the experienced worker is contaminated by the idea, of which she is usually unaware, that psychiatrists are "next to God" and therefore do not have the right to have personal or professional shortcomings. When a worker experiences the emotional impact of the reality that they are fallible, her disillusionment can result in overgeneralizing the particular psychiatrist's shortcomings and becoming unreasonably critical of him.

Dynamic utilization of structure in the interest of the client is a skill requiring much effort and perseverance. To creatively use structure, one must acquire and integrate a satisfactory understanding of it and can be helped to do so by the supervisor.

The neuropsychiatric examination, one of the steps in the application (evaluation) process, is a piece of structure whose full value is not appreciated by many workers. To some, it is merely a technical requirement which is an obstacle to be overcome and is presented to the patient as a necessity. To others, it is a means for better understanding the patient and is presented to him as such. But even the latter view does not indicate that the examination will be used dynamically. All too often, it is handled routinely as simply one part of the total evaluation. *Its potential dynamic value lies in its meaning to the patient.* This value does not obviate the importance of the data acquired. How can the examination be used to introduce or strengthen thoughts and feelings which are conducive to achieving the patient's constructive goals? First, it is necessary to help the patient recognize and express the meaning to him of both the neuropsychiatric examination and his experience in it. What did the questions, comments, nonverbal communication, and recommendations of the examining psychiatrist imply to the patient? What effect did their interaction have on him? Did it confirm his worst fears about himself? Did it further reduce his poor self-image? Too frequently, there is a wide disparity between intent and results. Was there any positive meaning to the patient of the examination experience? Did he learn that his worst fears were unfounded and that he is not as sick as he thought, he is not crazy, he does not require hospitalization, he can be helped? Or was the patient so sick or well defended that the examination had no impact on him?

It is the supervisor's job to help the worker be aware of the potential value of each part of the evaluation and treatment process and to use each one dynamically. The means utilized by the supervisor are a reflection of his self, whether it be pedantic, socratic, dialectic, a combination thereof, or a different approach. Just as the worker must be "tuned in" with clients, so must the supervisor be "tuned in" with his workers. Process reports, audio-tape recordings, video tapes, and observation of interviews are all aids to this goal of open access to staff members' practice. The supervisor should be receptive to hearing about the worker's accomplishments, fruitful interviews, and other areas of job satisfaction and share with her the pleasure derived from such achievements.

The administrative aspect of supervision has as its aims to facilitate service for the agency's clients and to provide the means and atmosphere which are conducive to the most effective and economical functioning of the staff. These are other integral and indispensable contributions the supervisor makes to agency operations and to the staff's professional growth and advancement. When a supervisor's job is well done in these respects, it leads to high staff spirit. Pride in one's job, satisfaction in one's accomplishments, identification with the purpose and function of agency, being free enough to suggest improvements in agency operations, a feeling of being an important part of the agency, a sense of being appreciated and valued—all contribute not only to a job well done and high morale but also to reducing staff turnover. Stability of staff is economically sound and enhances the quality of service rendered as each worker continually develops increasing competence in the tasks she performs and remains with the agency long enough to merit raises and promotions.

New, Now World

Clinical social work practice, supervision, and administration all must be understood in the light of present reality—the *now* world. Society, community, family, and individuals all have changed drastically in the past decade. "If one were to pick the chief trait which characterizes the temper of our time, it would be impatience. Tomorrow has become a dirty word" (Hoffer, 1967, pp. 99–100). The time necessary for many processes to occur is rejected by many adherents of the now world.

Today, there is a flood of condemnation of established values, morals, institutions, services, and our economic and political systems. In some groups, there is a rising tide of interest in, concern for, appreciation of, and dedication to each individual. The meaning of all this to social work is staggering. In an era when emotion frequently rules reason, when generalizations and categorizations abound, where action often is taken impulsively based on erroneous premises, the consequences often lie in the opposite direction from the perceived constructive goals. "However noble the intentions and wholehearted the efforts of those who initiate change, the results are often the opposite of that which was reasonable to expect" (Hoffer, 1967, p. 99).

The above phenomena are specifically but not exclusively a part of today's youth culture. Many social workers graduating from professional schools in recent years are part of that culture and have the same values, thoughts, and feelings and act in expression of them. It is the supervisor's responsibility to help workers examine their own values, philosophies, and premises to determine which are consistent with current reality. The natural question is "Whose reality?" Who determines reality? What makes the supervisor any more of an expert or any more likely to be right in answering these questions than the experienced worker or the new worker? The number of years' experience is not a valid criterion by itself. Twenty years' experience may, in fact, merely be one year's experience twenty times! Whether these critical questions can be answered satisfactorily depends on numerous elements. One factor is how sincere the worker is in seeking to comprehend and define reality objectively rather than maintaining his self-vested interest by rejecting, consciously or unconsciously, anything which contradicts his own predilections. The same is true for the supervisor. Where two people working together seek descriptions of truth and reality because they are positively motivated and their intent is constructive, the probability of approximating this goal is increased immeasurably.

When the supervisor is seen as "the establishment," a power which defends the status quo right or wrong, as biased and prejudiced, and perhaps even evil, then much must change if there is to be a basis for constructive joint endeavors. Rationalizations and vested interests do not serve healthy needs, nor do they contribute to the resolution of real, pressing problems of service users.

Those who conceive of authority figures as being automatically wrong are fundamentally no different from those who hold that authority figures are automatically right. Although there are few who would actually admit to such stereotyping, in effect many act in that manner. Such party-line thinking[8] and action have no place in any of the helping professions and only destroy teaching-learning opportunities.

> Probably, there is no single explanation of tabloid[9] thinking. There is the difficulty of grasping a complex proposition. The most finely developed brain reaches at some point the limit of the complexity it can grasp. With the majority of men, this limit is reached rather easily. Long before it is reached, however, mental idleness steps in, making us tend to accept mental food well below the limits of our digestion. . . . So, through idleness or indifference such tabloid thinking is accepted even by those easily capable of making a more complex judgment if they chose to make the necessary mental exertion [Thouless, 1939, pp. 95–96].

If that is the now world, how is it different from what existed not many years ago? Differences and change are two realities with which social workers deal every day, in direct practice, on the supervisory and administrative levels, and in their personal lives. That change and difference are hard to accept is an irrefutable fact underscored by life experience. But what are the reasons for this difficulty in

[8] Party-line thinking is the acceptance as true, out of blind loyalty, of whatever is said by the party or person.

[9] Tabloid thinking is characterized by oversimplified statements which distort the facts and thus preclude clear thinking.

accepting and utilizing change and difference constructively? What do they mean to us? What is the emotional impact? Why?

> In the case of drastic change, the uneasiness is, of course, deeper and more lasting. We can never really be prepared for that which is wholly new. We have to adjust ourselves, and every radical adjustment is a crisis in self-esteem; we undergo a test, we have to prove ourselves. It needs inordinate self-confidence to face drastic change without inner trembling; . . . passionate intensity may serve as a substitute for confidence. . . . A workingman sure of his skill goes leisurely about his job and accomplishes much though he works as if at play. . . . The workingman new to his trade attacks his work as if he were saving the world and he must do so if he is to get anything done at all [Hoffer, 1963, pp. 1–2].

All too often, when one speaks of "acceptance of difference" what is meant is that "*my* difference must be accepted but not yours." When speaking of change, we mean that "*you* must change, not I." Although at first glance it may appear that these clichés apply to the old and those steeped in tradition, a careful look will reveal that they apply equally to the new and the young. The attempt to throw out everything old and initiate and promote only the new, though it be untested and unproven, is a philosophy and an approach championed by many, some of whom do not even realize it. Neither extreme makes sense as a philosophical base for thought and action.

"The greater a person's awareness of himself, the more he can acquire the wisdom of his fathers to make it his, . . . the more profoundly he can confront and experience the accumulated wealth in historical tradition, the more uniquely he can at the same time know and be himself" (May, 1953, pp. 208–209).

But what does all of this have to do with social work supervision, particularly in a large federal psychiatric setting? Because no agency operates at maximum effectiveness, and because to many workers the supervisor *is* the agency, the "guilt by association" phenomenon occurs. If one succumbs to the tendency to hold the supervisor responsible for the agency's shortcomings (an elementary oversimplification), this becomes a significant obstacle to the worker utilizing the assistance of her supervisor.

Traditionally, supervision has included weekly hour-and-a-half conferences to analyze case material on specific interviews, separately or as a series. Process reports and tape recordings were an integral part of the data used to examine the direct practice of workers. The focus of conferences was on a thorough, critical examination of the worker's practice in terms of her understanding of psychosocial diagnosis, the approaches and techniques used in helping, and the relationship she established. The latter was related to the ability and degree of identification with a patient. In psychiatric clinics, psychological conflicts, the client's assets and liabilities, and health and pathology received primary attention. Although the social and environmental aspects were considered and handled in sound practice, these frequently were viewed as secondary. Looking analytically at the worker and her internal psychological processes in relation to her clients and her overall practice was a generally accepted part of supervision in spite of the discomfort and resistance it engendered. In past decades, such regular conferences continued indefinitely as long as there was a social worker on a higher level to do the supervision. This also applied to supervisors, assistant chiefs, and everyone in the stratification scale up to the highest rungs.

And what is supervision like today? Some of the above continue, but not without considerable questioning and even greater resistance. The argument runs that if society (systems, institutions, organizations, agencies, various levels of government, "the establishment," and so on) is primarily at fault, then logically, the locus of change must be the institutions rather than the individual. Thus, the problem is located outside of the self of the client or worker, and the goal is social change brought about by social action, not personal growth and change fostered through insight development. The danger here is accepting the rationalization which subtly wipes out the crucial role played by the individual, denying his ability and potential to change, grow, and exert reasonable mastery over his behavior and life. The supervisor's help with this can make a crucial difference in results.

There has been a trend for a number of years to minimize the importance of supervision following graduation with a master's degree in social work. A parallel has been drawn between social work and other professions such as medicine, law, teaching, and engineering, none of which requires supervision of graduate practitioners. All of these arguments have made inroads in social work supervision as it is practiced today, although the arguments by those minimizing the importance of supervision are not undergirded by documented evidence. These shifts in philosophy are reflected in this book in the chapters by Richan, Kaslow, and Perlmutter.

The Future: Beginning Now

The future begins now. The challenge is to combine all that is valid in social work supervision, the old and the new, and make it a relevant, dynamic, effective, realistic, growth- and independence-producing process. The theoretical framework on which supervision is predicated is one important factor. Another is the human factor, that is, the people involved (workers and supervisors) and the relationships which they form. In part, each person's practice is based on his philosophy. What we do today shapes what we do tomorrow. We can no longer rationalize a justification for either the idealization or the vilification and undermining of supervision without fearful cost. Stagnation and deterioration of practice, and thus of service given to clients, would result from the removal of supervision, one of the most effective means of stimulating the growth and learning of practitioners and thus of the profession itself. The entire field of social work is in a state of flux—adding, eliminating, changing, sometimes thoughtfully and planfully and other times confusedly and impulsively. Some changes are founded on positive motivations while others are based on negative motivations such as evasion, hostility, and guilt. I am convinced that supervision is a necessity and provides continuity and perspective amidst turmoil. When properly practiced, it is a means for stimulating growth and progressively increasing autonomy through fostering greater self-awareness and skill. Supervision facilitates the continuing process of self-evaluation which is an integral part of professional responsibility. It also represents one of social work's greatest potential contributions to other professions.

Where supervision will take its place in this potpourri is yet to be answered. But we social workers must be the ones to furnish that answer. We are best suited to determine the nature and role of supervision in social work, although we need to adapt concepts and suggestions developed by other professions.[10]

[10] The applicability of management principles and techniques to the field of social work has been amply demonstrated. The literature is replete with such experiences and examples.

Furthermore, serious attention needs to be given to providing meaningful training for potential supervisors as well as for those already supervising. Too often, supervision courses have been superficial, brief, and inadequate.

When two people of good will come together to accomplish a constructive purpose and focus on that purpose instead of defending their own shortcomings and vested interests, then a goal can be achieved which will be a distinct contribution to human well-being. "What we must reach for is a conception of perpetual self-discovery, perpetual reshaping to realize one's best self, to be the person one could be" (Gardner, 1971, p. 162). Supervision offers the worker assistance in developing her ability to achieve this goal professionally and also, in that process, personally.

Epilogue

What of the preceding applies specifically to social work supervision and what has implications far beyond our profession? I am struck by how much this chapter embodies my own personal philosophy of life, my views about people, values, standards, experiences with my superiors as well as my own experience in supervising. All of these have coalesced into my portrayal of supervision, emphasizing some aspects while merely mentioning others, thus demonstrating that the author of a work is in his work.

The literature reviewed herein and the analysis made in writing this chapter converge to reveal how generic social work principles are to life and to all relationships. The ideas expressed also apply specifically to social work supervision. What we integrate personally and professionally, what we believe in, and what we practice, although not always consistent, combine and reflect all that we are and believe.

With all of the life forces which impinge upon us, and without minimizing their great importance, *we* determine what we are and create what we become. But there is room for assistance. How we use that help, or whether we reject it, makes a difference in what we are and what we will one day be and do. Supervision in social work can supply information, energy, and sustenance to workers engaged in learning to more effectively and consciously use the self to offer improved service to clients.

CHAPTER 12

Supervision in a Public-Welfare Agency

Sidney S. Eisenberg
Wilbur A. Finch

What specifics in the public-welfare agency affect the practice of supervision and the activities of the supervisee, beyond the generics discussed in Part I of this volume? To set forth these particulars and elaborate on how the supervisor can cope with the problems they create is the purpose of this chapter.

Legislative reforms, such as those separating money payments from social services, have changed public welfare so rapidly in the recent past that the operations of a district office do not stand still long enough to be effectively analyzed. Although basic change in the family assistance plan (FAP) was postponed by President Nixon in August

1971, that plan or a similar minimum-income maintenance scheme, long overdue, will sooner or later be enacted, totally changing public assistance as we have known it since its institution under the Social Security Act of 1935.

Thus, it may seem an unlikely time to be concerned about the public-welfare agency supervisor and the practice of supervision. Yet, in spite of what may lie ahead, many thousands of social workers, supervisors and administrators among them, are concerned with the present and the near future of public welfare. It is more than likely that our society's concern for the well-being of the family and for individualizing its members and their needs will continue to be institutionalized. Such service is the heart and soul of social work. One future possibility is a kind of public family agency devoted to preventive and remedial activities including the administration of whatever special funds are required to meet the needs of families and individuals.

Factors Which Influence Practice and Supervision

In the public-welfare agency, nothing seems to remain the same from one day to the next. Practice is regulated and modified by federal legislation, HEW regulations, regional interpretation of HEW regulations, state legislation, regulations, and state staff interpretation of all of these. For states that have quasiindependent county or other local agencies to administer assistance and services, yet another level of legislation, regulation, and interpretation is added. The same counties which complain about red tape add their own local rulings to the blizzard of paper work. In addition, state and local fiscal units frequently have the final word on the delivery of financial aid, no matter what the social work staff may think policy is. Did we neglect to mention advisory commissions in this hierarchy of policy- and regulation-making bodies? If so, it was only because they are advisory, although they have a way of capturing public attention and of adding to pressures and to change.

Another potent factor influencing practice and supervision is structure. The hierarchies already mentioned are responsible for the rigid and highly structured nature of public welfare. For example, sit in a courtroom and listen to a bright, young social work administrator explain to a superior court judge the steps an eligibility worker must take to satisfy laws and regulations in determining whether or not an applicant is entitled to an aid-to-the-disabled grant. It takes the well organized young man (who is not loquacious) a full two hours to state, describe, and explain each step and the forms used. In another vein, when one of the authors of this chapter began to conduct workshops for supervisors and middle-management a decade ago, he learned not to use the word "structure"; it made participants shudder and stop listening.

It is urgent that workers give clients the "right" interpretation of policy directives. In a constantly changing scene, which demands accuracy and conformity to the dictates of each day, the financial aid worker is often uncertain and perennially prone to make errors. Because of the typically rigid authority structure, the supervisor is often unable to provide an answer until he receives assurance from the next in command that his interpretation of the new policy or regulation is correct. There are, alas, similar hierarchical fears and rigidities even in the administration of social services.[1]

There are good reasons behind much of the fussiness about correct interpretation of regulations, aside from conscientiousness and a sense of responsibility. There are members of each agency's hierarchy with seemingly little else to do but see that the operating units follow every provision of the regulations assiduously. Outside of the agency, legislators and newsmen are prone to call attention to exceptional errors: errors that make good copy or gain votes. Some localities, or even states, also fear that their claims for reimbursement from the next higher level of government may be denied because they are out of conformity. In some places, members of the Welfare-Rights Organization keep the staff on their toes by challenging agency decisions using their own substantial knowledge of policy and regulation.

Another factor which characterizes the public-welfare worker's task is overwork and related job pressures. The public is, to say the least, ambivalent about public assistance and in times of inflation, rising

[1] In a study of the New York City Department of Social Services, Ronald Miller and Lawrence Podell (n.d., p. 4) describe the staff thus: "They were . . . employees of a large, multifaceted, hierarchical, relatively impersonal organization, with ubiquitous regulations and specified procedures, narrowing the range of permissible discretion . . . [such a bureaucracy] involves emphasis upon uniformity of procedures, categorization of clients, and obedience to rules and superiors."

taxes, and unemployment, our representatives are increasingly loath to provide adequate relief budgets or staffing. This has been so since 1935, inflation or no inflation. Consequently, the pressures of too many relief applications and too many continuing social service cases means simply that it is impossible to do an adequate job free from error. If we were courageous enough to face it, perhaps the question should really be: what percentage and kind of mistakes can we tolerate?

Another characteristic of public welfare which influences the supervisor, but which need be only briefly discussed, is the public's attitude—the atmosphere in which public assistance is administered. The public is against higher taxes, against "reliefers" and other idle feeders at the public trough, but does not want the "worthy poor" to suffer. Worker and supervisor alike pay the price for this public hostility in pressures, tension, and frayed nerves. The efforts of the agency staff are often unrewarded, unrecognized, and even condemned.

The senior author of this chapter learned from social work staff before he first began to write on supervision in the fifties that an important task of the line supervisor is giving support and encouragement to the worker. This raises the companion question: where in the public welfare agency does the supervisor get the wherewithal, the support and encouragement, to continue doing his very difficult job, for often there is more pressure on the supervisor than on the worker.

Finally, attention rivets on a relatively recent development. The "awakened" college student of the sixties, undergraduate and graduate alike, began to appear in public welfare jobs in the latter part of that decade and in the seventies. They create a special problem for their line supervisors. (See Walz, 1971, pp. 19–23.) Having yearned for or tasted the heady wine of "participatory democracy," they want "a piece of the action": they want to have something to say about the rules of the game under which they and their clients must "play." But alas, rarely or never are those same supervisors asked to contribute to decision making, much less are their workers asked. Rather, top officials use them as a nominal part of administration when that suits their purposes, usually to get a particular, often an unpleasant, task done. The rules, including worker assignment and transfers, changes in the unit's task, and changes in paper work and other procedures are too often made without the line supervisor, except after the fact. Both worker and supervisor may be, or feel, shut out. In this book, we have attempted to offer some possible ways supervisors can deal with the yearnings, discontent, and pressures of the "new breed" of social worker for reform of the system, including his participation in it.

Now, let us briefly summarize. We have the line supervisors functioning under a complex and seemingly immovable hierarchy within a rigid yet constantly changing system of laws, regulations, procedures, and a storm of paper work about which they have little or nothing to say. The community atmosphere in which they work is ambivalent about the purposes of the agency and frequently bitterly critical of policy and case decisions; there is often blame, but never praise for a job well done. Understaffed, overworked, and often undertrained practice units are expected to do a wide range of tasks without error, a patent impossibility. The worker is expected, by the recipients and the profession, to administer social services and financial aid with decency, warmth, humanity, consideration of feelings, and even generosity, within the law. On the other hand, the public-assistance worker is pressed by others to be as punitive, rigid, and denying as possible: to discourage applicants, and to push people off the rolls. And under these same pressures, the supervisor has to help the worker stay in one piece emotionally and get the job done without error!

Supervisor's Unique Contribution

There are no high principles or secrets of supervisory practice that will change these special characteristics of public welfare. The supervisor cannot himself change federal law, the thinking of HEW officials, or the hierarchical superstructure of his own state and local agency. Neither can he change the tax structure to provide more funds without paining the taxpayer, or change the attitude of the public toward welfare. And yet, we believe that supervisors stay in public welfare because they can, given a certain devotion to clients, workers, and the task, and a perseverance and perhaps some greatness of soul, ameliorate to some extent the negative impact of public assistance on the client through enabling the worker to learn and grow and practice with as much freedom as present laws allow. Within what many regard as a wholly impossible system, we have seen clients served with dignity and respect, given every advantage that the law allows, and in partnership with the social worker, open up doors of opportunity for self-realization and fulfillment; and we have beheld clients happy to turn to "my caseworker" for support, resources, understanding, and ideas. Needless to say, such social workers also feel self-actualized and rewarded. They tend to remain in the field so that their expanding experience adds to their own capacity to be creatively helpful to recipients (Miller and Podell, n.d., pp. 67–71).

The most important consideration leading toward such an end is one's style of supervision. Included here are a variety of factors associated with the leadership role of the supervisor: leader versus boss for example.

Within a structure as rigid and bureaucratic as a welfare department, it is vital that the worker be allowed room to breathe; to be a sensate human being rather than a computer; to try out her own approaches to problems she encounters; and to have her views respected. In other words, the worker must have the freedom to find some areas of flexibility and an opportunity to be creative with her client and community contacts. And she should be able to do so because it suits agency purposes.

The supervisor who has no experience other than that of social work practitioner or eligibility worker will tend to do what comes naturally, that is, by fair means or foul to see to it that the worker carries the case as he would; such a supervisor is a boss, not a leader. Today, we realize that it is important to meet the program objectives of the agency (or of the district, bureau, or specialized service) but that no two people will practice in the same way and it is not the business of the supervisor to "protect" the client by trying to get the worker to do a job as the supervisor would do it. It *is* the task of the supervisor, on the other hand, to teach the worker, or see that she is taught, the basic knowledge and skills appropriate to her assignment; it is also the job of the supervisor to support the worker in the creative use of that knowledge.

The implication of such a style of supervision is that the supervisor is the organizer and the educator but not the policeman or psychotherapist (Towle, 1969, pp. 164–186). This style is worker oriented rather than client oriented, even though the applicant or recipient is indeed the ultimate beneficiary. This style keeps the supervisor from carrying the case at second hand.

Douglas McGregor, in explicating his "X" and "Y" theories

(1960), pointed out that the capacity to exercise a high degree of imagination, ingenuity, and creativity in the solution of organizational problems is more widely distributed in the population than supervisors (and higher management) think. Over the years, organizations tend to kill these qualities in workers until the worker becomes a laggard and a dullard who waits to be told what to do. If management can develop shared objectives and a sense of mutual responsibility for realizing them, they can free the desired characteristics in the operating staff—supervisors and workers alike. The role of the supervisor, then, is to see that the worker learns her tasks sufficiently well that her work need not be overseen to the point that it is no longer her own responsibility.

A balance between the teaching-enabling role and that of overseer is not easily achieved. This balance can emerge with some degree of sureness if the supervisor can make use of an informal kind of authority beyond that which his position in the agency contractually permits him to exercise.

We identify authoritarian supervision and formal organization with the "scientific" school of administration theory (Taylor, 1911), or what McGregor called the "X" approach. These efficiency experts invented factory piecework and the carrot and stick means of prodding those naturally indolent human beings into a decent level of performance. However, careful observation as well as hard-nosed research (Blau and Scott, 1962, ch. 6) show that reliance on formal authority alone, particularly in an organization employing professionals, not only may not get the job done, but may breed covert or open revolt. It may also breed continuing dependency which, it must be acknowledged, some supervisors welcome. At best, sheer authority will wring from workers that minimum standard of performance called for in their job specifications, the level which provides the paycheck and assures at least satisfactory evaluations. But, of course, worker and supervisor are then back in the welfare department straight jacket again.

Informal authority, which extends the influence of the supervisor beyond that granted by the position alone, is known as leadership. Leadership is based on the assumption that people have the capacity to take responsibility, are able to work toward organizational goals, and can be motivated by factors beyond those of basic security.

Man needs bread but, as McGregor points out, once he has bread, it no longer acts as a motivator of behavior. For a high quality of performance, we must rely on the staff's capacity for self-control and self-direction as manager-supervisors and organize the social work job so that it can meet the needs described by Maslow (1968, pp. 135–145): self-esteem, independence, competence, knowledge, status, recognition, the respect of one's fellows and, finally, the highest level of all, self-fulfillment.

The supervisor who relies on his formal authority alone closely directs the work of his subordinates, checks on their total performance, and reads all of the records of all of his workers, whether they are experienced and reliable or not. By contrast, the leader-supervisor trusts his staff to come to him when problems arise. He has challenged their best by establishing high standards, and he spot checks performance as experience directs. He permits and expects innovative solutions to problems, not solutions he would necessarily have chosen. There was one second-level supervisor who, despairing of being able to loosen up the four line supervisors in his bureau, met with their twenty social workers. He called upon them to try to produce in the ensuing month some case solution that was different from any they had ever tried before: "Let yourself go and try something different and I'll back you." A handful dared to take him at his word, and his peers at a management workshop could hardly believe their ears when he described some of the ingenious and innovative problem solving that resulted. For instance, an elderly lady on leave from a state mental hospital was able to return to her beloved tree house in a pleasant canyon in rural Southern California. The worker arranged for attendant care to be provided by a resident of a commune (yes, hippies!) further along in the canyon. The whole little community saw to it that her needs were met, including her need for acceptance and sympathetic company.

Fortunately, such leadership (although it comes to some fortunate ones easier than to others) can be learned and does not depend on a mysterious quality of charisma. Scott and Blau (1962, pp. 141–145) show that certain behavior of the supervisor tended to produce loyalty and thus commitment to high-quality production by subordinates. The liberating, yet responsible, supervisory style we are advocating includes: (1) teaching workers how to do their job (or seeing to it that training staff does so) and being available for help in enabling them to do it; (2) expecting high performance and trusting that standards will be met in accordance with the level of training and experience without closely checking on staff; (3) providing essential services that workers need in order to function well, namely, seeing that cars, typewriters, dictating machines, forms, secretarial help, and the like are available when needed; (4) backing his own unit in interdepartmental disputes; (5) obtaining responses to workers' suggestions, requests, and complaints from higher levels of management; (6) being flexible in scheduling vacations and overtime. This list could be greatly extended, of course. In performing these "services," the supervisor is likely to find that his workers respond in a way which substantially extends his formal authority. That is, in response to the supervisor's investment of himself, the workers expend more of themselves than their formal "contract" requires. The experience of being part of the work group becomes satisfying to a degree that to insure its continuance the group itself tends to enforce and spread the high standards of performance to newcomers.

Such an approach of mutual involvement may enable today's social worker, and perhaps her supervisor, too, to partly solve the existential dilemma of "being one's own man," that is, being a whole person versus being partly erased through subordinating oneself to a particular system, in this instance the welfare system. Howard Polsky points out (1969, p. 22): "A work system can be functional in maximizing profits (for "profits" read: "number of cases disposed of") and dysfunctional in destroying human potential in the process." But we are trying to envision a system that is functional in maximizing human potential.

Framework for Training

Probably the greatest challenge facing the line supervisor in public welfare is how to prepare his workers to handle constant change. The worker needs to be able to develop a sense of mastery over his job assignment and to serve clients effectively within the changing agency environment. His ability to do so will partially determine the degree to which public welfare can be responsive to client need. Perhaps it is for this reason that the role of the line supervisor has been changing, particularly his increasing role as a member of public welfare's management team. In the present as well as the future public-welfare agency, the line supervisor should be capable of four things. He should understand the program objectives of his agency. He should be able to explicate these to his workers in a way that will give meaning to their actions and activities. He must know how his workers can most effectively be organized in order to accomplish these program objectives. And he must be able to recognize dysfunctioning when it occurs so that he can redirect those activities of the worker which do not contribute to achieving agency goals.

The line supervisor in public welfare is probably the most critical person in deciding whether or not program objectives will be reached. Regardless of what management may say a worker's job should be, what a line supervisor does will be the determining factor in deciding the direction of a particular worker's activity (Fine, 1968, p. 309). Thus, unless a supervisor clearly understands what his agency wants to achieve, it will be difficult for him to marshal his workers in this direction. And, even when he has such an understanding, the line supervisor has much more to accomplish. Having had the opportunity to visit a large number of public-welfare agencies, we have become increasingly aware of one basic problem which many of these agencies appear to share: lack of agreement as to the agency's purpose and objectives.

Any employee of a public-welfare agency who gives thought to his agency sees it in his own image and carries in his mind a picture of how he would like it to be. However, public or administrative expectations can conflict with the employee's image. All too often, in order to survive in such a complex and confusing agency, an individual worker has had to be guided by his own image of what he would like the agency to be because public-welfare goals have not been stated clearly enough to be understood. The problem with this kind of situation is that an individual employee's goals may or may not be compatible with what an agency administratively decides it wants to do.

One of public welfare's core problems is its tendency to continue pretending to offer a wide range of services even after reductions have been made in financial and staff resources. As a result, it purports to do many things which, in fact, it cannot do. Staff frequently find themselves in the fiction that no matter what their caseload size or their own ability, they will continue to be all things to all people. Little wonder, then, that workers must choose their own direction in order to survive. Of course, the distinction between what the agency would like to do and what it can do is an urgent necessity, and a basic requirement if the line supervisor is to fulfill his managerial role.

Although welfare agencies generally recognize that conflicting messages often are communicated down through the agency structure to line workers, there appears to be less understanding of how to achieve individual worker identification with the function of a particular agency. The group for the Advancement of Psychiatry has suggested (1960, p. 127): "The administrative ideal is that each member of the organization shall fully understand its goals and fully share its purposes, for only in this way does identification become inevitable; and only with identification is the pursuit of the superior purpose made possible." However, such understanding and identification with the objectives of public welfare cannot be viewed as some abstract virtue or wishful hope. Identification will result only from management's deliberate attempt to achieve consensus about a shared objective. In other words, the process of determining agency direction requires staff participation and willingness to recognize what it is capable of doing within its many constraints and limitations. Of course, federal and state rules and regulations must be followed, but within these there is considerable discretion which can be exercised, particularly in the provision of social services.

What is a program objective and how can it be stated so as to guide a line worker's actions and activities? A program objective is a clear, factual statement of an end result which an agency can plan to achieve within a reasonable period of time. As such, it must be worded in such a way as to give order and direction to a worker's actions. It should assist him in judging his own accomplishments with clients (Wiley, 1969, pp. 11–12). Program objectives answer such questions as what will be done, for whom will it be done, when will it be done, and under what circumstances it will be done. For example, one current area of program emphasis in public welfare relates to the provision of family-planning services. In this area an agency might decide that one of its objectives is to provide an opportunity for all persons eligible for services to decide whether or not to seek family-planning services. However, if such a program aim is to be achievable, many public-welfare agencies will need to modify this statement further. For example, is it realistic to expect an agency to provide such a service to all eligible persons? Because of separation of eligibility from service functions, there may be many persons who no longer automatically come in contact with a service worker. (See McEntire and Hayworth, 1967.) How will this objective be fulfilled in relation to this client group? Similarly, there may be other groups of persons who the agency may feel need not receive priority in this service area (for instance, old-age–assistance recipients). Through the process of deciding what an agency can realistically do, a clear, concise statement can be formulated, one that is readily understandable by staff and can guide them in their activities with clients.

The task of making program objectives explicit in terms which will give meaning to a worker's actions and activities with clients is more complex. This is particularly true for the new worker who is not equipped with either undergraduate or graduate education in social work. He must learn, through agency training and experience, what he is to do with clients. One way to accomplish this is to determine what activities are required of a worker in order to accomplish a particular objective (Wiley, 1969, pp. 13–14). Using the previously cited program objective of family planning, one could ask: What will a worker do to accomplish this objective in his work with clients? He: (1) greets client and exchanges introductions in order to put the client at ease; (2) listens to the client's statement of problems or wishes, encouraging his expression with occasional comments, in order to learn his desires, concerns, and questions in relation to family planning; (3) asks client questions and assesses responses in order to learn what previous attempts he has made to limit or space his children and to determine his present understanding of and attitudes toward family planning.

Additional task statements could be made, but these three are sufficient for our purposes. As is evident, the words used are descriptive of "what workers do," and each is a reflection of the objective. They not only provide a clear means of describing what the worker will do with clients but they provide the means of assessing where, and under what circumstances, a worker will need additional help and supervisory guidance to assure achievement of the agency and consumer's objective. The last part of the task statement, which answers the question "to accomplish what purpose," provides a guide or list of questions which a supervisor will want to answer in determining a worker's need for additional training. Does he put the client at ease? Is he aware of the client's wishes, concerns, and questions in relation to family planning? Does he know what previous attempts the client has made to limit or space his children, as well as his present understanding of family planning? In this process, both the worker and supervisor will learn much about the clients whom the agency is seeking to serve.

The way in which jobs have been designed has tended to hamper rather than contribute to task achievement in many public-welfare agencies. Most welfare agencies have multiple classification levels for social service and eligibility workers. Despite job descriptions which emphasize increasing responsibility being assumed by workers as they advance to these higher levels, one can observe little change in activity in what these workers do with clients as they advance. Yet, does it make sense to give the same tasks to a beginning worker that one would assign to his more experienced counterpart? Would it not make more sense to design jobs in such a way that, with experience and increased skill, a worker would be given more complex tasks to perform?

In deciding how workers in a supervisory unit can be most effectively organized to accomplish agency goals, many agencies are moving to redesign and redistribute job functions as well as to create new organizational models in which line supervisors carry responsibility for joining different kinds of workers together into a mediating staff unit through which a variety of social services or financial-assistance functions are made available to a group of clients. Other agencies, using workers with differing kinds of education and training, have moved in the direction of specialization by unit. No matter what model is used, the supervisor ideally must be able to adjust the work load to meet each staff member's capabilities. Too often, where worker assignments cover too broad a span of activity, one finds that workers have learned to perform some tasks very well while minimally handling others which may, under the pressure of too much work, appear less critical. Yet, these incomplete tasks may be equally critical to the agency's being able to reach its objectives. If these tasks are not really important, then their inclusion as part of the work load should be questioned. Instead, jobs must be viewed more flexibly and they should be altered and grow with the worker as his capabilities expand.

Where supervisory units are comprised of workers who perform more than one function, the teaching responsibilities of the line supervisor are correspondingly expanded. He can no longer focus his teaching exclusively upon the individual skills which the worker needs to perform his job assignment. It may appear obvious that the improvement of a worker is, in part, a function of his learning to interact with others with whom he works. However, such interdependencies have received little attention prior to this volume. Thus, training must also focus upon the ability of the worker to use his knowledge and skill in conjunction with the expertise of other persons in the agency, who will also have contact with the client.

Teaching Responsibility

There have been some confusion and occasional conflict in welfare departments about the allocation of training responsibilities between training staff and the line supervisor. This confusion exists despite the clear criteria for the division of the training function proposed by HEW in the 1968 publication *Staff Development and Practice Supervision* (Bell, 1968), which assigns to training staff primary responsibility for all training: induction, orientation, and continued in-service training. Joanne Bell argues that line supervisors carry responsibility for *enabling* workers to make use of the training provided by central staff but not for the training per se.

The welfare departments on the West Coast with which we have worked have not found it possible to divide training chores in this way. In some places, agencies feel that the line supervisor is close to the worker and her caseload and therefore knows what the training needs are and how they can be met. This view is held even though it may be acknowledged that the training staff is better equipped by education and experience to do the teaching. Whatever current local opinions on this matter may be, the central staff rarely has the manpower to do the entire training job. This leaves to the supervisor, by default, major responsibility for much of the training. Formally and realistically assigning training tasks would prevent conflict, overlap and, most important, would avoid gaps in training which each "side" expects the other to meet. With the clear assignment of primary training responsibility (following orientation and induction) to the line supervisor, training staff can plan to help by training the trainers, thereby enabling the supervisors to do a good job.

Supervisors need such help. Too often, what passes for in-service training under their jurisdiction is the periodic unit staff meeting at which administrative announcements are read and changes in policy and procedure are discussed. But these meetings can also be used to discuss training needs with the unit staff and to plan with them how these needs can be met. The learning deficits of individual staff members are also made known to the supervisor through conferences and record reading. "Planning with" can avoid the most frequently heard worker complaints about training: that supervisors waste valuable time because sessions are repetitive, are not related to their particular job assignments, and are in the form of boring lectures. Such planning would tend to minimize resistance to staff development.

To carry out his responsibility for in-service training, the supervisor would do well to utilize the principles and concepts spelled out in educational psychology. Because social work practice itself is based partly on learning theory, the supervisor's own teaching of the helping process would be enriched by a knowledge of learning theory.[2] (In an earlier chapter, Alex Gitterman demonstrated the interrelationship of learning theory and social work supervision.) Devising a training program with staff participation takes into account what is known about how people learn. We know, for example, that people learn what they are interested in, such as when they recognize their own need stemming from the demands of the job and can have something to say about how the need is met. We are not suggesting that the supervisor desert his responsibility for assessing learning needs, but he cannot and should not do it alone.

Once the supervisor and his group find that there is a need for learning a particular set of skills or area of knowledge, training sessions are organized as separate from other unit meetings. Administrative announcements and changes in policy and procedure are important enough to merit their own time. So are the sharing of field experi-

[2] Most colleges and universities offer course work in learning theory. Application of theory calls for careful thinking through of its use in an agency because personnel join agencies to become workers, not students.

ences (resources uncovered, unmet needs identified, an outmoded service) that should influence agency policy. At any rate, the unit staff meeting is the channel for input by those most familiar with the grass-roots operation of the agency.

By the same token, training is also important and deserves a special time slot. There is a process in learning just as there is in helping. Advantage must be taken of motivation to change accustomed ways of doing things, or effort must be made to stimulate increased motivation.[3] Enough, but not too much, time must be spent on clarifying the teaching points and assuring that there is beginning mastery of the subject being discussed and that doubts and questions have been freely aired. The supervisor should try to build gradually on the skills of the staff members, trying to avoid the paralysis welfare departments experienced when "services" as a separate function were suddenly dropped on an unprepared staff.

The supervisor who takes the training aspect of his job seriously should assess with his own supervisor his skills in this practice area just as he does with respect to his role as enabler and his administrative duties. In addition, he should turn to the training supervisor as a resource for filling in the gaps in his own knowledge. The hardest part is acknowledging one's need for such new learning.

Is group supervision versus individual supervision still an important issue in public welfare? Practice varies enough so that this question is still discussed in some quarters. Florence Kaslow's chapter indicates that the adoption of group supervision has been slow. To clarify this issue, focus should be placed on the enabling aspect of the teaching role. The supervisor teaches the individual worker or, preferably, the group the meaning of, let us say, aggressive behavior. But there is still difficulty with a worker who cuts short an interview when a client becomes angry and demanding, or perhaps she summons the supervisor to deal with such a client. Problems like these are not usually dealt with in a group, although devotees of the encounter-group approach would say that there is no better way for a worker to learn how to cope with aggression than by way of the peer group. If

[3] See Hunter, *Motivation Theory for Teachers* (1971). This concise, programed statement is one of a series by Dr. Hunter. It has been found useful by the many training supervisors in California who have discovered it. The others in the series are: *Reinforcement, Retention,* and *Teach More, Faster.*

the staff is willing to risk it and informed sensitive leadership is available, that may be the method of choice for a particular group.

For most supervisors we have worked with, teaching is done in the group whenever the learning required is a group need. Individual conferences for the teaching or enabling function are scheduled regularly or arranged for as needed depending on the individual educational assessment developed at the previous evaluation. The central concern, of course, is to meet most appropriately the needs of the worker for learning to do a skillful and dependable job while building toward her independence from close supervision from her first day in the agency. Regarding the issue being discussed, we note that what has been abandoned in the last decade is total reliance on the individual weekly conference as the sole teaching, enabling, and overseeing medium, no matter what the degree of competence achieved by the worker, and without consideration of her learning pattern and learning needs. (There is always room for improvement, so one should keep prodding whether or not a stable and high level of performance is achieved!) We note an increasing flexibility regarding these vital matters in the field.

Another issue of significance in the public-welfare setting is the implication for training of the separation of services from financial assistance. During the shakedown period when social service workers and their supervisors were trying to clarify their statuses, stake out a meaningful role in public welfare, and overcome anxiety and self-doubts about their new function, they zealously attempted to make the separation complete: Don't play in my yard, and I won't play in yours. It has since been realized that it is usually the income-maintenance worker who needs to identify problems requiring the attention of the service worker and make the necessary referral.

Many public-welfare workers still need to learn that identifying problems and making referrals are in themselves "services" and require skills in addition to those needed in helping applicants establish eligibility. Helping Mrs. Jones to realize that she and her troublesome teenage daughter need not continue quarreling and that, if they wish, there is help available for them is in itself a helping process, a service. The eligibility worker should be able to decide whether the quarreling is a thing of the moment. Or, if she has been taught to listen and observe carefully and to recognize when people are really troubled, she will be able to discuss with them whether the quarreling is disturbing enough to consider seeking help in order to change it. An absence of pressure from the worker, who projects the feeling of hopefulness that the Jones' may indeed be helped to make things different, is essential. These and similar components of the helping process should be part of the training of the income-maintenance worker.[4] Anticipating objection to this view, let us point out that it is not only preventive or ameliatory, but economical of the service worker's time. Appointments not kept are expensive and wasteful, and someone whose need is great may have had to be put off.

We observe that learning and relearning the content of eligibility is so time consuming that the supervisor feels his job well done if that alone is accomplished and errors are minimized. For this and a variety of other reasons, training of eligibility workers to identify problems and make referrals is usually skimpy or ignored entirely. One of these reasons must be discussed: whether the eligibility supervisor is equal to undertaking such training. It is all too true that the pressures of the job may not permit time for this training. But lack of social work skills in eligibility supervisors constitutes a crucial gap, and this absence will become evident when promotional appointments are to be made from the ranks of the eligibility workers themselves.

What is the solution to this important problem? A finding and a decision have to be made by the supervisor and his superiors once it is agreed that eligibility workers should indeed possess these skills. The question is whether or not the supervisor possesses and can teach these skills. If he does not, someone else must be designated to do so if the service mission of the agency is to be effectively and economically accomplished.

The preceding has made amply clear that the teaching responsibilities of the supervisor are heavy. Recognition of this fact leads to the perplexing issue: What level of education should be required for appointment as a line supervisor? There seems to be general agreement that professional social work education should be required for the specialized child-welfare services. This does not seem necessary for the income-maintenance supervisor and, in the opinion of some, is even

[4] Indeed a case could be made for including these skills in the training of paraprofessionals, many of whom have assignments which require them to make responsible referrals.

contraindicated. However, if the social service branch of the agency is to accomplish its charge, the practitioners need to have professional know-how available to them. Ideally, their own supervisors would be professionally educated and able to perform both teaching and enabling functions. Failing this, professional social work competence should be easily accessible at the next level of supervision. From this level, training and consultation can be made available to a group of supervisors and to their workers. Under these circumstances, much of what we have already said regarding the continuing in-service training of social workers would apply to the line supervisors; the supervisor of services with education limited to the bachelor's degree needs on-going training in the social work practice part of the job and in supervision as well.

Challenge

Within a seemingly immovable hierarchy, how does a supervisor provide his workers with the freedom to be creative? This question, more than any other, represents the basic task of the line supervisor in public welfare. In discussing many of the problems and frustrations that workers and supervisors experience, we have also seen the power which the innovative supervisor can release in his workers. In doing so, he becomes a leader rather than a boss, a teacher rather than an overseer, a spokesman for his workers rather than one who transmits orders to them.

Increased participation by workers and line supervisors is an urgent necessity in developing new directions, new programs, and new modes of helping clients deal with their problems. However, in placing emphasis on worker participation, we do not want to imply that either top management or the line supervisor will find themselves making fewer decisions. As a matter of fact, the number of choices will probably increase. We have seen some agencies attempt to achieve staff involvement through establishment of myriad committees, even to the point where there is very little time left for workers to devote to achieving agency goals. And, all too frequently, workers may continue to feel that they have little voice in the destiny of the agency. To us, participation is a state of mind and not a state of physical involvement. It is the feeling a worker has that when she has something important to say, someone will listen to her and pass her information on to whomever makes the ultimate judgment. The judgment may not be to her liking, but if she knows her information was weighed, along with the input from others, the resolution can be accepted. The secret of participation is good communication: from line worker to supervisor, from supervisor to middle management, from middle management to top administration and back down. Good communication requires of the line supervisor a knowledge of what must be passed on through the chain of command as well as what should be shared with workers on its way back down. For all concerned, and especially for the ultimate recipient of the service, the client, the game is worth the candle.

References

ABELS, P. *Agency-Trained Workers in Professional Agencies.* Paper delivered at the National Conference on Social Welfare, New York. May 1969.

ABELS, P. "On the Nature of Supervision: The Medium Is the Group." *Child Welfare,* 1970, *49* (6), 307.

ABRAHAMSON, A. C. *Group Methods in Supervision and Staff Development.* New York: Harper and Row, 1959.

ABRAHAMSON, M. *The Professional in the Organization.* Chicago: Rand McNally, 1967.

Ad Hoc Committee on Advocacy. "The Social Worker as Advocate: Champion of Social Victims." *Social Work,* 1969, *14,* 16–22.

ADAMS, J. *Herbartian Psychology Applied to Education.* Boston: D. C. Heath, 1897.

ALMY, F. "The Problem of Charity." *Charities Review,* 1895, *4.*

American Jewish Year Book, 1905, *6.*

APAKA, T., HIRACH, S., AND KLEIDMAN, S. "Establishing Group Supervision in a Hospital Social Work Department." *Social Work,* 1967, 54–60.

APPLEBY, J., BERKMAN, V., BLAZEJACK, R., AND GORTER, V. "A Group Method of Supervision." *Social Work,* 1958, *3*(3), 18–22.

ARGYRIS, C. *Integrating the Individual and the Organization.* New York: Wiley, 1964a.

ARGYRIS, C. "T-Groups for Organizational Effectiveness." *Harvard Business Review,* 1964b, *42,* 60–74.

ATKESON, P. "Alternative Career Opportunities for the Neighborhood Worker." *Social Work,* 1967, *12*(4), 81–89.

AUFRICHT, E. "Control and Freedom in the Caseworker's Growth." In *Administration, Supervision, and Consultation.* Papers from the 1954 Social Welfare Forum, National Conference of Social Work, 1955.

AUSTIN, L. "Some Notes About Casework in Probation Agencies." *The Family,* Dec. 1937, 283.

AUSTIN, L. "Supervision of the Experienced Caseworker." In C. Kasius (Ed.) *Principles and Techniques in Social Casework.* New York: Family Service Association of America, 1950.

AUSTIN, L. "Basic Principles of Supervision." *Social Casework,* 1952, *33*(10), 411–419.

AUSTIN, L. "An Evaluation of Supervision." *Social Casework,* 1956, *37*(8), 375–382.

AUSTIN, L. "Supervision in Social Work." *Social Work Yearbook, 1960.* New York: National Association of Social Workers, 1960.

AUSTIN, L. "The Changing Role of the Supervisor." *Smith College Studies in Social Work,* 1961, *31.*

AUSTIN, L. "The Changing Role of the Supervisor." In H. J. Parad and R. R. Miller (Eds.) *Ego Oriented Casework.* New York: Family Service Association of America, 1963.

BABCOCK, C. G. "Social Work as Work." *Social Casework,* Dec. 1953.

BARBER, B. "The Sociology of the Professions." *Daedalus,* Fall 1963.

BARNARD, C. *Functions of the Executive.* Cambridge, Mass.: Harvard University Press, 1938.

BARNETT, E. Class papers and discussion in social administration seminar. University of Pennsylvania, 1971.

BECK, B. "Nonprofessional Social Work Personnel." In C. Grosser, W. E. Henry, and J. G. Kelly (Eds.) *Nonprofessionals in the Human Services.* San Francisco: Jossey-Bass, 1969, 66–77.

BECKER, D. G. "The Visitor to the New York City Poor, 1843–1920." *Social Service Review,* Dec. 1961.

BEDFORD, C. "An Analysis of the Problem of Case Supervision." *The Family,* Feb. 1930.

BELL, J. I. *Staff Development and Practice Supervision.* Washington,

D.C.: Government Printing Office (HEW, Social and Rehabilitation Service), 1968.

BENNIS, W. G., BENNE, K. D., AND CHIN, R. *The Planning of Change.* New York: Holt, Rinehart, and Winston, 1961.

BENNIS, W. G. *Organization Development: Its Nature, Origins, and Prospects.* Boston: Addison-Wesley, 1969.

BERG, R. "Social Work Practice and the Trend Toward a Legalistic Juvenile Court." *Social Casework,* 1966, *47*(2), 93–97.

BERNE, E. *Games People Play.* New York: Grove, 1964.

BERNE, E. *Principles of Group Treatment.* New York: Oxford University Press, 1966.

BIGGE, L. M. *Learning Theories for Teaching.* New York: Harper and Row, 1964.

BILLINGSLEY, A. "Black Students in a Graduate School of Social Welfare." *Social Work Education Reporter,* 1969, *17*(2).

BLACKWELL, J., AND HANG, M. R. *Black Bosses: Black Workers; Or Are Black Bosses Beautiful?* Paper presented at the American Sociological Association, Denver, Colorado. Sept. 1971.

BLANK, M. L. *Implications of Recent Research Results for Social Work Practice with the Aging.* Paper presented at National Conference on Social Welfare, Chicago. June 1970.

BLAU, P., AND SCOTT, W. R. *Formal Organizations.* San Francisco: Chandler, 1962.

BOEHM, W. "Relationship of Social Work to Other Professions." In *Encyclopedia of Social Work.* New York: National Association of Social Workers, 1965, 644.

BOGEN, B. D. *Jewish Philanthropy.* New York: Macmillan, 1917.

BRACKETT, J. R. *Supervision and Education in Charity.* New York: Macmillan, 1903.

BRADFORD, L. "The Teaching-Learning Transaction." In W. G. Bennis, K. D. Benne, and R. Chin, (Eds.) *The Planning of Change.* New York: Holt, Rinehart, and Winston, 1961.

BRADFORD, L., GIBB, J. R., AND BENNE, K. D. (Eds.) *T-Group Theory and the Laboratory Method.* New York: Wiley, 1964.

BRAGER, G. "The Indigenous Worker: A New Approach to the Social Work Technician." *Social Work,* 1965, *10*(2), 33–40.

BRENNAN, E. C. "Nonprofessionals and the Planned Replacement Model." W. C. Richan (Ed.) *Human Services and Social Work Responsibility.* New York: National Association of Social Workers, 1969, 202–211.

BRODY, E. M. *Educational Needs as Viewed by Practice.* Paper prepared for seminar on gerontology and higher education, sponsored by New Jersey Division on Aging, Feb. 1968.

BROOM, L., AND SELZNICK, P. *Sociology.* New York: Harper and Row, 1963.

BROUDY, S. H. "Historic Exemplars of Teaching Method." In N. Gage (Ed.) *Handbook of Research in Teaching Education.* Chicago: Rand McNally, 1963.

BRUNER, S. J. *Toward a Theory of Instruction.* Cambridge, Mass.: Belknap Press, 1967.

BRUNER, S. J. "Learning and Thinking." In Shober (Ed.) *Problems and Issues in Contemporary Education.* Glenview, Ill.: Scott, Foresman, 1968a.

BRUNER, S. J. *On Knowing: Essays on the Left Hand.* New York: Atheneum, 1968b.

BURNS, MARY E. "Supervision in Social Work." In *Encyclopedia of Social Work.* New York: National Association of Social Workers Press, 1965, 785.

CAHN, M. "Preliminary Report of the Committee of Nine." In *Proceedings, National Conference of Jewish Social Service, 1923.* Washington, D.C., 1923.

CALNEK, M. "Racial Factors in the Countertransference: The Black Therapist and the Black Client." *American Journal of Orthopsychiatry,* 1970, *40*(1), 39–46.

CANTOR, N. *Dynamics of Learning.* Buffalo: Henry Stewart, 1961.

CANTOR, N. *The Learning-Teaching Process.* New York: Holt, Rinehart, and Winston, 1966.

CARNER, L. P. *The Settlement Way in Philadelphia.* Philadelphia: Delaware Valley Settlement Alliance, 1964.

CARTER, R. M. "The 'Authority Problem' Revisited." *Federal Probation,* 1961, *25*(4), 52–56.

"Case Conference on the Neighborhood Subprofessional Worker." *Children,* 1968, *15,* (1) 7–16.

CAUDILL, W. *The Psychiatric Hospital as a Small Society.* Cambridge, Mass.: Harvard University Press, 1958.

CAYTON, C. "Relationship of the Probation Officer and Defense Attorney." *Federal Probation,* 1970, *36*(1).

CHAPPEL, R. A. "Probation: Casework." In R. S. Carven (Ed.) *Readings in Juvenile Delinquency.* Philadelphia: Lippincott, 1964.

Charity Organization Society of the City of New York Tenth Annual Report for the Year 1891. New York, 1892.

CHRISTMAS, J. J. "Group Methods in Training and Practice: Nonprofessional Mental Health Personnel in a Deprived Community." *American Journal of Orthopsychiatry,* 1966, *36*(3), 410–419.

CLARK, B. R. "Organizational Adaptation and Precarious Values: A Case Study." *American Sociological Review,* 1956, 21, 327–328.

CLAYTON, C. "Relationship of the Probation Officer and Defense Attorney." *Federal Probation,* 1970, *36*(1), 8–13.

CLOWARD, R. A., AND EPSTEIN, I. "Private Social Welfare's Disengagement from the Poor: The Case of Family-Adjustment Agencies." In M. N. Zald (Ed.) *Social Welfare Institutions: A Sociological Reader.* New York: Wiley, 1965.

COHEN, N. E. "Social Work As a Profession." *Social Work Yearbook.* New York: National Association of Social Workers, 1957.

COHEN, R. "Graduate Social Work Training in a Multipurpose Geriatric Center." *The Gerontologist,* Fall, 1971.

COMESS, L. J., AND O'REILLY, P. J. "Private Practice Approach in A Family Service Agency." *Social Work,* 1966, *2*(2), 82.

CONRAD, J. P. *Crime and Its Correction: An International Survey of Attitudes and Practices.* Berkeley: University of California Press, 1967.

"COS Statistics for December, 1897." *Charities,* 1897, *1,* 14.

CREMIN, A. L. "What Happened to Progressive Education?" *Teachers College Record.* New York: Columbia University, 1954, *61.*

CUDABECK, D. "Case Sharing in the AFDC Program: The Use of Welfare Aides." *Social Work,* 1969, *14*(3), 93–99.

CZAJKOSKI, E. H. "The Need for Philosophical Direction in Probation and Parole." *Federal Probation,* 1965, *39*(3), 24–28.

DE FOREST, R. W. "The Federations of Organized Charity." *Charities,* 1904, *12,* 20.

DENHAM, W. H., AND SHATZ, E. O. "Impact of the Indigenous Nonprofessional on the Professional's Role." In W. C. Richan (Ed.) *Human Services and Social Work Responsibility.* New York: National Association of Social Workers, 1969.

DEVINE, E. T. "The Relief and Care of the Poor in Their Homes." *Charities Review,* 1900, *10,* 180.

DEVIS, D. A. "Teaching and Administrative Function in Supervision." *Social Work,* 1965, *10*(2), 83–89.

DEWEY, J. *Democracy and Education.* New York: Macmillan, 1922.

DEWEY, J. *The Theory of Inquiry.* New York: Holt, Rinehart, and Winston, 1938.

DEWEY, J. *Experience and Education.* New York: Macmillan, 1947.

DEWEY, J. *The Child and the Curriculum and the School and the Society.* Chicago: Phoenix, 1966.

DIMOCK, H. S., AND TRECKER, H. B. *The Supervision of Group Work and Recreation.* New York: Association Press, 1949.

DRUCKER, P. F. *Managing for Results.* New York: Harper and Row, 1964.

EBY, F. *The Development of Modern Education.* Englewood Cliffs: Prentice-Hall, 1952.

EISENBERG, S. *Supervision in the Changing Field of Social Work.* University of Pennsylvania: Jewish Family Service of Philadelphia, 1956.

EMERY, F. E., AND TRIST, E. L. "The Causal Texture of Organizational Environment." *Human Relations,* 1965, *18,* 21–32.

ETZIONI, A. *Complex Organizations.* New York: Holt, Rinehart, and Winston, 1961.

ETZIONI, A. *The Semi-Professions and Their Organization.* New York: Free Press, 1969.

"Executive Officers and Employees." *Sixty-First Annual Report of the New York Association for Improving the Condition of the Poor for the Fiscal Year Ending September 30, 1904.* New York: United Charities Building, 1904.

FANT, F. D. "The Impact of the Gault Decision on Probation Practice in Juvenile Courts." *Federal Probation,* 1969, *33*(3), 14–18.

FARRAR, M., AND BLOOM, M. *Social Work Education and the Reduction of Stereotypes about the Aged.* Paper presented to the 20th Annual Meeting of the Gerontological Society. Nov. 1967.

FINE, S. A. "Up From Poverty." In F. Reissman and H. I. Popper (Eds.) *Guidelines for the Design of New Careers.* New York: Harper and Row, 1968.

FINK, A. E. "Authority in the Correctional Process." *Federal Probation,* 1961, *25*(3), 34–40.

The First Annual Report of the New York Association for the Improvement of the Condition of the Poor, for the Year, 1845. New York: 1845.

FISHER, B. C. "Juvenile Court: Purpose, Promises, and Problems." *Social Service Review,* 1960, *34,* 75–82.

FISHER, G. "What to do Until the GAI and Universal Services Arrive: Early Lessons of Separation." *Public Welfare,* 1971, *29*(4), 468–474.

FITZDALE, R. "Peer Group Supervision." *Social Casework,* 1958, 39 (8), 443–450.

FLEXNER, A. *Is Social Work a Profession?* New York: Columbia University Press, 1915.

FRALEY, Y. L. *The Role of the Professional Social Work Practitioner in Social Policy Formation.* Unpublished Doctoral Dissertation, University of Pennsylvania, 1966.

FRAMO, J. L. "Rationale and Techniques of Intensive Family Therapy." In I. B. Nagy and J. Framo (Eds.) *Intensive Family Therapy.* New York: Harper and Row, 1969.

FRENCH, D. G. *Objectives of the Profession of Social Work.* Bangkok: United Nations Economic Commission for Asia and the Far East, 1967.

FROEBEL, F. *The Education of Man.* New York: Appleton-Century-Crofts, 1887.

GARCIA, A. "The Chicano and Social Work." *Social Casework,* 1971, 52 (5), 274–278.

GARDNER, J. W. *Excellence.* New York: Harper and Row, 1971.

GETZEL, G. S., GOLDBERG, J. R., AND SALMON, R. "Supervising in Groups as a Model for Today." *Social Casework,* March 1971, 154–163.

GLASGOW, D. "The Black Thrust for Vitality: The Impact on Social Work Education." *Journal of Education for Social Work,* 1971, *7*(2), 9–18.

GOLDBERG, G. "Untrained Neighborhood Workers in a Social Work Program." In A. Pearl and F. Riessman (Eds.) *New Careers for the Poor.* New York: Free Press, 1965.

GOLDBERG, G. S. "Nonprofessionals in Human Services." In C. Grosser, W. E. Henry, and J. G. Kelly, (Eds.) *Nonprofessionals in the Human Services.* San Francisco: Jossey-Bass, 1969.

GOLEMBIEWSKI, R., AND BLUMBERG, A. (Eds.) *Sensitivity Training and the Laboratory Approach.* Illinois: Peacock, 1970.

GORDON, M. M. *Assimilation in American Life.* New York: Oxford University Press, 1964.

GROSSER, C., HENRY, W. E., AND KELLY, J. G. *Nonprofessionals in Human Services.* San Francisco: Jossey-Bass, 1969.

Group for the Advancement of Psychiatry. *Administration of the Public Psychiatric Hospital,* 1960, *46,* 127.

HALLOWITZ, E. "Use of Nonprofessional Staff: Issues and Strategies." In W. C. Richan (Ed.) *Human Services and Social Work Responsibility.* New York: National Association of Social Workers, 1969, 166–177.

HALPERN, K. S. "Navajo Health and Welfare Aides: A Field Study." *The Social Service Review,* 1971, *45*(1), 37–52.

HANLAN, A. "From Social Work to Social Administration." In *Social*

Work Practice, 1970. New York: Columbia University Press, 1970, 41–55.

HANLAN, A. "Casework Beyond Bureaucracy." *Social Casework,* 1971, 52 (4), 198.

HANNERZ, U. *Soulside.* New York: Columbia University Press, 1969.

HARDCASTLE, D. A. "The Indigenous Nonprofessional in the Social Service Bureaucracy: A Critical Examination." *Social Work,* 1971, *16*(2), 56–64.

HARDMAN, D. G. "Authority is My Job." *National Probation and Parole Association Journal,* 1957, *3*(3), 215–221.

HARDMAN, D. G. "Constructive Use of Authority." *Crime and Delinquency,* 1960, *4*(3).

HARE, P. *Handbook of Small Group Research.* New York: Free Press, 1962.

HARE, P., AND EFFRAT, A. Personal working papers, 1968.

HARFORD, J. "Integration of the Teaching and Administrative Aspects of Supervision." In *Administration, Supervision and Consultation.* Papers from the 1954 Social Welfare Forum, National Conference of Social Work, 1955.

HENRY, C. S. "Criteria for Determining Readiness of Staff to Function Without Supervision." In *Administration, Supervision and Consultation.* Papers from the 1954 Social Welfare Forum National Conference of Social Work, 1955.

HERBART, F. J. *A Textbook in Psychology.* New York: Appleton-Century-Crofts, 1895.

HERBART, F. J. *Outlines of Educational Doctrine.* New York: Macmillan, 1901.

HIGHET, G. *The Art of Teaching.* New York: Random House, 1950.

HILGARD, R. E., AND BOWER, G. H. *Theories of Learning.* 3rd ed. New York: Appleton-Century-Crofts, 1966.

HILL, J. G., AND ORMSBY, R. "The Philadelphia Cost Study." *Social Work Journal,* 1953, *34,* 168.

HOFFER, E. *The Ordeal of Change.* New York: Harper and Row, 1963.

HOFFER, E. *The Temper of Our Time.* New York: Harper and Row, 1967.

HOUSTON, L. P. "Black People, New Careers and Humane Services." *Social Casework,* 1970, *51*(5), 291–299.

HOWARD, J. *Please Touch.* New York: McGraw Hill, 1970.

HUNTER, M. *Motivation Theory for Teachers.* El Segundo, California: TIP Publications, 1971.

HUTCHINSON, D. "Supervision in Social Casework." *The Family,* 1935, *16,* 45.

INDIK, B. P. *People, Groups, and Organizations.* New York: Teachers College Press, 1968.

JAMES, W. *Talks to Teachers.* New York: Holt, Rinehart, and Winston, 1899.

JONES, H. "The Use of Indigenous Personnel as Service Givers." In H. H. Weissman, (Ed.) *Individual and Group Services in the Mobilization for Youth Experience.* New York: Association Press, 1969.

JUDD, J., KOHN, R., AND SCHULMAN, G. L. "Group Supervision: A Vehicle for Professional Development." *Social Work,* 1962, *7,* 96–102.

KADUSHIN, A. "Games People Play in Supervision." *Social Work,* 1968, *13*(3).

KAHLE, J. H. "Structuring and Administering a Modern Voluntary Agency." *Social Work,* 1969, *4*(4), 21–28.

KATZ, D., AND KOHN, R. L. *The Social Psychology of Organizations,* New York: Wiley, 1966.

KELLOGG, D. O. "The Function of Charity Organization." *Lend-A-Hand,* 1886, *1,* 452.

KENNEDY, A. J., AND FARRA, K. *Social Settlements in New York City.* New York: Columbia University Press, 1935.

KENNEDY, A. J., AND WOODS, R. A. *Settlement Horizons.* New York: Russell Sage Foundation, 1922.

Kerner Commission. *Report of the National Advisory Commission on Civil Disorder.* New York: Bantam, 1968.

KEVE, P. *Imaginative Programing in Probation and Parole.* Minneapolis: University of Minneapolis Press, 1967.

KIDNEIGH, J. C. "Social Work as a Profession." *Social Work Year Book,* 1960.

KILPATRICK, W. H. *Foundations of Method.* New York: Macmillan, 1926.

KLEIN, D. C. *Community Dynamics and Mental Health.* New York: Wiley, 1968.

KNEZNEK, E. *Supervision for Public Welfare Supervisors.* Chicago: American Public Welfare Association, 1966.

KNOLL, F. "Casework Services for Mexican Americans." *Social Casework,* 1970, *52.*

KOFFKA, K. *Principles of Gestalt Psychology.* New York: Harcourt Brace Jovanovich, 1935.

KOHN, R. "Differential Use of the Observed Interview in Student Training." *Social Work Education Reporter,* 1971, *3,* 45.

KRAFFT, L., AND HOWE, L. "Guidelines for Sensitivity Training in Your School." *Phi Delta Kappan,* Nov. 1971.

KRAMER, J. R., AND LEVENTMAN, S. *Children of the Gilded Ghetto.* New Haven: Yale University Press, 1961.

KUTZIK, A. J. *Guidelines for Student Training in the Philadelphia Settlements.* Philadelphia: Delaware Valley Settlement Alliance, 1967.

LEADER, A. "Supervision and Consultation Through Observed Interviewing." *Social Casework,* 1968, *49.*

LEFTON, M., DINITZ, S., AND PASAMANICK, B. "Decision-Making in a Mental Hospital: Real, Perceived, and Ideal." *American Sociological Review,* 1959, *24*(6), 822–828.

LEVINSON, D. J., AND KLERMAN, G. L. "The Clinician Executive." *Psychiatry,* 1967, *30*(1), 3–15.

LEVINSON, P., AND SCHILLER, J. "Role Analysis of the Indigenous Nonprofessional." *Social Work,* 1966, *11*(3), 95–101.

LEWIN, K. *Principles of Topological Psychology.* New York: McGraw-Hill, 1936.

LEWIN, K. *Field Theory in Social Science.* New York: Harper and Row, 1951.

LEWIN, K., AND LIPPITT, R. "An Experimental Approach to the Study of Autocracy and Democracy." *Sociometry,* 1938, *1,* 292–300.

LIEBOW, E. *Tally's Corner.* Boston: Little-Brown, 1967.

LIKERT, R. *New Patterns of Management.* New York: McGraw-Hill, 1961.

LOCKE, J. "Some Thoughts Concerning Education." In J. W. Adamson (Ed.) *Educational Writings of John Locke.* New York: Longmans, 1912.

LOCKE, J. *An Essay Concerning Human Understanding.* New York: Dover, 1959.

LOOMIS, C. P. *The Social System.* New Jersey: Van Nostrand, 1960.

LOWENBERG, F. M. "Social Workers and Indigenous Nonprofessionals: Some Structural Dilemmas." *Social Work,* 1968, *13*(3), 65–71.

LOWREY, L. G. "Foreword." In S. Swift, *Training in Psychiatric Social Work.* New York: Commonwealth Fund, 1934.

LOWRY, F. "A Philosophy of Supervision in Social Casework," *Proceedings, National Conference of Social Work.* Atlantic City, 1936.

LUBIN, B., EDDY, W. B. "The Laboratory Training Model: Rationale, Method, and Some Thoughts for the Future." *International Journal of Group Psychotherapy,* 1970, 20 (3), 305–339.

LUBOVE, R. *The Professional Altruist.* New York: Atheneum, 1969.

MAAS, H. S. "Social Casework." In W. S. Friedlander (Ed.) *Concepts and Methods of Social Work*. Englewood Cliffs, New Jersey: Prentice-Hall, 1958, 66–72.

MC CONNELL, J. W. "Problems of Method in the Study of Human Relations." *Industrial and Labor Relations Review,* 1950, *3*(4), 549.

MC ENTIRE, D., AND HAYWORTH, J. "The Two Functions of Public Welfare: Income Maintenance and Social Services." *Social Work,* 1967, *12*(1).

MC GREGOR, D. *The Human Side of Enterprise*. New York: McGraw-Hill, 1960.

MC GREGOR, D. *The Professional Manager*. New York: McGraw-Hill, 1967.

MC LEAN, F. H. "The State Conferences-Illinois." *Charities and the Commons,* Oct. 1908.

MC LEAN, F. H. *The Family Society: Joint Responsibilities of Board, Staff, and Membership*. New York: American Association for Organizing Family Social Work, 1927.

MARCUS, G. "How Casework Training May Be Adapted to Meet the Worker's Personal Problems." In *Proceedings, National Conference of Social Work, 1927*. Chicago: University of Chicago Press, 1927.

MARENHOLZ-BULOW, B. VON. *Reminiscences of Friedrich Froebel*. Boston: Lee and Shepard, 1895.

MARROW, A. J., BOWERS, G. D., SEASHORE, S. E. *Management by Participation*. New York: Harper, 1967.

MASLOW, A. H. *Toward a Psychology of Being*. Princeton: Van Nostrand, 1968.

MAUSS, M. *The Gift: Forms and Functions of Exchange in Archaic Societies*. New York: Norton, 1967, 63–72.

MAY, R. *Man's Search for Himself*. New York: Norton, 1953.

MEEKER, B. S. "The Curriculum Study: Implications for the Field of Corrections." *Social Casework,* 1960, *61,* 28.

MERTON, R. *Social Theory and Social Structure*. New York: Free Press, 1957.

MEYER, H. J. "Professionalism and Social Work." In A. J. Kahn, (Ed.) *Issues in American Social Work*. New York: Columbia University Press, 1959, 336.

MILES, A. P. "The Reality of the Probation Officers' Dilemma." *Federal Probation,* 1965, *39*(1), 21–22.

MILES, M. B. *Learning to Work in Groups*. New York: Bureau of Publications, Teachers College, Columbia University, 1959.

MILLER, D. C., AND FORM, W. H. *Industrial Sociology*. New York: Harper and Row, 1951.

MILLER, I. "Distinctive Characteristics of Supervision in Group Work." *Social Work,* 1965, *5*(1), 69–76.

MILLER, I. "Supervision in Social Work." In *Encyclopedia of Social Work,* 1971.

MILLER, R. AND PODELL, L. *Role Conflict in Public Social Services.* New York: State of New York, Office for Community Affairs, n.d.

MILLER, S. M., AND RIESSMAN, F. *Social Class and Social Policy.* New York: Basic Books, 1968.

MURPHY, G. *Historical Introduction to Modern Psychology.* New York: Harcourt Brace Jovanovich, 1949.

NAPIER, R., AND GERSHENFELD, M. *Groups: Theory and Practice.* Boston: Houghton Mifflin, 1972.

NATHANSON, T. "Self-Awareness in the Educative Process." *Social Work,* 1962, *7*(2).

National Association of Social Workers. *Handbook on the Private Practice of Social Work.* New York, 1967.

National Association of Social Workers. *Personnel Information Bulletin.* New York, July 1971.

NEUGEBOREN, B. *Evaluation of Unified Social Services.* New Haven: Community Progress Incorporated, 1967.

NEUGEBOREN, B. "Developing Specialized Programs in Social Work Administration in the Master's Degree Program: Field Practice Component." *Journal of Education for Social Work,* 1971, *7*(3), 35–47.

OHLIN, L. E., PIVEN, H., AND PAPPENFORT, D. M. "Major Dilemmas of the Social Worker in Probation and Parole." *The National Probation and Parole Association Journal,* July, 1956.

PAINE, R. T. "Address." March 12, 1874. In *Writings* (bound by the Boston Public Library).

PARSONS, T. *The Social System.* London: Glencoe, 1951.

PARSONS, T. *Essays on Sociological Theory.* New York: Glencoe, 1964, 374–375.

PARSONS, T. "On the Concept of Value-Commitments." *Sociological Inquiry,* 1968, *38,* 135–160.

PARSONS, T., AND SMELSER, N. J. *Economy and Society.* New York: Free Press, 1965.

PEARL, A., AND RIESSMAN, F. *New Careers for the Poor.* New York: Free Press, 1965.

PILIAVIN, I. "Restructuring the Provision of Social Services." *Social Work,* 1968, *13,* 34–41.

PINS, A. M. "Changes in Social Work Education and Their Implications for Practice." *Social Work,* 1971, *16*(2), 5–15.

PIVEN, F. F., AND CLOWARD, R. A. *Regulating the Poor: The Functions of Welfare*. New York: Pantheon, 1971.

POLANSKY, N. A. "The Professional Identity in Social Work." In A. Kahn (Ed.) *Issues in American Social Work*. New York: Columbia University Press, 1959.

PRAY, K. L. M. "Social Workers and Partisan Politics." *The Compass,* 1945, *26,* 3–6.

"Preliminary Report of the Committee of Nine." *Proceedings, National Conference of Jewish Social Service*. Washington, D.C., 1923.

PRUGER, R., AND SPECHT, H. "Establishing New Career Programs: Organizational Barriers and Strategies." *Social Work,* 1968, *13*(4), 21–32.

PUMPHREY, R. E., AND PUMPHREY, M. W. *The Heritage of American Social Work*. New York: Columbia University Press, 1961.

RABINOWITZ, C. "The Caseworker and the Private Practitioner in Psychotherapy." *Jewish Social Service Quarterly,* Winter 1953.

RAPPOPORT, L. "In Defense of Social Work." In P. Weinberger, *Perspectives on Social Welfare*. New York: Macmillan, 1969.

REECE, A. S. "Social Work Practice: An Exploratory Study." *Social Work,* 1961, *6*(3).

REYNOLDS, B. C. *Learning and Teaching in Social Work*. New York: Russell Sage, 1965.

REYNOLDS, R. "Relationship of Field Placement to Classroom Teaching." *Social Casework,* 1952, 33.

RICHAN, W. C. *Human Services and Social Work Responsibility*. New York: National Association of Social Workers, 1969.

RIESSMAN, F., AND HALLOWITZ, E. "The Neighborhood Service Center: An Innovation in Preventive Psychiatry." *American Journal of Psychiatry,* 1967, *23*(11), 1408–1413.

ROBINSON, V. P. *Supervision in Social Casework*. Chapel Hill, N.C.: University of North Carolina Press, 1936.

ROBINSON, V. P. *Dynamics of Supervision Under Functional Controls*. Philadelphia: University of Pennsylvania Press, 1949.

ROSZAK, T. *The Making of a Counter Culture*. New York: Doubleday, 1969.

ROUSSEAU, J. J. *Emile, or Education*. New York: Dutton, 1911.

SAUL, S. *Learning About Aging*. Address to the Board of Directors meeting, Central Bureau for the Jewish Aged, June 1970.

SAUNDERS, M. K. "Social Work: A Profession Chasing Its Tail." *Harpers,* 1957, *214,* 56.

SCHEFFLER, I. "Philosophical Models of Teaching." *Harvard Educational Review,* 1965, *35*(2).

SCHEFFLER, I. *The Language of Education.* Springfield, Ill.: Charles Thomas, 1968.

SCHEIN, E. H., AND BENNIS, W. G. *Personal and Organizational Change Through Group Methods: The Laboratory Approach.* New York: Wiley, 1965.

SCHERZ, F. H. "A Concept of Supervision Based on Definitions of Job Responsibility." *Social Casework,* 1958, *39*(8), 435–443.

SCHWARTZ, W. *The Classroom Teaching of Social Work with Groups: Some Central Problems.* Paper presented at Council on Social Work Education Faculty Day, Toronto, Canada, Jan. 1964.

SCHWARTZ, W. *Comments.* New York: United Neighborhood Houses, 1968.

SELZNICK, P. *Leadership in Administration.* Evanston, Ill.: Row, Peterson, 1957.

SHANNON, B. E. "Implications of White Racism for Social Work Practice." *Social Casework,* 1970, *51.*

SHARKANSKY, I. *Public Administration.* Chicago: Markham, 1970.

SHAW, M. E. *Group Dynamics.* New York: McGraw-Hill, 1971.

SILVERMAN, E. "Lawyers and Social Workers in Juvenile Proceedings." *Crime and Delinquency,* 1960, *11,* 263.

SIMON, H. *Administrative Behavior.* New York: Macmillan, 1957.

SKINNER, B. F. "The Science of Learning and the Art of Teaching." *The Harvard Educational Review,* 1954, *24*(2).

SKINNER, B. F. "Teaching Machines." *Science,* Oct. 1958, 969–977.

SKINNER, B. F. *Cumulative Record.* New York: Appleton-Century-Crofts, 1959.

SMALLEY, R. E. "Values and Directions in Social Work Education." *Journal of Social Work Process,* 1969, *17,* 33.

Social Work. "Letters." 16(4), 3.

STANSKY, J. F. "In Re: Gault: Children are People." *California Law Review,* 1967, *60,* 1204–1218.

STOTLAND, E., AND KOBLER, A. *The Life and Death of a Mental Hospital.* Seattle: University of Washington Press, 1965.

STUDT, E. "An Outline for Study of Social Authority Factors in Casework." *Social Casework,* 1954, *25*(6), 231–238.

STUDT, E. *Education for Social Workers in the Correctional Fields.* Vol. 5. Project report of the curriculum study. Council on Social Work Education: New York, 1959, 20–21.

STUDT, E. "Fields of Social Work Practice: Organizing Our Resources for More Effective Practice." *Social Work,* 1965, *10*(4), 156–165.

SULLIVAN, H. S. *The Interpersonal Theory of Psychiatry.* New York: Norton, 1953.

TANEBAUM, S. *William Heard Kilpatrick: Trail Blazer in Education.* New York: Harper and Row, 1951.

TANNENBAUM, R., WESCHLER, I. R., MASSARIK, F. *Leadership and Organization: A Behavioral Approach.* New York: McGraw-Hill, 1961.

TAYLOR, F. W. *Scientific Management.* New York: Harper and Row, 1911.

THIS, L. E., AND LIPPITT, G. L. "Learning Theories and Training." *Training and Development Journal,* Apr.-May, 1966.

THOMPSON, J. D. *Organizations in Action.* New York: McGraw-Hill, 1967.

THORNDIKE, L. E. *Educational Psychology.* New York: Teachers College, Columbia University, 1913.

THOULESS, R. H. *How to Think Straight.* New York: Hart, 1939.

TIMMS, N. *Language of Social Casework.* London: Routledge and Kegan Paul, 1968.

TOLLEN, W. *Study of Staff Losses.* Washington, D.C.: Department of Health, Education, and Welfare, Children's Bureau Publication 383, 1960.

TOREN, N. "Semi-Professionalism and Social Work: A Theoretical Perspective." In A. Etzioni (Ed.) *The Semi-Professions and Their Organizations.* New York: Free Press, 1969, 177–178.

TOWLE, C. *The Learner in Education for the Professions.* Chicago: University of Chicago Press, 1954.

TOWLE, C. "The Place of Help in Supervision." In H. H. Perlman (Ed.) *Helping.* Chicago: University of Chicago Press, 1969.

TRECKER, H. B. *Group Process in Administration.* New York: Women's Press, 1946.

TREGER, H. "Reluctance of the Social Agency to Work with the Offender." *Federal Probation,* 1965, *39*(1), 23–28.

U.S. Commission on Civil Rights. *Hearing Before the United States Commission on Civil Rights: Cleveland Ohio, April 1–7, 1966.* Washington, D.C.: Government Printing Office, 1967.

U.S. Commission on Civil Rights. *Racial Isolation in the Public Schools.* Washington, D.C.: Government Printing Office, 1967. 2 vols.

U.S. Department of Health, Education, and Welfare. *An Introduction to Mental Health Consultation.* Public Health Service, Monograph 69. Washington, D.C., 1962.

Veterans Administration, Department of Medicine and Surgery. *Program*

Guide Social Work Service, Standards for Clinical Social Work in Veterans Administration Hospitals, Outpatient Clinics and Domiciliaries G-1, M-2, Part XII. Washington, D.C., August, 1957.

VINTER, R. D. "The Social Structure of Service." In A. Kahn (Ed.) *Issues in American Social Work.* New York: Columbia University Press, 1959.

WALZ, T. H. "New Breed of Social Workers: Fact or Fancy?" *Public Welfare, 29,* 19–23.

WASSERMAN, H. "The Professional Social Worker in a Bureaucracy." *Social Work,* 1971, *16*(1), 89–95.

WATSON, B. J. *Psychology from the Standpoint of a Behaviorist.* New York: Lippincott, 1924.

WATSON, F. D. *The Charity Organization Movement in the United States: A Study in American Philanthropy.* New York: Macmillan, 1922.

WAX, J. "Time-Limited Supervision." *Social Work,* 1963, 8(3).

WEBER, M. *The Theory of Social and Economic Organizations.* New York: Oxford University Press, 1947.

WIDEMAN, P. "Organizational Structure for Casework Supervision." *Social Work,* 1962, 7(4), 78–85.

WILENSKY, H., AND LEBEAUX, C. *Industrial Society and Social Welfare.* New York: Russell Sage Foundation, 1958, and Free Press, 1965.

WILEY, W. "Six Steps to New Careers." *A Systems Approach to New Careers: Two Papers.* Kalamazoo: W. E. Upjohn Institute for Employment Research, 1969.

WILLIAMSON, M. *Supervision.* New York: Woman's Press, 1950.

WILLIAMSON, M. *New Patterns and Processes.* New York: Association Press, 1961.

WILSON, G., AND RYLAND, G. *Social Group Work Practice.* Boston: Houghton Mifflin, 1949.

WITTMAN, M. *What Changes are Needed in Social Services for Older People.* Paper presented at annual meeting of the Jewish Home in Buffalo. New York, Oct. 1968.

WOODS, R. A., AND KENNEDY, A. J. *The Settlement Horizon: A National Estimate.* New York: Russell Sage Foundation, 1922.

World Book Dictionary. Chicago: Field, 1968.

YOUNG, R. *Supervision—Challenges of the 70's.* Unpublished paper presented at Family Service Association of America conference. Philadelphia, Spr. 1971.

YOUNG, W. M., JR. *Beyond Racism.* New York: McGraw-Hill, 1969.

ZALD, M. N. *Organizational Change: The Political Economy of the YMCA.* Chicago: University of Chicago Press, 1970.

Name Index

Subject Index